BORN IN BLOOD
AND FIRE

Latin American Voices

BORN IN BLOOD AND FIRE

Latin American Voices

Second Edition

JOHN CHARLES CHASTEEN

W · W · NORTON & COMPANY
NEW YORK · LONDON

W. W. Norton & Company has been independent since its founding in 1923, when William Warder Norton and Mary D. Herter Norton first published lectures delivered at the People's Institute, the adult education division of New York City's Cooper Union. The firm soon expanded its program beyond the Institute, publishing books by celebrated academics from America and abroad. By midcentury, the two major pillars of Norton's publishing program—trade books and college texts—were firmly established. In the 1950s, the Norton family transferred control of the company to its employees, and today—with a staff of four hundred and a comparable number of trade, college, and professional titles published each year—W. W. Norton & Company stands as the largest and oldest publishing house owned wholly by its employees.

Editor: Jon Durbin
Editorial Assistant: Travis Carr
Project Editor: Caitlin Moran
Production Manager: Eric Pier-Hocking
Photo Editor: Trish Marx
Permissions Manager: Megan Schindel
Composition: Westchester Book Group
Manufacturing: Maple-Vail Book Manufacturing Group

Library of Congress Cataloging-in-Publication Data

Names: Chasteen, John Charles, 1955– compiler. | Chasteen, John Charles, 1955– Born in blood and fire.
Title: Born in blood and fire : Latin American voices / [compiled by] John Charles Chasteen.
Description: Second edition. | New York : W.W. Norton & Company, 2016. | Documentary companion to: Born in blood and fire : a concise history of Latin America.
Identifiers: LCCN 2016014212 | ISBN 9780393283068 (pbk.)
Subjects: LCSH: Latin America—History—Sources.
Classification: LCC F1410 .B697 2016 | DDC 980—dc23 LC record available at http://lccn.loc.gov/2016014212

ISBN 978-0-393-28306-8 (pbk.)

W. W. Norton & Company, Inc., 500 Fifth Avenue, New York, N.Y. 10110
www.wwnorton.com
W. W. Norton & Company Ltd., Castle House, 75/76 Wells Street, London WIT 3QT

1 2 3 4 5 6 7 8 9 0

Contents

CHAPTER 6 | REACTIONS AGAINST NEOCOLONIALISM 184

CHAPTER 7 | CULTIVATING NON-EUROPEAN ROOTS 216

CHAPTER 8 | COLD WAR VISIONS 250

PREFACE

And now for something rather different. It is true that many of the authors here are the usual suspects—las Casas and Guaman Poma, Humboldt and Sarmiento, Rodó and da Cunha. The themes are familiar for any teacher of Latin American history, from the Encounter to neoliberalism. But there are a lot of fresh sources here, stuff rarely seen in English (or, in many cases, never before translated), and even classic texts appear in new translations. There is a rare Jesuit account of music and festivals in the Guaraní missions of Paraguay; fascinating Inquisition transcripts; a new sampling of nineteenth-century local color from Mexico, Colombia, Brazil, Peru, and Argentina; and a wealth of fiction, including a number of complete short stories. Unusual sources include the diary of an independence-era patriot, a nationalistic puff about the tango's European apotheosis in the 1910s and 1920s, an outrageous declassified "story" by the CIA (written for radio broadcast during the Guatemalan intervention of 1954), and the 1994–95 confessions of an unrepentant Chilean torturer.

Narrative sources read best, of course, and they have been favored here. Each selection has been chosen and excerpted with maximum emphasis on the coherence of the resulting text, then translated and edited to read lucidly and naturally in contemporary English. Baffling allusions and extraneous detail were sacrificed to clarity, without littering the text with brackets and ellipses. In other words, these texts have been carefully and thoroughly adapted for the classroom.

The selections span the gamut chronologically and originate in countries all over the region, but they have been grouped thematically in each chronological chapter. Therefore, despite their diversity and geographical distribution, these Latin American voices speak to one another. It was a delight to excerpt and translate them with a view to making students of Latin American history conversant with them as well. After all, what could be more exciting than working elbow to elbow—as a translator and author always do, somehow—with such great masters of Spanish and Portuguese prose as El Inca Garcilaso or the incomparable Machado de Assis? I only hope that reading these texts will be as much fun and as illuminating as choosing, editing, and translating them has been.

John Charles Chasteen
February 2016
Chapel Hill, North Carolina

Chapter 1

CHRONICLES OF THE ENCOUNTER

[handwritten margin note: we only know about even of involved]

The first contact between Europeans and indigenous Americans, populations totally isolated from each other for millennia, was among the most momentous and fascinating encounters in world history. Virtually all our direct evidence of the Encounter comes from the European side, unfortunately, yet it can still help us think about how each side viewed the other. This chapter presents excerpts of eight accounts of the Encounter, all written during the 1500s.

This early date of writing makes these excerpts *primary sources*—the term that historians use for evidence generated more or less contemporaneously with the events they describe. Primary sources are the raw materials interpreted by historians and are the necessary starting points of all serious historical research. Historians believe that all students of the past should be exposed to primary sources, and so this book is devoted to them. Of course, students also (and mostly) need to read the writings of historians who have devoted years of study to particular topics. The writings of historians are termed *secondary sources* to distinguish them from primary sources.

Primary sources must be read with particular care. Often, the available primary sources offer no semblance of objectivity, and their biases must be taken into account when interpreting them. However, we cannot simply put primary sources aside because they are biased. All evidence, in fact, has a bias, its own point of view that must be considered. Bartolomé de las Casas, the great Spanish champion of indigenous people, tended to exaggerate in their favor,

1

◆ importance of different narrative

while Francisco Cervantes de Salazar exaggerated his bitterly prej-
udiced criticisms of them. If we keep point of view in mind, we can
learn something from any primary source, particularly when we
compare various primary sources to each other, noting where they
seem to agree and disagree.

Because primary sources (which we will also call documents)
are defined, above all, by the timing of their creation, this book
arrays them basically in chronological order. The present chapter,
for example, begins with an excerpt from *The Caminha Letter* written in 1500, and moves toward *A General History of New Spain*,
written during the middle 1500s. And because consideration of
their point of view is so important, each of the primary sources is
introduced by a header (a secondary source, written by a historian—
me, in fact) that identifies who wrote the document, when, and
more or less why. Students should consider the information in the
header carefully before reading the document that follows it and
should never confuse the two, because their status as sources is
worlds apart.

Let us turn, then, to the matter at hand. What was the Encounter
like? The sources collected in this chapter help us visualize it. The
first four sources describe the meeting of Europeans with nonsedentary people who lived in family groups and then semisedentary
people who lived in villages of a few hundred inhabitants. Such people
were typically exterminated by the Europeans after only a few years
of contact. Like the *Caminha Letter,* the account of Cabeza de Vaca
allows us to see them still intact. The writings of Las Casas, especially, provide a sense of the appalling process by which they were
destroyed—a process so appalling, in fact, and so unexpected, that
indigenous peoples seem to have needed to make sense of it, afterward, by fitting it retrospectively into their own traditions. Both
López de Gómara and Sahagún record indigenous "premonitions"
of conquest that actually arose after the fact.

The rest of the excerpts in this chapter deal with the Spanish
takeover of the fully sedentary Nahua peoples of what is today
central Mexico. Shortly before the arrival of the Spaniards, the
Nahuas had been gathered under the dominion of the Aztec
Empire, with its splendid capital city of Tenochtitlan. The people of

Tenochtitlan—the Mexicas, as they called themselves, though they tend to be called "Aztecs" in common parlance—had developed the most impressive and elaborate urban society in the New World. Their emperor Moctezuma ruled in splendor and with great authority, as strongly suggested by two documents included here: the eyewitness account of Bernal Díaz del Castillo and the later account authored by Sahagún, who drew on the testimony of indigenous informants, thus giving us a rare sense of how the Mexicas themselves viewed the Encounter.

[handwritten: he knew about the indigenous ppl' their lives) non-Euro perspective (Portugal)]

THE CAMINHA LETTER

Pero Vaz de Caminha

Pero Vaz de Caminha was a royal official on the Portuguese expedition that discovered Brazil in 1500. His letter dated May 1, 1500, reporting to the Portuguese king on the newly discovered territory, constitutes the earliest narrative of Portuguese contact with the semisedentary native people of what is today Brazil. To Caminha, the Island of the True Cross (as the expedition named what was not yet called Brazil) seemed a tropical paradise, an impression underlined by the fact that its inhabitants wore very little clothing. But the paradisiacal vision, no less than the jaundiced view of those who rabidly condemned the indigenous people, contained considerable self-delusion. Readers of the following excerpts of the Caminha letter should consider that Caminha wished not only to report on but also to promote the newly claimed territory. *[handwritten: advertising]*

We headed ashore in a small boat, and as we approached the mouth of the river, natives gathered there to meet us in groups of two or three, until eighteen or twenty of them awaited.

SOURCE: adapted from Pero Vaz de Caminha, *A Carta de Pero Vaz de Caminha* (Rio de Janeiro: Livros de Portugal, [1943]); folios 1–14 contain a facsimile and transcription of the original manuscript from 1500.

They had brown, rather reddish, skin and went completely naked, without any covering at all over their private parts, and they had bows and arrows in their hands. When we landed, they walked rapidly toward our boat, and Nicolau Coelho, the leader of our group, signed to them to lower their weapons, which they did. There was no way to speak with them or make ourselves understood in any way, however, because of the noisy surf. So Coelho merely gave them a few small gifts, such as a red cap, a black hat, and a linen bonnet that he took off his own head. In return, one of them gave him a feather headdress; and another gave him a string of tiny white pearl-like beads which, I believe, has been sent to Your Majesty. And then, because it was getting late and there was no way to talk to them, we returned to our ship.

These people have attractive, well-made features and take no thought of covering their bodies. They seem entirely unconcerned about concealing their genitals and display them with no more embarrassment than they feel in showing their faces. They wear a bit of pointed bone though their pierced lower lips, inserted from inside the mouth, which somehow poses no obstacle to their talking, eating, and drinking. They have straight hair and wear it cut short and shaved close above the ears. One of them wore something like a wig composed of yellow feathers several inches long around the back of his head, covering his ears. It was very thick and even, attached directly to his hair with a substance like wax, although it was not wax, and it was easily cleaned without removing it from his head.

When two of them later came aboard the flagship to speak with the admiral, he greeted them sitting down and dressed in finery, with a very large gold chain around his neck. The admiral's feet rested on a piece of carpet, and others of us (Sancho de Tovar, Simão de Miranda, Nicolau Coelho, Aires Correia) sat on the carpet around his feet. We lit torches and the visitors entered the cabin, but they made no courteous gestures nor did they signal a desire to speak to the admiral or to anyone else.

One of them fixed his eyes on the admiral's gold necklace and began to gesture toward it and, alternately, toward the ground, as if saying that there were gold there. Likewise, he spied a silver candlestick and did the same, pointing to the ground and then the candlestick, as if saying that there were silver in that country, as well. Seeing an African grey parrot that the admiral had with him, one of the visitors took it onto his hand and pointed at the ground, indicating that parrots lived there also. We showed them a sheep that we had aboard, but they paid no attention to it. We showed them a hen, and they seemed almost frightened of it and refused to hold it at first, finally accepting it with trepidation. We gave them food—bread, fish, dried figs, and sweets—which they hardly touched, and anything that they did put in their mouths they quickly spat out. We offered them wine, which they scarcely tasted and liked not at all, refusing to try any more after the first sip. We brought them water, which they refused to drink, merely rinsing their mouths and spitting it out.

One of them spied a rosary of white beads and signed that we should give it to him, whereupon he played with it for a long time. Finally, he put the rosary around his neck but soon took it off and, wrapping it around his arm, pointed at it, then at the admiral's gold necklace, then at the ground, as if saying that they would give gold for the rosary. That is how we preferred to interpret his gestures, in truth. If he were actually asking for both the rosary and necklace, saying they should stay there, we pretended not to understand because we had no intention of making such a gift. Eventually he returned the rosary to its owner.

Finally, the two visitors stretched out on the carpet to sleep, face up, making no effort to cover their private parts, which were uncircumcised. Their pubic hair was neatly trimmed and groomed. The admiral ordered that cushions be placed under their heads, and the one with the yellow-feather wig carefully arranged it on the cushion so that his headgear might not be damaged. We spread a cloak on top of them, which they accepted, and they soon fell asleep.

On Monday we went ashore to get water, and the natives again appeared, a goodly number, although not as many as on other occasions. This time very few of them carried bows. At first they kept their distance, but little by little they came nearer and mixed with us. They hugged us playfully. Some disappeared after a short time, but others stayed and traded us bows and arrows for trifles such as a sheet of paper or an old cap. Twenty or thirty of our men went with them to a place where there were many others, including girls and women, and they came back with more bows and feather headdresses, both yellow and green, of which I believe the admiral will certainly send a sample to Your Highness.

The admiral ordered a man called Afonso Ribeiro, and two other men who, like Ribeiro, were to be exiled on this shore as punishment, to go and mix with the natives, along with one Diogo Dias, whom he likewise ordered to mix with them, simply because he was good at amusing them. The three exiles were ordered to spend the night among the natives. They all went and did so. The village lay a good league and a half away and was composed of nine or ten high wooden dwellings with thatched roofs, each as long as a large sailing vessel. Each had only two small doors, one at each end. These long dwellings were each inhabited by thirty or forty people, but they were without interior subdivisions, being completely open with the exception of beams between which hung, at a considerable height, many hammocks for sleeping. Fires burned inside these dwellings and the people gave our men many kinds of food, especially manioc. But they would not let any of our men spend the night there and even wanted to come back to our ships. Our men had gone well provided with trinkets and they traded them to the natives for two beautiful large red parrots and two small green ones, as well as several feather bonnets and a quite beautiful sort of fabric woven of feathers, which the admiral is sending to Your Highness.

One day four hundred or four hundred and fifty of them came down to the beach, many with bows and arrows that they were willing to trade for an ordinary sailor's cap. By now they were willing to eat with us, whatever we gave them, and some drank wine. Not all of them were able to do so, but I believe that, once accustomed, they would drink it with a good will. They were so well put together, these natives, so carefully groomed, so striking in their body paint, as to have a pleasing appearance. They gladly helped us load our firewood into the boats. They seemed even more relaxed and self-assured among us than we did among them.

The admiral led us to the place where the large wooden cross that we intended to erect the following day stood leaning against a tree beside the river bank. He had us all kneel and kiss the cross so that they could see our reverence for it. We signed to the ten or twelve who had come with us, indicating that they, too, should kneel and kiss the cross, and they quickly did so.

These people seem so innocent that, if it were possible to understand their tongue, or if they could understand ours, they would become Christians immediately, because it seems that they have no faith of their own. Therefore, if the Christian exiles that we intend to leave on these shores learn the language of these people well and make themselves understood, I cannot doubt that the wishes of Your Highness will be achieved and with little difficulty they will come to belief in our Holy Faith. And God willing that it may be so, because they are truly a good and innocent people and can easily be shaped by us. I believe that Our Lord brought us to these shores for that very reason.

Analyzing the Sources: Where can one detect in Caminha's report his desire to promote the settlement of Brazil? What role does religion play in it?

SHIPWRECKS AND COMMENTARIES

Álvar Núñez Cabeza de Vaca

The Spanish explorer Cabeza de Vaca was shipwrecked on the coast of the Gulf of Mexico in 1527 and, barely surviving along with a few companions, made his way from Texas across northern Mexico to the Pacific Coast, leaving a priceless account of his adventures, the earliest European experiences in that part of the world. In this passage, he finds himself still near the Gulf of Mexico, among nonsedentary peoples who lived in small groups, often on the move. Here we get the Spanish explorer's skeptical description of hunter-gatherers, whose life involved difficult physical challenges. From the sixteenth through the nineteenth centuries, the rippling dislocations of European invasion and disease increased intertribal competition and warfare up and down the Americas. At the time of Cabeza de Vaca's visit in the 1520s, enormous American bison still grazed as far south as the Gulf Coast of Texas. Cabeza de Vaca was the first European to describe them.

These people's victuals are primarily roots of two or three kinds, which they search for wherever they go. They are very bad to eat and make you swell up. It takes two whole days to roast them, and even then many are bitter. To make matters worse, the things are hard to dig, too. But these people are so hungry for roots that they'll walk many miles to find them. Occasionally they hunt a deer or catch a fish. But they're so hungry that they eat all manner of insects and reptiles, and even man-killing venomous vipers and deer droppings and other things that I won't list. They even keep the bones of animals and fish to grind them up and eat them. But they don't plant any crops at all.

Nor do the warriors carry heavy loads, leaving that to the women and old men. Some of them habitually commit the Crime against Nature. And furthermore, they lie, steal, and cheat, and they use a certain thing to get intoxicated. They abduct their enemies' daughters for wives and scarcely attend to raising their own children. They are great runners. They can chase a deer without stopping from morning to night, without resting or getting tired, until the animal is exhausted. Sometimes they can take it alive. Their dwellings made of reed mats laid over arched poles. Every few days, they just pick of their dwelling and move them to a new location. Meanwhile, the women do all the work, sleeping only six hours out of every twenty-four. The rest of the night they spend tending the ovens where they dry their roots, and at dawn they commence to carry wood, haul water, and take care of everything else that needs doing.

SOURCE: Álvar Núñez Cabeza de Vaca, *Naufragios y Comentarios* (Madrid: Espasa-Calpe, 1971), pp. 52–54, 59–60, 106–08, 114.

They are spirited people, and no matter how hungry they might be, do not neglect their dances (*areitos*) and ceremonies. Their favorite time for gatherings is when the cactus ripens and they eat them and dance day and night. They eat them and drink the juice and dry others to eat when they leave that place. Many times when we had nothing to eat, the Indians told us not to worry, when the cactus ripened we would be happy, with our bellies full. They told us that five or six months beforehand. When the time came, though, it was so hot where the cactus grows, with so many kinds of biting mosquitoes, that we had to make great smouldering fires of damp wood all night to keep from being eaten alive, and we slept in the smoke, or tried to. Some of us went to sleep on the beach.

[*Eventually Cabeza de Vaca and his remaining three companions from the shipwreck made their way west to the Pacific Ocean. Their years among the Indians had taught them how to live off the land. Finding that many Indian groups expected healing magic from strangers such as themselves, Cabeza de Vaca's companion Castillo did his best to provide it, in which he was imitated by the other survivors of the shipwreck.*]

We found a place with many cactus, where we could satisfy our great hunger, and we gave thanks to Our Lord who never failed to provide for us. One day in the morning there appeared many Indians, five of them quite ill, and each of the five offered his bow and arrows, desperate for a cure. Castillo received them solemnly, and, just at sunset, he made the sign of the cross over each of the sick men and blessed them in the name of Our Lord, and all the rest of us prayed as best we could, that the Indians be healed. And Our Lord heard our prayers, because the next morning each of the sick men awoke in fine condition. The Indians were amazed, and we gave thanks to Our Lord, hoping this was a sign that He intended to rescue us from so many trials and tribulations. Our fame as healers spread far and wide, and Indians of many tribes came to us seeking cures. Castillo was called to heal an Indian who was about to die, but he was afraid to go, saying his sins might limit his healing powers, and so he sent me. When I arrived, it seemed that the patient had already died because people were around him crying, and they had already taken apart his dwelling, which is their custom when someone dies. His eyes were rolled back in this head, and he had no pulse. I prayed to Our Lord to heal the patient and anyone else who might be sick. After I'd made the sign of the cross and whispered my prayers many times, the Indians gave me the sick man's bow and took me to heal others.

[*Whether by luck, skill, or the power of placebo, Cabeza de Vaca's handful of survivors continued to heal the sick across northern Mexico until they finally made contact with other Spaniards. The first account of Cabeza de Vaca's adventures began to circulate almost immediately, in 1537.*

Within a few years, Cabeza de Vaca became the leader of a new Spanish expedition to the New World, this time to the Río de la Plata and Paraguay. His expedition landed on the Atlantic shore in what is today the Brazilian state of Santa Catarina and marched west to Paraguay, the first Europeans to do so. Cabeza de Vaca's previous experience had made him, in the view of many other Spanish adventurers, entirely too sympathetic to the indigenous people that he encountered now. These were the Guaraní people, a group related to the semisedentary Tupís, who existed throughout Brazil. Unlike the shipwreck narrative, with its intimate first-person detail, his account of the 1540–45 expedition to the Río de la Plata and Paraguay is a formal report, drafted by a secretary, and directed to the king. It calls Cabeza de Vaca "the Governor," because he had been granted that office by the king. Unfortunately for Cabeza de Vaca, his friendly attitude toward the indigenous people made him so unpopular with the other Spanish adventurers that his governorship was short lived.]

On second day of November 1541, the governor called everyone together, asking that each of us carry supplies for the road, in addition to what the Indian carriers had, and forthwith he marched out, followed by two hundred and fifty men armed with muskets and crossbows, twenty-six men on horseback, two friars, and a lot of Indians from the place of our landing. For nineteen days they marched through a mountainous and unpopulated terrain, until all their provisions were consumed, and it pleased God that they emerge then on a high plateau where there were many villages and prestigious chiefs, Añiriri, Cipoyay, and Tocanguanzu by name. And as they had heard that the governor was coming, these chiefs came out to greet us on the road, with food for us to eat, and gave us a most enthusiastic reception, to which the governor responded with enormous pleasure and affection. He insisted on paying them for the food and, furthermore, made many gifts to their headmen, and treated them with respect, which plainly delighted them.

These people are called Guaraníes. They are farmers who plant two crops of corn a year. In addition they plant manioc and keep birds similar to our chickens and ducks, as well as parrots in their houses for companions. There are many villages of them, all speaking the same language. In some ceremonies, they eat human flesh, mostly war captives. The captives come from on-going feuds among villages, for from raids against other tribes, or against Christians. And the governor took possession of these villages in the name of Your Majesty, a newly discovered land, that he called the Province of Vera. The name was inscribed in the official Act of Possession, penned on the spot by the royal notary Juan de Araoz. Then the governor was anxious to continue west to the river that the Indians call "big water," in their language, Iguazú.

The governor treated the Guaraníes so well that soon people were bringing supplies to us from all sides. He always paid for them, and then distributed the food among us so that we would not be tempted to steal from the Indians. The governor took great care to prevent his men from mistreating anyone, and so the Indians bought their women and children to see the Christians and especially the horses, which they found terrifying. We were "a sight to see," in their eyes, as they were in ours.

[*Cabeza de Vaca's expedition, like his subsequent governorship, was troubled not by threats emanating from the indigenous people but rather by dissension among various groups of Spaniards quarreling over the spoils of conquest.*]

We were now eager to arrive at Asunción. From the sixth to the tenth of January the expedition passed through several Guaraní villages, and at each the headmen came out to greet us as had become customary, offering food and surrounded by women and children. This time, however, the two friars went ahead of the rest and took all the food for themselves and the Indians who accompanied them. When the governor and the main party arrived there was no more food. The governor's men were angered by the friars' actions and complained that this was not the first occurrence of it, and that the friars had gathered around them too many useless Indian mouths to feed. These Indians ought to be left behind, they argued, but the friars refused to leave them. The men would have taken matters into their own hands had the Governor not prevented it, in the service of God and Your Majesty. Eventually the friars left us, in disobedience to the Governor's wishes.

Analyzing the Sources: What sorts of information are more likely to show up in a shipwreck narrative than in an official report?

A BRIEF ACCOUNT OF THE DESTRUCTION OF THE INDIES

Bartolomé de las Casas

The best-known and most efficacious of all Spanish spokesmen for the indigenous victims of the Spanish conquest of America was a Dominican friar, Bartolomé de las Casas (1484–1566). As a young man, las Casas witnessed the devastation of the semisedentary Taíno people of the island of Hispaniola (today divided between Haiti and the Dominican Republic), which he recounts in the following excerpt from his Brief Account of the Destruction of the Indies *(1552). After participating in the conquest of Hispaniola and Cuba, las Casas became an impassioned defender of the indigenous people of the New World and spent the rest of his life working in that capacity. His most important achievement was promoting passage of the New Laws of the Indies (1542), which protected the indigenous people against the practice of* encomienda, *whereby Spanish conquerors received legal rights to indigenous labor as a reward for conquest. Las Casas wrote the* Brief Account of the Destruction of the Indies *as part of that reform campaign. Translated into many languages, it became one of the most often-published diatribes in European history.*

Everything that has happened in the Indies between the moment of their remarkable discovery and the present day has been so astonishing that no one who did not see it all with his own eyes would be likely to believe it. Indeed, the happenings of the Indies seem to have obscured the fame of all other worldly deeds ever seen or heard of, however bold and notable they might have been. Some of the things that have occurred in the Indies, however, are quite terrible—the slaughter of innocent people, the depopulation of entire villages, provinces, and kingdoms, and many other acts no less horrifying. And for that reason Don Bartolomé de las Casas, after having been made a friar and finally a bishop, came to the royal court of Spain to inform our lord the Emperor, who had formerly looked with approval upon the happenings of the Indies, and when las Casas narrated the awful truth, it caused the most profound impact upon all who heard him, and his hearers begged him insistently to put these horrors succinctly into writing. And so he did. But seeing in later years many unfeeling men, their humanity degraded by their greed, ambition, and evil deeds, not content with the wickedness that they had already committed when they depopulated the Indies with the most exquisite forms of cruelty—seeing these same men petition the king for license to commit more such acts, and others yet worse (if worse could exist), las Casas decided to offer the present summary of the earlier treatise, so that his Highness would be reminded to refuse those petitions.

Las Casas has thought it appropriate to publish this summary in printed form so that his Highness might read it with greater ease. And that is the origin and purpose of the following, highly abbreviated account.

* * *

SOURCE: Bartolomé de las Casas, *Breuíssima relación de la destruyción de las Indias* (Seville: Sebastián Trugillo, 1552), pp. 2–3, 7–14.

The Indies were discovered in the year 1492. Christian Spaniards began to settle there in the following year. Therefore, it has been only forty-nine years since Spaniards in great numbers arrived, which they did first at the large and lovely Island of Hispaniola, which is six hundred leagues around. There are infinitely many other islands, some exceedingly large, everywhere around Hispaniola, all populous and filled with native-born peoples, the Indians. When we came upon the Indies, it was as well populated a land as any upon the earth. The seacoast of Venezuela remains filled as though with a beehive of people. It would appear that God set forth upon these lands an entire multitude, the greatest part of all humanity.

God made these people open and straightforward, without malice or guile, most obedient and most loyal to their native lords and to the Christians whom they serve. Of all the people of the earth, these natives are the most humble, most patient, most peaceful, the least quarrelsome or troublesome, the slowest to take offense, and most tranquil in demeanor. Hatred, rancor, and vengeance are utterly foreign to them. They are likewise physically slight and delicate, and unable to endure hard labor, perishing easily of any illness or disease. Not even the children of princes and lords raised among us are more physically delicate than the Indians, and I refer even to the humblest ones. Among nations, these people possess, and desire to possess, the fewest earthly goods of any. And, thus, they are never ambitious and never greedy. No saintly hermit ever satisfied himself with food more simple and meager than that which the Indians eat. Most go naked, covering only their private parts, and their most lavish clothing is a small cotton shawl. They sleep on straw mats or suspended in contrivances like fishing nets, and they call these "hammocks."

These people are among the purest, the most innocent, and the most intelligent imaginable, very receptive to good teachings, virtuous customs, and our holy Catholic faith. As soon as they learn a bit of Christian doctrine, they become eager to learn more, and I have been told by many Spaniards other than clergy, men who have dwelled in the Indies for years, that they see undeniable goodness in the Indians. "In truth," they say, "these people would be the most blessed on earth if they only knew God."

Upon this herd of gentle sheep, imbued by their Creator with all the aforesaid qualities, the Spaniards descended like starving wolves and tigers and lions. And what they have done for the last forty years, and continue to do, right down to today, is slay, torment, persecute, dismember, and destroy the Indians with refinements of cruelty never before seen, heard of, or read about in books, and so horribly, that on the Island of Hispaniola, of the over three million native people who lived there when the Spanish arrived, no more than two hundred remain. The island of Cuba—almost as lengthy as the distance from Valladolid to Rome—is today virtually depopulated. Puerto Rico and Jamaica, both of them large, lovely, and fertile islands, have been totally devastated. Not a living soul remains of the five hundred thousand who once dwelt in the Bahama Islands, which lie to the north of Hispaniola and Cuba, all of them more lovely than our king's gardens. These innocent victims perished while being brought to the island of Hispaniola when the Spaniards realized that the native population there was dying off. Another thirty small islands in the vicinity of Puerto Rico now lie deserted and uninhabited for the same reason. On the mainland to the south, there can be no doubt that our Spaniards, by their cruel and wicked acts, have depopulated and laid waste more than ten kingdoms, an area larger than the entire Iberian Peninsula—twice the territory between Seville and Jerusalem, a distance of more than two thousand leagues.

Beyond question, during the forty years in which Christians have devastated the Indies, more than twelve million souls, including men, women, and children, have died unjustly, and I do believe that a truer number would be above fifteen million.

Two principle methods have been employed by those who, calling themselves Christians, have annihilated these unfortunate Indians from the face of the earth. The first is war—unjust, cruel, bloody, and tyrannical war. The other method—applied after having slain all those who have resisted or tried to escape, which is to say, all the adult males, for the Spaniards customarily allow only young boys and females to live—the other method is the harshest bondage ever afflicted on man or beast.

The reason that the Christians have slain such an infinite number of souls has been the desire to take the Indian's gold, to enrich themselves quickly, and to raise themselves up to a high social rank that bears no relation to their humble origins in Spain. This insatiable greed and ambition knows no limits. These lands were so rich and favored by God, and the inhabitants so humble and easy to subjugate, that the Christians should have respected them, and yet they treated the Indians worse than beasts (to beasts they might have been more gentle), with less regard than one treats a pile of manure in the road. I speak as a firsthand witness, for I was present during the entire time. And with like disregard have the Christians mistreated the Indians' souls, for all these millions have died without our Christian faith and without the sacraments of the Church. And it is a widely known and undisputed truth, acknowledged by one and all, that the Indians never once did anything to hurt the Christians, but instead believed them to be descended from heaven, until becoming victims of so much robbery, savagery, and murder at their hands.

*　　*　　*

The Island of Hispaniola was the first where the Christians began their depredations, not content with what was freely given, taking the women and children of the Indians to serve them and eating the food produced by the Indians' hard work. The Indians have little, seldom more than they need, and in truth what suffices several Indian households for a month a Christian will consume in one day. The Indians soon realized that these newcomers had not come down from heaven, and some hid their provisions, others their women and children, while still others took refuge in the wilderness. The Christians struck them with clubs and seized the village chieftains. And such was their shameless temerity that a Christian captain raped the wife of their greatest king, lord of the entire island. Then the Indians began seeking ways to rid themselves of the Christians and took up arms. But their weapons are weak and ineffectual—so much so that their wars resemble a fight with wooden swords or a children's game in Spain—and at that, the Christians, with their horses and swords and lances, began the slaughter.

They entered villages and spared neither children nor old people, neither pregnant women, nor those with nursing infants. They made bets to see who could, with a single sword stroke, slice an Indian in half, spill his entrails, or cut off his head. They ran swords through a mother and child at once, or flung infants into rivers, laughing and making fun. They pulled babies from their mothers' breasts and swung them by the feet to smash their heads on rocks. They split open women's bellies and hacked them apart as though butchering lambs. They erected long gallows high enough to dangle thirteen Indians just above the ground, putting firewood around them to burn them alive—all in honor, or so they said, of our Redeemer and the twelve Apostles. They encased other Indians' bodies in dry straw to burn them that way. If they desired to let an Indian live, they cut both his hands nearly off, but left them dangling by the skin, as an example to those who had fled and hidden themselves. They killed the Indian nobles and lords by tying them on a grate over a slow fire, to roast them little by little until they died howling in agony.

On one occasion, I saw four or five Indian leaders being burned on grates in this way, with terrible screams, and perhaps the Spanish captain took pity on them, or possibly their cries were disturbing his sleep, because he ordered them strangled, but the executioner (whose name I know and whose kinsmen I have met in Seville) did not want to take the trouble, and so he simply shoved branches into their mouths to silence them and then stirred up the fire. And because some Indians fled and hid in the mountains, escaping from this pitiless savagery, the Spaniards trained fierce dogs to find them and tear them to pieces. These hounds did terrible carnage. And because sometimes—though seldom and for good reason—the Indians slayed a Christian, the Spaniards made a law that for every Christian slain, a hundred Indians would die.

I saw all the things that I tell of here and an infinity of similar things.

Analyzing the Sources: In addition to their gruesome nature, what other aspects of the events in the Indies would presumably displease the king of Spain?

GENERAL HISTORY OF THE INDIES

Francisco López de Gómara

Francisco López de Gómara (c. 1511–c. 1566) was a Spanish chronicler who, very unlike las Casas, never visited the Indies. Nonetheless, Gómara talked extensively with various conquerors upon their return to Spain, most notably with Cortés himself, whose personal chaplain he became. It is no surprise, then, that Gómara's writing was highly laudatory of the Spanish conquest in America and of Cortés in particular. Gómara's General History of the Indies (1552) attracted many readers because of its stylistic elegance, which is evident in the following excerpts from the opening dedication and from a brief chapter titled "Prophecies among the Indians of Hispaniola Concerning the Coming of the Spaniards." Gómara's distant vantage point and overemphasis on the role of Cortés inspired Bernal Díaz del Castillo, a veteran of the Cortés expedition, to respond with his own eyewitness account of events, which is also represented in this chapter.

DEDICATION

To Carlos, Holy Roman Emperor, King of Spain, Lord of the Indies and the New World

Sovereign Lord: The greatest event since the creation of the world, leaving aside the earthly incarnation and crucifixion of He who created it, has been the discovery of the Indies, and for that reason they are called a New World. The name comes not so much from the newness of their discovery as from their immense size, almost the size of the Old World, which comprises Europe, Africa, and Asia. This is also a New World because it is so different from our old one. The animals in general are not the same—the fish that swim, the birds that fly, the trees, fruit, herbs, and grains that grow—a remarkable thing for the Creator to have done, given that

---

SOURCE: Francisco López de Gómara, *Historia general de las Indias y Vida de Hernán Cortés* (Caracas: Biblioteca Ayacucho, 1979), pp. 7–8, 52–53.

the elements are the same there and here. The men, however, are like us, except for their color, for otherwise they would be beasts or monsters who could not possibly descend, as the Indians do, from Adam. They do not have writing or money or beasts of burden—things necessary for the well-ordered life of mankind—but it is not so unusual that, living in a hot climate and lacking wool and linen, they go naked. And as they do not know Our Lord, the true God, they commit the great sins of idolatry and human sacrifice, eating human flesh and conversing with the devil, as well as committing sodomy, intercourse with throngs of women, and such things.

On the other hand, all the Indians who have become your subjects have been converted to Christianity, by the goodness and grace of God and thanks to the efforts of Your Majesty and Your Majesty's parents and grandparents. In preaching and conversion no less than in discovery and conquest, the people of Spain have gladly shouldered the burden of this great work and its attendant dangers. No other nation has ever extended its customs, language, and armed might as Spain has, nor travelled so far, by land and sea, to make its conquests. And Spain would have discovered, conquered, and converted even more had Your Majesty not needed to pursue other wars in Europe. God chose to reveal the existence of the Indies to Your Majesty's vassals, as many wise men say, precisely to insure the work of conversion, because the Spaniards, who have ever fought against infidels, began their conquest of the Indians as soon as they had finished conquering the Moors.

ON PROPHECIES AMONG THE INDIANS OF HISPANIOLA CONCERNING THE COMING OF THE SPANIARDS

When Christopher Columbus was on the island of Hispaniola, certain caciques*—along with the wise men who, among the Indians, conserve the people's memories—told him about what their idols in years past had predicted concerning the coming of the Spaniards. The Indians had inquired of their idols about the future and had

---

Cacique means local indigenous chieftain. The Spanish picked up the word in the Caribbean and then applied it elsewhere.

fasted for five days, without eating or drinking anything, and they had cried and mortified their flesh in supplication and burned the great quantities of incense that the ceremonies of their religion require. And finally the idols answered that, although they normally conceal the shape of things to come, and do so for the good of men, they would reveal the future in recognition of such fervent devotion. Then the idols predicted the coming of bearded men with bodies entirely covered by clothing, men who carried shining swords capable of splitting someone in two with a single blow. These bearded men would cast down the idols, they predicted, and punish those who performed their rites, and they would spill the blood of the Indians or carry them away in captivity. And hearing this horrifying prediction, the people had composed a sad and mournful song to be sung in the dance ceremony that they call an *areito*, and remembering that song, the Indians had fled from the Spaniards upon their arrival. Let each reader form his own opinion of this story, which I no more than report as the Indians told it.

However that may be, all these things did come to pass in exactly the manner foretold in the areito, because the Spaniards did indeed slice apart many Indians with their swords, both in wars and later, in the mines, and they cast down all the idols, so that not a single one remained, also prohibiting all their rites and ceremonies. The Spaniards enslaved the Indians and made them labor for their new masters harder than they were able to endure, so that some simply died and others killed themselves. That is why, of a hundred and fifty thousand inhabitants on that island alone, no more than five hundred remain today. Some died of overwork, others of hunger, and many of smallpox. Some killed themselves by drinking poison and others by hanging themselves from trees, women as well as men, and they found ways to abort their pregnancies so as not to bear children who would be forced to serve the Spaniards. God must have been punishing the Indians for their sins, but it is also true that the Spaniards were guilty of treating them very badly, valuing gold over the welfare of their fellow men.

Analyzing the Sources: What about Gómara's comments gains credibility since his overall purpose is to praise Spanish conquest of the New World?

CHRONICLE OF NEW SPAIN

Francisco Cervantes de Salazar

Francisco Cervantes de Salazar was born around 1514 in Spain, where he studied at the prestigious University of Salamanca and published a number of works on philosophical and theological topics before traveling to New Spain (as Mexico was called in the colonial period) at mid-century to become one of the first professors at the University of Mexico City. Cervantes de Salazar's Chronicle of New Spain *(written in about 1560 but not published until the nineteenth century), like the work of Gómara, assigns a heroic role to Cortés, and it presents a notably negative portrait of the indigenous people, whose supposed general characteristics are outlined in the following excerpt. Obviously, the author is quite biased against the indigenous people, but this primary source is not useless if we read it "against the grain," looking for meanings that the author did not intend to communicate.*

There is no nation so barbarous, so riddled with defects, that some virtuous and intelligent men cannot be found in its midst. Nor, to the contrary, is there any nation so wise and politic as to harbor none who are dishonorable or inclined toward vice. Thus, although the inhabitants of this enormous land were in general barbarous, as I will indicate, nonetheless there were among them some wise men, as will become evident in my later discussion of their laws.

Overall, however, one may say of the Indians that they are gullible, pusillanimous, and attracted by any sort of novelty. They pay scant heed to their honor and reputation. They are so fond of ceremonies of all kinds, that many authorities have affirmed on that basis that the Indians must somehow descend from Jews. Most are cowardly, and although some among them are called *tiacanes*, which is a way of saying "brave," their bravery is remarkable only in comparison to the cowardice of the majority. They are extremely vindictive

---

SOURCE: Francisco Cervantes de Salazar, *Crónica de la Nueva España* (Madrid: The Hispanic Society of America, 1914), pp. 30–31.

and commonly spend in suing one another much more than the value of the object of their lawsuits. They cannot keep a secret at all. Furthermore, as servants they respond only to threat of punishment, and fear alone motivates them to do a job well, so they have little respect for any master who is not stern enough or who treats them affectionately. They are such ingrates that even when they have been raised in the households of Spanish masters from whom they have received many benefits over the years, they quite easily abandon those masters when the opportunity arises. They are so fickle that they change their minds for the slightest reason. Most of them are simple-minded and have little to say, and therefore although some have managed to learn Latin, none can advance in the study of any science requiring a higher level of intelligence. They are so greedy as to be willing, when the reward is sufficient, to take their own parents prisoner (when caught in the crime of drunkenness or some other) and turn them in to the authorities by force. They are completely lazy and tend to remain inactive whenever not impelled to labor by the need to provide themselves with shelter and sustenance, and they can easily spend an entire day sitting on their heels, as they commonly do, and hardly speaking, even when in the company of others. The cause of this behavior is a predominance of phlegm in their physical composition, rendering them excessively phlegmatic, which, while in general not a good thing, does suit them for certain crafts that, no matter how experienced the craftsman, are only done well when done slowly.

The Aztec emperor Moctezuma knew his subjects very well and thus governed them more effectively than any other heathen prince. Moctezuma often told Cortés that, as emperor, he kept his people in line and imposed justice principally through physical discipline and corporal punishment. They quite willingly attend dance ceremonies that last all day without a rest, and there is not a single one of them, no matter how elevated his status, who does not act proud of getting totally drunk, and scarce one who does not behave badly and even commit serious crimes when under the influence of alcohol. They are generally clumsy at everything except for archery and tend to behave dishonorably on the battlefield. They are quick to follow bad examples and slow to follow good ones. They are disloyal even with their friends, and so much so, that all kinds of contracts suffer more frequent violations among them than among us. They eat sparingly in their own houses, but gobble up everything when eating at someone else's expense and seem never to get full, no matter how much food they are given. They earn more than they deserve to and then do not spend it on property or dowries for their daughters, but rather, on alcoholic drink, whether Castilian wine, or worse, something called *pulque*, a foul-smelling, foul-tasting wine that they make from agave. This pulque makes them drunk and senseless faster and more violently than wine from grapes, and the more that we prohibit it, the more they insist on consuming it.

> **Analyzing the Sources:** *This selection arguably tells us more about the self-image of the colonizers than about the true characteristics of the colonized. Explain by reading against the grain.*

THE TRUE HISTORY OF THE CONQUEST OF NEW SPAIN

Bernal Díaz del Castillo

Bernal Díaz del Castillo was among the Spanish adventurers who accompanied the Cortés expedition that entered and, with the eventual collaboration of thousands of indigenous allies, ultimately destroyed the Aztec capital, Tenochtitlan (here called the City of Mexico). Díaz del Castillo was of humble background and objected to accounts of the expedition that gave too little credit to rank-and-file members of the expedition, especially the account written by Francisco López de Gómara (author of a previous selection). Therefore, in his old age, decades after the Cortés expedition, now resident in Guatemala, the aging conquistador wrote his own True History of the Conquest of New Spain, *which is excerpted here. Eyewitness accounts, such as this one, have their own biases, of course.*

We proceeded along the causeway eight paces wide that ran straight as an arrow across the water toward the City of México ahead of us. And because it was so sturdy and well-made, the causeway was thronged with people, some entering the city and some coming out to see us, so many that we were hardly able to pass, crowds of people everywhere, on the towers and pyramids and in canoes, people who had come from all over the lake. And it was not to be marveled at, for they had never before seen horses nor men like us. We beheld such wondrous sights that we hardly knew what to say or whether what we saw ahead of us was real—large buildings standing along the shore and many others rising from the waters full of canoes. And along the causeways were many bridges at intervals, and before us stood the great City of Mexico.

We numbered not even four hundred and fifty soldiers, and we well remembered the warnings that we had received about not entering the City of Mexico because, once inside, we would surely be killed. Let curious readers ponder what I am writing here. Have men ever shown greater daring than this? But let us go on down this causeway and continue the tale.

When we reached a point where another, smaller causeway branches off in the direction of Coyoacán, where there are towering buildings for prayer, we found the pavement crowded again with great caciques clad in fine mantels, each distinct from the others, all sent to greet us by the great Moctezuma. And when they came before Cortés they bade us welcome in their language, and as a sign of peace each touched and kissed the ground with his hand. Then the great Moctezuma approached, carried in a rich litter and accompanied by lords and caciques with vassals of their own. And the great Moctezuma got down from his litter and the surrounding caciques supported him with their arms beneath a splendid canopy that was a delight to look upon, the color of green feathers embroidered with gold and silver and bordered with a fringe of pearls and other precious things. The great

Source: adapted from Bernal Díaz del Castillo, *The True History of the Conquest of New Spain*, trans. Alfred Percival Maudslay (London: Hakluyt Society, 1910), pp. 2:39–44.

Moctezuma was richly attired in his manner, wearing the sandals that they call *cotaras*, their normal footwear, except that the soles of these were golden, and the uppers were adorned with precious stones. And the four lords at his sides were likewise richly dressed in garments that they had donned especially for this moment. Many other lords came ahead of Moctezuma sweeping the path where he would tread and spreading cloth upon it so that his feet would not touch the ground. Not one of all these caciques thought for a moment of looking their Moctezuma in the face, but rather, kept their eyes lowered with great reverence, excepting only those who supported him with their arms, for these were members of his family.

And when Cortés was told that the great Moctezuma was approaching, and when he saw him coming, he dismounted from his horse, and when he was near Moctezuma, the two paid reverence to one another. Moctezuma offered words of welcome and our Cortés responded through his interpreter, doña Marina, desiring Moctezuma good health. Moctezuma offered his hand and Cortés brought out a necklace that he held ready for that moment, glass beads of many colors and patterns strung on a golden cord and sweetly scented with musk, and he placed it around the neck of the great Moctezuma. And when he had so placed it, he was going to embrace him, but the lords who accompanied Moctezuma held Cortés back for they considered it an indignity. And then Cortés said to Moctezuma through doña Marina, his interpreter, who stood close at his side, that his heart rejoiced at seeing so great a prince and that he considered it a great honor, among many others, that Moctezuma had come to greet him in person. And Moctezuma answered Cortés with similar courtesies, and he instructed his two nephews, who were among the lords who stood at his elbows, the Lord of Coyoacán and the Lord of Texcoco, to go with us and show us to our lodgings. And Moctezuma, with the other two relations, the Lord of Cuitlahuac and the Lord of Tacuba, who accompanied him, returned to the city, and all the rest who had come out with him, all the other lords and caciques with their entourage, returned with him. And as they turned back after their prince we stood watching them and observed how they all went with their eyes fixed on the ground without looking at their lords, but only following as inconspicuously as possible, with great reverence.

Thus space was made for us to enter the streets of Mexico without being so much crowded. But who could count the multitude of men and women and boys who filled the streets and rooftops and floated in canoes on the canals to see us enter the city? It was indeed a wonderful thing, something that even now as I write this years afterward, appears before my eyes as if it happened only yesterday. And such was our daring and fortunate entrance into Tenochtitlan, the great City of Mexico, on the eighth day of November, in the year of our saviour Jesus Christ, 1519.

> *Analyzing the Sources: What interest did Díaz del Castillo have in writing, and how is it represented in the excerpt that you have just read?*

A GENERAL HISTORY OF NEW SPAIN

Bernardino de Sahagún

Franciscan friar Benardino de Sahagún, born in 1499, was one of the most significant of the early missionaries to the New World. During the middle 1500s, Sahagún interviewed indigenous elders in their own language, Nahuatl, to reconstruct aspects of pre-Encounter Aztec life and culture. The results of this investigation were recorded in a body of work of enormous importance, the trilingual Florentine Codex, the Spanish-language portion of which became the General History of New Spain, *excerpted here. While Sahagún's works indubitably represent an indigenous point of view, readers must consider that his informants were interviewed many decades after the events that they recounted and had been raised and educated in a postconquest, Christian context. Moctezuma's confusing welcome to Cortés as a returning deity is almost certainly a retrospective addition of Sahagún's informants, who wanted to explain how the Aztec emperor was misled by false prophecy.*

As the Spaniards approached Tenochtitlan, Moctecuzoma arrayed himself in his finery to go out to receive them. Many great lords and princes accompanied him to receive Cortés and the other Spanish captains in peace and with honor. They took with them large, painted trays upon which were heaped strings of beautiful and fragrant flowers and necklaces of gold and precious gems. Moctecuzoma himself placed a necklace of gold and precious gems around the neck of Cortés, and he put the garlands of flowers around the necks of the other Spanish captains, according to our customs of greeting.

Then Cortés asked him if he were indeed the great king Moctecuzoma. And the king replied, "I am Moctecuzoma," and he made a great reverence before Cortés, and then he stood proudly and moved close, face to face with Cortés, and he spoke to him this manner, saying: "Oh, great lord! Welcome! Be at home in this land, among our people, in this city of Mexico. You have come here to sit on a throne that belongs to you, a throne that I have possessed in your name for merely a few days, a throne that other kings who came before me also possessed in your name, awaiting your coming, one who was called Itzcoatl, and another, Moctecuzoma the Elder, and another, Axayacatl, and another, Tizoc, and another Ahuitzol. I am the last among those who has ruled the people of Mexico in your name. Would that the others, who are no longer among the living, could witness your presence! They cannot see you, my lord, but I can see you, for I am not asleep, nor is this a dream. I have waited many days for this occasion. For days my heart has looked in the direction of your coming, and now you have emerged from the clouds, from the mists, from the most hidden of places, to stand among us. It is just as was foretold by the kings who came before me, saying that you would return to rule over us, that you would return to sit upon your throne. And behold, it is true. Welcome! Long roads have you trod to come to us! Rest, now. You have returned to your home, to occupy your palaces. Take them and rest with these, your captains, who have made the journey with you."

SOURCE: Bernardino de Sahagún, *Historia general de las cosas de Nueva España* (Mexico City: Editorial Nueva España, 1946), pp. 3:41–45.

When Moctecuzoma had finished his speech, Marina, who was his interpreter, an Indian woman who could speak both Spanish and Nahuatl, translated it for Cortés, and Cortés replied: "Tell Moctecuzoma to have no fear, that I love and esteem him greatly, and that my men will do no harm to anyone. Tell him that we have desired for a long time to see his face and come to know him, that we are very pleased finally to have done so. We are happy to have arrived at his city, where we will have time to speak at length." Cortés took Moctecuzoma by the hand, and together they entered the city and went to the royal palace.

And the great lords who were present with Moctecuzoma on this occasion were the lord of Texcoco, whose name was Cacamatzin; the lord of Tlacopan, whose name was Tetlepanquetzatzin; the governor of Tlatelolco, whose name was Itzquauhtzin; and Moctecuzoma's treasurer, whose name was Topantemoctzín. Many lesser figures were also present, such as Cuappiatzin, Atlixcatzín tlacateccatl, Tepeoatzin tlacochcalcatl, Quetzalaztatzin ticociaoacatl, and Totomotzin hecatempatiltzin, but when the Spaniards made Moctecuzoma a prisoner, all of these abandoned him and hid themselves.

No sooner had the Spaniards entered the royal palace than they placed Moctecuzoma under guard and never afterward let him out of their sight, and along with him, Itzquauhtzin, the governor of Tlatelolco. These two the Spaniards kept with them, and they let the rest go. And then they fired off their cannon, and the roar and smoke stunned the Indians, who stumbled around as if drunk and then scattered, horrified, in all directions. A mortal terror crept through the city that night, and early the next morning orders came from the palace in the name of Cortés and Moctecuzoma, commanding the city to furnish provisions of food for the Spaniards and fodder for their horses. Moctecuzoma insisted greatly that these things should be brought, and certain officials of the city did not want to obey his detailed instructions, nor to talk to Moctecuzoma while he was a prisoner of the Spaniards. Nonetheless, they did supply the necessary provisions.

When the Spaniards had thoroughly installed themselves in the royal palace, they began to question Moctecuzoma about the royal treasure, where it was located, and he sent them to the treasure house called Teucalco, which was full of priceless feathers, jewels, and gold, and this treasure was spread before the Spaniards. The Spaniards began to tear the gold from the feather adornments and ornamental shields used in the ceremonial dances. They tore these things to pieces, and they melted the gold down into bars. They took the most precious jewels, as well, leaving the lesser ones for their Indian allies from Tlaxcala. The Spaniards also looted the royal palace, taking everything that they desired for themselves.

And having done all of this, they asked to see Moctecuzoma's private chamber, and he took them to it. The Spaniards were overjoyed, knowing that they would find much gold there, and when they arrived they looted the entire contents of the royal chamber and stripped the gold and jewels from all its feathered adornments, and they threw the feathers into the patio for the benefit of their Indian allies. Then Cortés gave orders to Marina, his interpreter, and she began to shout to the officials of the city, commanding them to bring food to feed the Spaniards, but no one dared come close to them because the entire city was so terrified. The men who finally took them food trembled as they carried it to the palace, and as soon as they had delivered it, they hurried away in fright.

[Weeks later, the Aztecs prepared one of their most important religious festivals, Tóxcatl, celebrated on behalf of their chief deity, Huitzilopochtli, the hummingbird god. On Tóxcatl, the idol representing Huitzilopochtli would not spend the day atop a pyramid. Instead, his people would dance before him. Many great nobles of Tenochtitlan would enter a special temple courtyard to take part. The Spaniards, too, asked to be invited. The massacre that ensued was similar to other events around the Americas during which Europeans used previously unknown, and therefore terrifying, weapons against the indigenous people.

On the morning of the Tóxcatl festival . . .]

The priests unveiled the face of the idol, which they had adorned with precious feathers, and then they formed a line before it. There they raised a cloud of incense and placed before the god a variety of delicacies, perhaps including human flesh. All the men, our strongest, most beautiful warriors, were called to dance before Huitzilopochtli. They desired with all their hearts to show their guests the splendor of their festival, the power of their deity, and the greatness of their city.

At a given hour, people flooded into the courtyard. There, before the idol, they readied themselves for the snake dance. And so it began, when all were present, so began the singing, so began the snake dance. The people formed a line. Those who had fasted to purify themselves for Tóxcatl, directed the others. Those who had fasted during an entire year, had shown themselves most worthy and were called "brothers of Huitzilopochtli." The purified ones carried long wooden staffs to assure the most decorous order among the multitude. At the head of the column went our valiant war captains, then mature warriors followed, at a slight distance, by the younger warriors who had never taken a prisoner in battle, or never done it by themselves. The proven warriors taunted the inexperienced ones, saying, "let us see how brave you are!"

It was then, as people surrendered themselves to the festival of Tóxcatl, raising their voice of celebration higher and higher, each song overflowing the last, like crashing waves, that the Spaniards decided to start killing. They blocked the entrances to the sacred courtyard, pulled out their swords, and stepped immediately among the dancers and the musicians. One drummer who continued to play lost both arms at a single sword stroke. Then the sword sliced off the drummer's head, which fell far from his body. Then all the swords started cutting us apart. Approaching our warriors from behind, the Spaniard reached around and sliced open bellies, so that our warriors' entrails spilled out. Steel swords sliced our warriors' heads like melons, split shoulders, severed legs. Entrails spilled to the ground. Some tried to run and became entangled in them. Those who wished to save themselves found nowhere to turn. The entrances to the courtyard were clogged with gore. Some tried to climb the walls and were cut down. Others pretended to be dead to save themselves. Lying still among the corpses, they had a chance, but if any one of them stood up, he was spotted and finished off.

The blood of our warriors flowed like water at the festival of Tóxcatl.

Analyzing the Sources: What elements in the Sahagún/Nahua version of Cortés's arrival in Tenochtitlan contrast with Bernal Díaz del Castillo's account of the same event? What is the significance of the differences?

THE LAST DAYS OF THE SIEGE OF TENOCHTITLAN

Anonymous Nahual Poet

One of the very earliest pieces of evidence of Nahua responses to the destruction of Tenochtitlan is a poem written in the Aztec language, Nahuatl. While not dated, it was apparently written around 1524 while the ruins of the Aztec capital were still smoldering. It is therefore very much a primary source. On the other hand, the meaning of a poem translated from Nahuatl into Spanish and then from Spanish into English, at intervals of centuries, will survive only in basic outline. A basic gist is all we can be sure of in this text. Yet, the gist is meaningful and hard to miss.

All this we saw.
This amazing sorrow,
All this, befell us.
Bitter was our fate!

Broken bones in the streets,   5
And people's hair,
The houses, wrecked,
White masonry, reddened.

SOURCE: *Ms. Anónimo de Tlateloco*, 1528 (Biblioteca Nacional de México).

Maggots in the dirt.
Brains splattered on the walls.   10
Waters running red,
Tasting of saltpetre.

Great walls of our city,
Riddled with holes,
Our shields were your defense.   15
Bitter was your fate!

Analyzing the Sources: Whom does the poet seem to blame for what happened to Tenochtitlan?

Chapter 2

COLONIAL TRANSCULTURATION

Gradually, indigenous Americans and their new European overlords changed each other's ways and created new cultures that were neither indigenous nor European. Africans also played a role in the process, as will be documented in the next chapter. For now, however, we will explore the theme of indigenous/European interactions in South America after the Encounter, during the "mature colonial period" (the 1600s and afterwards).

The primary location of early colonization in South America was in the high Andes, especially Peru. Two things attracted colonizing energies into the Andes. Of these, large populations of fully sedentary farmers constituted the main attraction. The Spanish wanted, above all, to extend their control over prosperous, well-organized societies, and they found exactly that in the Inca Empire. Of secondary, but still enormous, importance, were the silver mines located in the same region, especially the fabulously productive "mountain of silver" at Potosí, probably the single greatest silver mine in the history of the world.

Two lengthy and valuable primary sources provide evidence about indigenous Peruvian understandings of colonization: the works of Garcilaso de la Vega (or "El Inca Garcilaso," as he is usually called) and Felipe Guaman Poma de Ayala (Guaman Poma, for short), excerpted for this chapter. Both men were of indigenous descent, each having one foot in the indigenous world and one in the Spanish world. Thus both exemplify the cultural process of give and take that scholars of Latin America called *transculturation*. Guaman Poma (whose name is entirely indigenous) spoke the two major indigenous languages of the Andes, Quechua and Aymara, but his Spanish was shaky, and he never left Peru. El Inca Garcilaso (whose name echoes that of a great Spanish poet) lived most of his life in Spain and wrote superb Spanish. Both Guaman Poma and El Inca Garcilaso were spokesmen for an indigenous perspective, though in contrasting ways. Guaman Poma wrote a white-hot denunciation of Spanish abuses, while El Inca Garcilaso wrote a tactful history designed to set Spanish readers at ease even as he insisted on the value and dignity of all things indigenous. Both authors were pious Catholics and loyal subjects of the Spanish Crown. In addition to these two documents, a third and final excerpt on colonial Peru offers a total contrast to both: the screed of a Spanish official who disregards, and even disdains, the indigenous perspective.

Two other primary sources in this chapter deal with the semisedentary peoples of South America, who had not been part of the Inca Empire and whose interaction with the European invaders led, in some cases, to the indigenous population's total annihilation. Because semisedentary people had to move, occasionally, in order to feed themselves, Europeans could not simply conquer and rule over them as they ruled over sedentary peoples. Instead, semisendentary peoples had to be captured and enslaved or, alternatively, attracted into mission settlements. Missions were, in fact, the principal form of colonization in much of Latin America, most of which—including such far-flung areas as northern Mexico and the Orinoco and Amazon Basins—was inhabited by semisedentary or nonsedentary peoples. The Guaraní missions of Paraguay (and surrounding areas) were among the most notable (and certainly the most famous) missions in South America. Jesuit Father Cardiel's description of mission life in this chapter will give some indication of larger patterns that extended through many parts of Brazil, where Jesuits were the principal missionaries. The missionaries were paternalistic, which means that they sincerely wanted to benefit the indigenous people but had no qualms about trying to "improve" indigenous ways. Still, given the large predominance of indigenous populations in mission areas, two-way transculturation was inevitable. The phenomenon is easily observable in Father Cardiel's discussion of church festivals in the missions.

Some semisendentary people resisted missionization and also eluded destruction. That was the case of the Mapuches of southern Chile, who battled Spanish conquerors to a stalemate that lasted for centuries. One Spanish captive, taken prisoner in this ongoing battle with the Mapuches, wrote an account of his "happy captivity," excerpted for this chapter. His narrative represents the common phenomenon of European captives or castaways who, finding themselves immersed in indigenous societies, learned the language of their captors and came to respect their cultures. The shipwrecked Cabeza de Vaca comes to mind. In addition, such captives usually married into the indigenous societies, something that the narrative of happy captivity clearly suggests as a possibility.

Finally, two expressions of colonial control. *The Book of Visitation of the Holy Office of the Inquisition* will amaze you with transcripts of testimony given to the Portuguese version of this famous institution. The testimony describes magical treatments for sickness that the Inquisition views as witchcraft, a true showcase of transculturation. *A Guide for Inexperienced Travellers,* on the other hand, treats us to the sneering, exploitative, supercilious attitude of a Spanish colonial bureaucrat. Like the racist vitriol served up by Professor Cervantes de Salazar in the last chapter, the guide's repellent attitude was only too common among his contemporaries. It's a short, bracing selection that, like that of Cervantes de Salazar, may serve as a salutary inoculation.

ROYAL COMMENTARIES OF THE INCAS

Garcilaso de la Vega

El Inca Garcilaso was the son of a Spanish conqueror and an Inca princess. Born in 1539 in Cuzco, the former Inca capital of Peru, he lived as a child with his mother and then traveled to Spain as a young man to seek his fortune and spent the rest of his life there, receiving a Spanish education, serving in the Spanish army, and becoming a great master of Spanish prose style. While thoroughly adapted to life in Spain, he nonetheless maintained a powerful identification with his mother's people, and his Royal Commentaries of the

Incas *(1609), excerpted here, is one of the most valuable histories of pre-Columbian and conquest-era Peru. Readers should note that he uses the word* Inca *to refer to the emperor and members of his family, not to the inhabitants of the empire generally. And here's yet another retrospective premonition of conquest.*

THE AUTHOR'S EXPLANATION CONCERNING THIS HISTORY

During my childhood I heard stories, told in the manner of fables recounted to children, about matters I narrate in this book. Afterward, when I was older, my elders related in detail the laws and government of the Incas, comparing them to the laws and government of the Spaniards, with particular attention to the rigorous punishment of various crimes. My elders told me of the Incas' actions in peace and in war, of how the Incas had treated their vassals and how these had served them. Moreover, with the candor proper to parents speaking to their own children, they related their idolatries, enumerating all the rites, ceremonies, and sacrifices, all the feast days, both major and minor, and how they were celebrated. They spoke of their superstitions and false beliefs, of their omens, good and ill, and of how they interpreted sacrifices and other signs. In sum, I learned from them everything about their state and society, so much that, were I to write it all here, this work would be even longer than it is.

In addition to having told me all of this, I saw with my own eyes many idolatrous and superstitious practices that still persisted in my childhood. I was born only eight years after the Spaniards seized control of our country, and I lived there until I was twenty years old. Some of the heathen ways of which I was witness did not fully disappear until I was twelve or thirteen years old. And even beyond what elders of my own family told me, beyond what I witnessed with my own eyes, I have acquired further knowledge of the Inca monarchs, of their deeds and conquests, by writing to men who studied

---

SOURCE: adapted from Garcilaso de la Vega, *Primera parte de los Comentarios reales* (Lisbon: Oficina de Pedro-Crassbeek, 1609), pp. 1:48–50; 2:249–51; 2:252–57; 2:267; 2:269–70; 2:278–79.

with me at school in Cuzco when I decided to write this history, asking each of them to supply information particular to their respective provinces of origin, because each province has its own annals and retains special memories of what transpired there. My former schoolmates, taking my request to heart, relayed it to family members in their provinces of origin, and their families, upon learning that an Indian, a son of Peru, wished to write a history of their native land, gladly supplied the requested information, and thus did I piece together a complete picture of each Inca emperor's rule.

From the apparently fabulous beginnings of Inca rule derive the great domains that Spain today possesses in Peru, for which cause the telling of these fables is permissible and worthwhile, and I promise to tell no more than what I heard at my mother's knee and afterward learned in the manner that I have indicated. And I promise further not to omit anything condemnable or invent anything praiseworthy to augment the virtues of the heathens, who verily swim in a sea of error. And further yet, I will not write of new topics previously unheard of, but rather, will discuss the matters written about by Spanish historians who have chronicled the things of Peru and its Inca rulers, quoting their words when need be, to show that I am not improvising fictions in favor of my family and relations. For the most part, I will merely amplify elements that Spanish authors have left incomplete because their sources were themselves incomplete, and, occasionally, correct errors rooted in that same reason. Moreover, I will add facts of unquestionable truth omitted in earlier accounts but leave out apocryphal episodes that they may have inserted thanks to false reports or confusions of place and time or misunderstandings that have their origins in an imperfect comprehension of Quechua. In truth the most knowledgeable Spaniard knows only a fraction of the possible meanings of a given word and often confuses words of similar pronunciation.

THE LAST TESTAMENT AND DEATH OF HUAYNA CÁPAC AND HIS PREDICTION CONCERNING THE COMING OF THE SPANIARDS

One day during the royal Inca Huayna Cápac's stay in the Kingdom of Quito, he took a chill upon bathing for pleasure in a highland lake. The chill, which the Indians call *chucchu*, meaning "trembling," was followed by a fever, which they call *rupa*, meaning "burning," and on subsequent days, given that he felt ever worse and worse, the emperor believed that he was dying, because his death in this manner had been foretold years earlier by a sorcerer or *amauta*, a heathen "soothsayer," "priest," or "wise man." Omens such as these regarding the person of the emperor were accorded great authority in those idolatrous times because they were said to be revelations coming directly from the royal Inca's celestial father, the Sun. Aside from these demonic prognostications made by sorcerers, there appeared other omens, frightening comets in the skies (one of them green in color and horrifying in the extreme), and a bolt of lightning that struck the Inca's very house, as well as other prodigious signs that alarmed the amautas. They augured not only the death of Huayna Cápac but also the end of his royal bloodline, the destruction of his empire, and other great calamities destined to affect our society as a whole and to devastate each of its members. The amautas did not dare to publicize their predictions, however, lest the highly impressionable people, who were quick to believe in such things, become paralyzed with dread.

Huayna Cápac, feeling very ill, summoned his children and the other relatives whom he had near him, as well as the governors and military leaders of the surrounding provinces who dwelt near enough to be able to arrive in time. Speaking first to those of royal blood, he said: "I will soon go to rest in heaven with Our Father the Sun, who revealed to me years ago that a river or lake would cause my death. My having emerged from the waters of a lake with my current illness constitutes a sure sign that Our Father is calling me to him now. Once I am dead, you should open my corpse in the manner that we are accustomed to do with the bodies of deceased royalty. I command that my heart and entrails be buried in Quito as a sign of the love that I bear for that land. Take the rest of my body back to Cuzco to be interred alongside those of my parents and grandparents. To your care I entrust my beloved son Atahualpa, who will replace me as Inca in Quito and everywhere else that he is able to bring under his imperium, whether by the influence of his royal person or by the triumph of arms. I enjoin those of you who are my war captains, especially, to obey Atahualpa with the fidelity and love that you properly owe to your sovereign, in anything that he may command, and these very things I will reveal to him forthwith, by order of Our Father the Sun. Be just and merciful, all of you, with the vassals of our realm, so that we do not lose our reputation as true benefactors of the humble. I charge you to behave always as befits Incas, true Children of the Son."

Having spoken these words to his children and other relatives, he then addressed the captains and *kurakas** not of royal blood, citing the loyalty and obedience properly owed to the sovereign, and then saying: "For many years it has been known to us by revelation of Our Father the Sun that following the reigns of twelve of his children as royal Incas, new people, not hitherto known, would appear among us, and that the newcomers would conquer us and add this, our territory, to their own empire, along with many other territories. And I suspect that the strangers who have recently appeared on the shores of our sea are those whose coming is foretold and that they must be intrepid and powerful people who will have the advantage over us in all things. My rule is, as we know, the rule of the twelfth Inca, so I can say to you with certainty that within a few years of my death the new people will come to fulfill the revelation made by Our Father the Sun, to conquer our empire and become its overlords. And I command that you obey them and serve them as those who have advantage over you in all things. Their laws will be superior to ours, and their arms will be invincible. Abide in peace, for I go now to rest with My Father the Son, who calls me."

Spanish writers have indicated that the royal Inca's predictions became known throughout Peru. Pedro de Cieza de León, in chapter forty-four of his chronicle, touches on the predictions made by Huayna Cápac about the coming of the Spaniards and about his saying that newcomers such as those recently seen in ships would impose their rule over his empire. Cieza de León says that the dying Inca recounted these things to his people in Tumipampa, near Quito, where he further says that Huayna Cápac first learned of the coming

---

*Kuraka is an Andean word for a local indigenous chieftain, roughly equivalent to *cacique*.

of the Spanish discoverers of Peru. Francisco López de Gómara, in chapter one hundred and fifteen of his history, tells that Huayna Cápac's son Huáscar also made reference to his father's predictions of Spanish conquest in the following manner (which I quote word for word) saying that "his dying father Huayna Cápac had told him to befriend the bearded white men who would shortly arrive, for these men would become the new lords of the land."

The instructions that Huayna Cápac left as his last will and testament were regarded with veneration and faithfully obeyed by his subjects. I remember that one day during my youth in Peru, when an old Inca was speaking to my mother, describing the arrival of the Spaniards and how they had taken over our country, I inquired: "Inca, how is it that such a rough and mountainous land, defended by such numerous and warlike armies, was surrendered so quickly to so few Spanish invaders?" In response he explained Huayna Cápac's foretelling of the Spanish victory and how the emperor had instructed his subjects to obey and serve the Spaniards because they would have the advantage over our people in all things. And having explained these things, he addressed me angrily for having implied that the defenders of our lost empire had been pusillanimous and cowardly, saying: "The last words spoken to us by our Inca did more to defeat us and destroy our empire than did all the weapons that your Spanish father and his comrades brought with them to our land." His point was the immense esteem with which our people had always regarded the instructions of their Inca, and all the more so regarding the final instructions of Huayna Cápac, the most beloved Inca of them all.

Huayna Cápac died of his illness, and his people did as he had instructed them, opening his body and embalming it to take it back to Cuzco, except for his heart, which they interred in Quito as he had wished. During the journey to Cuzco, at every populated place the people came to pay their respects to the deceased Inca because of the love that they had borne him, and they did so with great sentiment, clamor, and crying. The funeral observances that were organized upon the arrival of his body in the imperial capital, according to the custom of the times, lasted an entire year. Huayna Cápac left more than two hundred sons and more than three hundred daughters, and almost all of them were killed by his would-be successor Atahualpa.

THINGS THAT DID NOT EXIST IN PERU UNTIL THE SPANISH BROUGHT THEM

Many readers will want to know what things did not exist in Peru before the Spanish conquered it, and I would like them to observe that many things they may believe utterly necessary to human life were absent in Peru, and yet people got along quite happily without them.

First of all, they did not have horses for war or celebrations until Spaniards arrived with horses and used them for their conquests. In the early days of conquest, therefore, horses were highly prized and generally not for sale. If one did find a horse for sale, because its owner had died or planned to return to Spain, the price was sure to be excessive—four, five, or even six thousand pesos. In the year 1554, for example, before the battle of Chuquinca, a rich gentleman approached Don Alonso de Alvarado, who was going to fight. Alvarado's black slave was there, too, leading a fine war horse, with a beautiful saddle and bridle, ready for his master to mount. The horse caught the rich gentleman's eye, and he said: "I'll give ten thousand pesos, right now, for the horse and slave together." Alvarado declined. He was then severely wounded in the battle, and his horse was killed. The point of this story is that a very rich gentleman with many Indians at his service could not buy a horse, even at a most exorbitant price. The owner of the horse did not have Indians at his service, but he was a famous soldier and required his horse for a battle. These men were both of noble Spanish blood, and I knew both of them. Many horses have been bred in Peru since that time, so the price has come down considerably. A good riding horse now costs three hundred or four hundred pesos, and an old nag, twenty or thirty.

The Indians had a notable fear of horses at first. Now they are much more used to horses, but still, one never finds an Indian shoeing horses, although Indians have shown great skill in all the other trades introduced from Spain. Shoeing requires close handling of a horse, and Indians do not want to do it. It is true that Indian servants do tend horses, but they never dare to ride. I can say, in truth, that I have never seen an Indian mount a horse. Indeed, to climb up and down the rugged mountains of Peru, Indian carriers are much more useful than horses, for they have been born and bred for such work.

Before the conquest, the Indians did not have cows or oxen to plow the earth to plant their crops. Cows seem to have arrived just after the conquest, brought by many different people, and they spread quickly throughout Peru. I first saw oxen plowing in the Valley of Cuzco more or less in the year 1550. A horde of Indians was rushing to see such a totally new and monstrous thing, and they took me along. They said in amazement that the Spaniards forced these enormous animals to do their work out of pure laziness. I remember the day well because I did not go to school and the escapade cost me two whippings, one from my father and one from the schoolmaster.

Horses and cows were not the only animals that the Indians lacked before the arrival of the Spaniards. They had neither camels, nor donkeys, nor mules to carry their loads; nor sheep, whether the common sort or fine merinos, for meat and wool; nor goats or pigs for meat and leather; nor dogs of the kind that hunt or care for livestock. Pigs and goats also arrived soon after the conquest in considerable numbers. I remember seeing them in Cuzco when I was very young.

As for crops, before the conquest the Indians of Peru had neither wheat nor barley, neither wine nor olive oil, neither fruits nor vegetables of the Spanish sort. Let us account for their appearance, then. The first person to introduce wheat into my country (by which I mean the entire empire once ruled by the Incas) was a noblewoman named María de Escobar, married to a gentleman called Diego de Chaves, both of them natives of Trujillo in Spain. I met her in Cuzco where she went to live long after her initial arrival in Peru, but I did not meet him because he died in Lima. No one was able to tell the year in which this good woman first planted wheat down on the coast. But I know that she had so few grains at first that for three years she saved the entire harvest for seed and did not make any bread at all. Each year of those first three she doled out twenty or thirty grains from her harvest to her friends so that each of them could begin to plant wheat in the new land.

Grapes and wine were likewise unknown in the Inca empire before the Spanish conquest. In the year 1560, during my journey from the highlands to the coast on my way to Spain, I met an administrator of a rural property, Alfonso Váez, a fine fellow and very knowledgeable about agriculture. Váez gave me a full tour of the establishment under his charge, including a vineyard that was quite loaded with grapes, and yet he did not offer a single bunch to me, his guest, a footsore traveler, although I clearly desired to taste the grapes. It would have been a magnificent gesture, and yet he did not make the offer. Aware of my puzzlement at his refusal to do so, he begged my pardon, explaining that the owner of the estate had forbidden him to touch even a single precious grape because he wanted every one of them for wine. Back then, even landowners with many Indians at their service did not offer wine to anyone, unless perhaps to a guest who needed a glass for reasons of health, because wine was not considered a daily necessity at all. Wine was still so rare in Peru that, out of politeness, guests sometimes refused a glass even when their hosts offered it, and sometimes there was not enough wine available to offer communion at mass, even in Lima.

As for fruit, Peru lacked pomegranates, oranges, apples, limes, pears, peaches, apricots, plums, and many other things that Spain has. It would be good to know just who brought each of these fruits to Peru and in what year, because each is a blessing and the person who introduced it deserves our praise and remembrance.

Finally, we have been forgetting the most important living things that have lately arrived in the Indies, the Spaniards themselves, and also the blacks that the Spaniards brought with them to serve as slaves, for blacks did not exist in the Indies until the Spaniards introduced them. Whites and blacks have combined with the Indians to produce a variety of mixtures, each of which has its own name. Let us consider these varieties of people. A person who goes to the Indies from Spain is called an *español* or a *castellano*, two names which in the Indies amount to the same thing. A son born to Spaniards in the Indies is called a *criollo*, and a daughter, a *criolla*. These names were first invented by blacks to distinguish those born in Africa from their children born in the Indies. The African parents consider it a point of honor to have been born in their original homeland, and they are offended if one calls them *criollos*. Therefore, the parents are called simply *negros* or *guineos*, whereas their children, born outside of the African homeland, are called *criollos*, as are the children of Spaniards born outside theirs. Children born of a Spanish-Indian combination are called *mestizos*, which indicates that they are a mixture of those two nations. This name was established by the first Spaniards to have children with Indian women. Here in Spain, I use the term proudly and feel honored by it. Back in the Indies, however, the term *mestizo* is considered scornful.

> *Analyzing the Sources: How does the author try to make his Inca history nonthreatening to his Spanish readership? As in the López de Gómara and Sahagún selections, this one contains a prophecy of conquest taken, ultimately, from indigenous sources.*

THE FIRST NEW CHRONICLE

Felipe Guaman Poma de Ayala

Guaman Poma was an indigenous noble born in Peru after the Spanish conquest, around the middle of the 1500s. He used his facility in several indigenous languages to compile a sustained and hard-hitting critique of Spanish colonial rule in Peru, The First New Chronicle and Good Government, *written between 1600 and 1615. Guaman Poma's book is especially notable for its almost four hundred drawings, two of which accompany this excerpt. In the excerpt, the author imagines himself in direct dialogue with the king of Spain, making his denunciation of colonial problems directly to the king's ear. In fact, the Spanish king never saw Guaman Poma's book, which remained unpublished until the twentieth century.*

MESSAGE TO HIS ROYAL CATHOLIC MAJESTY DON FELIPE III, MONARCH OF THE WORLD

PROLOGUE

I say to Your Royal Holy Catholic Majesty—shedding tears and crying out to heaven, pleading to God, the Virgin Mary, and all the

SOURCE: Felipe Guaman Poma de Ayala, *Nueva Corónica y buen gobierno, Compuesto por don Felipe Guaman Poma de Ayala, Señor y Príncipe,* digitized manuscript, Royal Library of Denmark, www.kb.dk/permalink/2006/poma/info/es/frontpage.htm, mspp. 982–89, 999.

saints and angels—I say that we, the poor, suffer untold punishment, ill fortune, and destruction. May God and Your Majesty not permit the end of us poor Indians or the depopulation of your kingdom.

DIALOGUE

Guaman Poma de Ayala: Your Royal Catholic Majesty, I tell you that in the kingdom of Peru the Indians are coming to an end, utterly to an end. In twenty years, there will be no Indians in this kingdom to serve your royal Crown and defend our holy Catholic faith, and without the Indians, Your Majesty will have nothing because, remember, the labor of the Indians has made Castile what it is today. Your grandfather and your father were monarchs of great power and renown because of the Indians, and Your Majesty also. And this valuable kingdom is already being depopulated. In places where there were a thousand souls, not a hundred remain, and all of them old men and women who can no longer multiply. Married women are being stolen away, and unmarried men will have to marry old women who cannot have children. Besides, the Indians suffer great woes. Their sons and daughters are taken from them, and they can do nothing because all conspire against the Indians: Spaniards and mestizos; judges, officials, and *encomenderos*;* inspectors and priests of the Holy Mother Church. All conspire against the poor. All have worked hand in hand to favor the Spanish *dons* and the lady *doñas*. They exploit the poor and enter their lands and houses by force. To write these things is to weep. No officials report these things to Your Majesty. Throughout the kingdom of Peru the Indians are losing everything, but I will tell the truth regarding the income and benefits which the Indians have enjoyed and should continue to enjoy. Your Majesty should know how you are being served by the Indians. Twice a year, they offer silver, corn, wheat, clothing, chickens, livestock, and other tribute. In addition, they serve in the mines and plazas and royal inns along the highways of the kingdom. They

---

*Encomenderos were Spaniards who possessed *encomienda* grants of indigenous labor and tribute. These grants were curtailed, but not completely eliminated, by the New Laws.

THIS PICTURE SHOWS GUAMAN POMA (in Spanish clothes) collecting information for his book. "Tell me," he asks in two Andean languages: Quechua ("MA VILLAVAI") and Aymara ("ACHAMITAMA"). *Snark / Art Resource, New York.*

maintain the roads and repair the bridges. They produce all sorts of revenues—the personal tax, the tithe, and the royal fifth. Your Majesty does not get as much revenue from all the mestizos, pardos, and Spaniards put together. Therefore, the Indians are worth an inestimable amount to Your Majesty: Take care that this kingdom should not lose these Indians. If a Spaniard steals away four Indian women to make little mestizos, he will bribe the judges and refuse to recognize his paternity. The Spaniards have many women and many mestizo children. They extract women from scattered settlements and pursue them day and night, both in the women's houses and in public gathering places. If the women's fathers and mothers try to defend them, they suffer mistreatment also. The Spaniards do not let Indian women marry or, if they are married, live with their husbands. So the married ones are unable to have children by their husbands and instead give birth to little mestizos. The kingdom of Peru is now full of mestizos who wander around dressed like Indians. And when a poor Indian woman has a child by a poor Indian man, the church and civil officials and *encomenderos* immediately descend on her to make her the servant of some lady or priest. Then they fornicate with her, and she soon gives birth to more little mestizos. And eventually she prefers to live that way, and on and on it goes.

His Royal Catholic Majesty: Tell me, author Ayala. You have told me many disturbing things about how the Indians are coming to an end and are suffering troubles and cannot multiply because Spaniards steal their wives and daughters and all their possessions, leaving them with nothing. I do not send my judges to rob or do harm; but rather to honor the nobles, *caciques*, local authorities, and poor Indians that they may thrive and multiply in the service of God and my royal Crown, and in the defense of the holy Catholic faith. Tell me now, author Ayala, how can these problems be remedied?

Guaman Poma de Ayala: I say to Your Majesty that the Spaniards ought to live like Christians, marrying ladies of equal status and leaving the poor Indian women alone so that they can have Indian children. They should leave the Indians' property alone, give back what they have taken, offer money for what they have used, and pay the legal penalty if they fail to do so. He who abuses an Indian virgin or gets a married woman pregnant or forces her to fornicate should pay the legal penalty and be banished to Chile or sentenced to six years of hard labor, and all his possessions should be confiscated to pay the Indian woman and the court expenses. And any judge who fails to do justice deserves the same punishment. Enforce the laws, and the Indians will multiply.

Your Royal Catholic Majesty, about the community lands belonging to the Indians and the churches, religious brotherhoods, and hospitals: in order that they may prosper, I recommend that the Indians be asked to give an accounting to me as your second-in-command in this kingdom. They could report to me twice a year, paying me a salary so that I will be able to devote myself to the service of God and your royal Crown and increase the public revenues. I further recommend that all the Indian and royal authorities report to me as your second-in-command in this kingdom, so that I may inform you of their needs and deservings, for I know all there is to know, all the whys and wherefores. Let me and my descendents have this power, by law and in perpetuity, and I assure you that then no Indian will go around wearing Spanish clothes, or assume the title of *don* or *doña*, or assume a title of authority that he does not deserve. That way, the Indian authorities will have to prove themselves loyal and faithful Christians, eager to serve God and Your Majesty and favor the poor.

Your Royal Catholic Majesty, if one Indian pueblo prospers and its population multiplies while another pueblo declines and only a few Indians remain there, then Your Majesty, as the new Inca king of Peru, should transfer the croplands, pastures, jurisdiction, and property of the declining pueblo to the prospering one, so that its inhabitants may serve God and Your Majesty. The names of Indians who have strayed from their pueblos without permission should go on a list, and the authorities should assign a Spaniard, mestizo, or mulatto to search for them, receiving a reward of one peso per Indian brought back in shackles. The prisoner should do forced labor to pay for the cost of his capture and then be returned to his pueblo.

"GOD MADE THE HEAVEN AND THE EARTH" is a translation of the picture title, given in Spanish. The paired representation of the sun and the moon in this illustration constitutes an Andean influence. Do you see any other elements that might have native overtones? *Department of Manuscripts and Rare Books, The Royal Library, Copenhagen, Denmark.*

So that the Indian pueblos might remain well populated and multiply, Your Royal Catholic Majesty should order the local authorities to be removed and the priests also, if they commit a single infraction, and that will remedy the problem. Also, prohibit *encomenderos* from entering the Indian pueblos, ever, for any reason, and let that prohibition be strictly enforced by royal authorities. Indian authorities should be descendents of the great Inca lords of this kingdom, reaching back to *Wari Wiracocha Runa, Wari Runa, Purun Runa, Auca Runa,* and *Incap Runa.* Let none be a drunk, a coca chewer, or a gambler. Good Indian leaders will recover the wanderers who have left their pueblos, and all will live at ease and multiply in the service of God and Your Majesty. Furthermore, Majesty, the Indians should not be forced to labor in the mercury mines for a year. The Indians should be allowed to rest, without the mines stopping their production, to serve Your Majesty.

His Royal Catholic Majesty: But tell me, author, how can the Indians rest and the mines continue working?

Guaman Poma de Ayala: I say to Your Majesty that the Indians who serve as laborers in the Spanish cities of this kingdom should go to the mines and trade places with the Indians who are there for one year, because working in the mercury mines is the most dangerous thing of all. Let Indians who have gone to the cities replace those in the mines and work hard for a year while the others rest. Remember, Your Majesty, the king who loses all his Indian vassals loses everything.

His Royal Catholic Majesty: Explain to me, author, exactly what you mean.

Guaman Poma de Ayala: I say to Your Majesty that the Indians provide all the income of this kingdom. Like you, I am a prince, and without my subjects, I would be nothing. Without Indians, the land will be left barren and empty. Therefore, let no Indian boy under the age of twenty be sent to the mines or sent to smelt ore or work in any way with mercury. The young ones get mercury poisoning very quickly, and, since there is no cure, they die, and that will be the end of all the Indians.

His Royal Catholic Majesty: Tell me, author. What is the remedy?

Guaman Poma de Ayala: Let only strong, full-grown Indians be sent to work in the mines, and let each work for one day at a time, no more, each alternating with others, so none will get sick and die. And Indians who are to go to the mines should be freed for one month from personal service before they go, so that they may commend their souls to God and Mary and all the saints and angels, singing and dancing and enjoying some time with their families. Also, they should go to confession, take Communion, and make a last will and testament. Finally, I say to Your Majesty that food and water should be stored in the mines so that if the miners become trapped inside, they can survive for a time with the help of God. And let those outside work day and night to open a way into the collapsed mineshaft and deliver the trapped miners from the mountain.

> *Analyzing the Sources: Like Caminha and las Casas, Guaman Poma was writing directly to the king. How does he seek to interest "the monarch of the world" in his denunciation of abuses? What is his overall attitude toward Spanish rule?*

HAPPY CAPTIVITY

Francisco Núñez de Pineda y Bascuñán

Francisco Núñez de Pineda y Bascuñán was a Spanish soldier born around 1607 on the southern frontier of Chile. In the early colonial period, the region was defined by the fierce resistance of the semisedentary Araucano people (today known more properly as the Mapuches). When Núñez was only about twenty-two, he was captured by the Mapuches and held captive for seven months. Nevertheless, he was well treated (in part because of the fame of his father Álvaro, an esteemed war captain) and decades later, in 1673, penned an account titled Happy Captivity, *a book not published until 1863. The following excerpt begins at a point when the "happy captive" has been deposited by his original captor in the house of a Mapuche chieftain, Tereupillán.*

After only two or three days, the children of Tereupillán had become so fond of me that they could scarce be without me for an instant. Altogether, there were seven or eight children of many mothers, for Tereupillán had four wives. My closest companions among his sons were two, about ten to twelve years old, who shared the wonderful bed that their father had given me, a mattress pad and covering of thirty fluffy and clean fur pelts sewn together for protection against the winter frost. Tereupillán asked that I teach his sons Christian prayers. Many of this chieftain's people knew some prayers, and the two boys, who had learned to say the Lord's prayer by heart from some old Spanish women, captives there before my time, repeated it perfectly each night before we went to bed and then again in the morning when we arose.

After a few nights, I asked if they understood what they were praying and they said no.

"Why should I teach you more prayers, then," said I, "if you won't understand them either?"

"We want to know them anyway," replied the boys, "because we are told that they are the word of God."

"All right," said I, "that is a good reason, and I will gladly teach you. Moreover, I will do so in your own language so that you can know the meaning of the prayers and better understand our sacred mysteries. Now, repeat after me . . ."

Sitting up in bed, they did so, thrilled to learn to pray in Mapuche. After only a few repetitions they had memorized a goodly portion of the Lord's Prayer in their own language and were immensely pleased to be mastering its meaning. After three or four days they

---

Source: adapted from Francisco Núñez de Pineda y Bascuñán, *El cautiverio feliz* (Santiago: Empresa Editora Zig-Zag, 1948), pp. 281–84, 319–21, 336–40.

had mastered it completely, and word got out to the boys who lived in the neighboring huts. Then, for many days I had fourteen or fifteen boys around me, sent by their parents so that they might learn our faith and be baptized. Then a grown woman came to learn Christian prayers, and she brought me a hen, in which others imitated her, bringing me hens, corn, eggs, potatoes, and other things to eat, which I told them that they need not do, and yet they insisted, thereby demonstrating their eagerness to become Christians. I noticed then, and have subsequently noticed elsewhere, that heathens embrace our holy Catholic faith with a better heart before we conquer them.

Soon Indians were coming to me from all around to prepare for baptism. I noticed that many came from districts where other Spaniards had resided for years. I wondered why the Indians had not learned prayers from these other Spaniards. An old man explained to me that these other Spaniards were not captives, but rather, renegades who lived among them by choice, adopting Indian ways and abandoning Christian ones. Various captives had told the people that these were heretics, because only heretics would choose to live among Indians, and they rightly judged that a heretic who had rejected our religion could not lead anyone to it.

*   *   *

The Mapuches open the ground and plant their crops in September, October, and November, and during this time a nearby chieftain, Quilalebo by name, invited surrounding groups to come help his people do their planting, for which he would provide food and diversion. Because my host, the chieftain Tereupillán, was Quilalebo's friend and ally, we accepted the invitation and went. Now, Quilalebo had been raised among Spaniards but hated them and had never spoken to any Spanish captive, and Tereupillán cautioned me not to speak to Quilalebo unless he spoke first.

We found about sixty Indians gathered at Quilalebo's settlement with the various implements that they use to open the ground for planting. The men use these implements to work the soil and make ridges onto which the women drop seeds. A chieftain who hosts such a gathering kills many calves and sheep to feed all the Indians who join in the work. The fields are dotted with pots of chicha* and campfires where meat roasts and women stir pots of stew, frequently supplying the workers with food and drink.

No one told me to join in the work, and when I did anyway, despite the Indians' insistence that I need not do so, they were very appreciative, and even Quilalebo softened toward me. I was digging alongside Tereupillán when Quilalebo approached and toasted his friend. Then turning toward me, he invited me, too, to drink, although wordlessly. I accepted the jar of chicha with the Mapuche salutation, "mari mari," and bowed with great respect. This display of humility and courtesy quickly undermined the chieftain's old rancor toward Spaniards, as I later confirmed.

That evening Quilalebo hosted the dance and celebration that customarily accompany collective planting. He now revealed his generous and demonstrative nature. After eating and drinking our fill of the magnificent feast, we went to the fire around which the dancing had already begun. A number of chieftains begged me to join their dance, and, desirous of pleasing them, I joined them. Now Quilalebo went to his daughter, who was dancing, and he took her by the hand and brought her to me, surrounded by the other maidens, and Quilalebo told his daughter to dance with me, for she was to be my wife. The maidens offered us chicha, as is the custom on such occasions, and each of the chieftains took one of the maidens by the hand and danced with her.

Never did I feel the devil so close to having me in his snare. The chieftains fervently encouraged my sensual appetites, as did the now-affectionate Quilalebo, who exercised total control over his daughter. Unable to extricate myself from the situation in any other manner, I took the girl's hand and spoke to her of the limitless gratitude that her father's expressions of esteem inspired in me. I said that the offer of her hand in marriage constituted the most wondrous gift I could ever hope to receive. I asked her nevertheless to forgive me—and here I released her hand—because I could not accept that gift. I explained that, because she was not a Christian, our union would be an offense to the Lord and a peril to my

---

*A fermented corn drink still popular throughout the Andes.

immortal soul. In addition, I expected to be ransomed in the spring, so how could I bind myself to her love and then leave so soon? I promised her that if the ransom did not occur as planned, I would attempt to return and learn to live among her people. The maiden replied with polite approval that she would obey her father's wishes, whatever they might be. Meanwhile, the rest of the company was dancing around us, not having heard my words and judging us already married.

Next the girl's mother appeared, offering me a jar of chicha, addressing me as her son-in-law, and proclaiming her pleasure at the match. The good woman was, in fact, Spanish, but had lived so many years among Indians that her language, clothing, and habits had become quite degraded and barbarous. Therefore, although she told me the name of her conquistador father, I did not bother to remember it. I explained my refusal to marry her daughter as courteously as possible, and she accepted my reasons. She said that Quilalebo would nevertheless expect me to dance with her and her daughter, and taking my hand and the girl's she obliged me to dance with both of them at once. I contrived to show a happy and satisfied expression, but inwardly, I begged God's aid in the trials and tribulations of my captivity. As soon as possible I withdrew and slept, while the sound of the festivities continued all night long.

The next morning, when I awoke, the sun was already high in the heavens, and the women of Quilalebo's family were busy at their chores. Accompanied by one of the chieftain's young mestizo sons, I went down to the stream for a morning bath, as is the Indians' custom. Several maidens were already there, playing naked in the water, among them, my erstwhile bride of the night before, who stood out for her beauty, her delicate manners, and her light mestizo coloring. Her brother encouraged me to approach her, and I confess to my readers that I was sorely tempted. I could not avert my gaze from her, and seeing us there, the girls called us over, with the free and high-spirited behavior of unmarried Indian maidens at such gatherings. Not wishing to seem rude, I declined cheerfully, saying that we were headed elsewhere and in a hurry. And even though they laughed and continued to beckon to us, we excused ourselves jokingly and continued along the bank to a more with-drawn and hidden place.

> *Analyzing the Sources: Why does this author (as well as others) empha-size the indigenous people's (supposed) inclination to convert to Christi-anity? How do attractive Indian maidens fit into this Spanish vision of colonization?*

AN ACCOUNT OF THE GUARANÍ MISSIONS

José Cardiel

José Cardiel (1704–1782) was a Jesuit missionary who provided a detailed description of the Guaraní missions in what is today Paraguay and neighboring areas of Argentina and Brazil. Like the Mapuches of southern Chile and the indigenous people of Brazil generally, the Guaraníes were originally semisedentary. Unlike sedentary indigenous people, whose pre-Columbian farming villages could be incorporated into the ordinary system of Catholic parishes, the mobile Guaraníes were gathered into missions by the Jesuit order. In the following excerpt from his 1747 Account of the Missions, Cardiel discusses the indigenous people's participation in various aspects of Catholic religious observance organized by the missionaries. Cardiel was forced to leave Spanish America in 1767 along with all other Jesuits.

Each church in these missions has thirty or forty musicians and might easily have more, except that their number is limited in order that enough laborers be available for economic production. The Indians regard it as a great honor to be a musician, just as they so too regard the exercise of any occupation associated with the church. Boys begin their musical training at the age of eight or nine under

SOURCE: adapted from Guillermo Furlong, *José Cardiel y su carta—relación (1747)* (Buenos Aires: Librería del Plata, 1953), pp. 165–68.

the supervision of a native teacher whose work is normally characterized by considerable seriousness and zeal. They learn quickly, and yet there are limits to the musical vocation among them. No matter how skilled a musician, no Indian ever becomes a composer, because Indians lack the creative faculty, their abilities being limited strictly to imitation. They are instructed in the following manner. The instructor plays or sings an example of what is to be learned and is imitated exactly by the pupils. The instructor strikes an erring pupil immediately with his hand, just as one does in training a dog. By dint of continual practice, even indifferent pupils memorize each piece of music that they are to perform in church, and good pupils with attentive instructors learn to sight read difficult musical scores flawlessly after looking them over two or three times.

Let us discuss their dances, which occur exclusively in a religious context and for a religious purpose, especially in festivities associated with particular saints. There is no dancing outside of a religious context, such as for courtship, as occurs in Europe, nor do women dance at all, whether in public or in private. Mission Indians also dance in the honor of visiting bishops or other dignitaries, either lay or ecclesiastical. Each village in the missions has an instructor who teaches and organizes these dances. Many are quite elaborate, and all present a religious story or drama. A few involve a single dancer, but most of their dances are performed by a large group who often present a cast of characters. Some dances, as in Spain, represent battles between opposing armies who swing their swords or fire guns in time with the music. Some dances dramatize struggles between angels and devils in their corresponding costumes. In others, dancers carry bits of a larger picture that, when held up together and assembled at some point of the performance, combine into a perfect image of the Virgin Mary or of San Ignacio, the founder of our holy order, or of some other saint. In another performance, twelve Indians of various ages, including children, play instruments and dance simultaneously, requiring no additional musicians. Such are the dances of the missions. Oh, that the rest of the Christian world danced in this way, rather than in the scandalous ways that have become so common!

After each dance a few Indians perform some sort of entertainment at the intermission while the large group changes costumes, and some of these entertainers demonstrate special talent, but never do their performances include anything immoral in the slightest, as often occurs elsewhere. To the contrary, everything that the Indians witness in these assemblies serves as a wholesome and edifying diversion, preventing them from straying in mind or body from teachings of the Church and adding to the attractions of mission life.

The most important public observances in the missions are Holy Week, Corpus Christi, and the feast pertaining to the patron saint of each village. The procession of Corpus Christi, celebrating the triumph of our holy faith, occasions the erection of triumphal arches over streets and the decoration of village squares with altars at all four corners. Leafy boughs and fragrant flowers adorn the arches and altars and line the streets along which the procession must pass, conveying the consecrated communion host. The arches also contain chattering parrots, other beautiful birds that sing delightfully, monkeys of many species with their wry expressions, and various wild animals that lend grace and vivacity to the scene. The lovely contents of the churches are brought out on those days, and so, too, do the people bring out the finest things of their houses (perhaps a painting of the kind they fancy here, perhaps a wall hanging of striped design) to beautify the street in tribute to the Lord—things that the Indians regard as precious, and which the Lord, who truly cannot but esteem these tokens of their affection and obeisance, must also therefore regard as precious. In their innocence and candor, the Indians contribute even brightly colored articles of clothing to the public display, and because they seem not to discern what things may be inappropriate, they sometimes bring out underclothing, so that the village priest must inspect the street ahead of the procession to make sure it will pass by nothing indecent.

Preparation for this celebration begins many days in advance and involves everyone, so that all lend their hands to the adoration of the Lord. During these days the Indians gather the leafy boughs and flowers and animals hitherto described. Individual families adorn the area in front of their houses, and the principal men of the village take responsibility for the large triumphal arches that span the street. The village priest plays no part in these preparations, leaving everything to the great devotion of the people.

Dancers accompany the procession that conveys the consecrated communion host through the streets during Corpus Christi, and so, too, do musicians who play both stringed and wind instruments. Soldiers are there, as well, wearing their dress galas, carrying lances, and making gallant displays in the style of old Spain. They wave their military banners in tribute to the consecrated host. The Indian leaders of the village bear upon their shoulders the portable platform that conveys the host in its richly bejeweled enclosure, and beside the platform walk numerous altar boys, in their clean and attractive robes. Two others walk before the platform swinging incense burners. And there, too, goes the priest, while the sacristan and others of the faithful strew flowers in his path. And all is done without rowdiness or even a trace of vanity, and to the contrary, executed with such devotion and received by the spectators with such respectful awe and silence, that I confess never to have been present at Corpus Christi in the missions without feeling deeply moved.

And consider that, even given the existence of these spectacles, celebrations, and festivities, many Indians leave the missions and wander through the land, seeking employment in the towns populated by Spaniards, seeking a livelihood in the vast, open, and almost uninhabited spaces, and drifting wherever their volatile spirit may lead them. How much less effective would the missions be if such entertainments did not exist?

Analyzing the Sources: According to Cardiel, what is the crucial evangelizing function of the music and pageantry that he describes? What part do you think it played in transculturation?

BOOK OF VISITATION OF THE HOLY OFFICE OF THE INQUISITION TO GRÃO PARA, BRAZIL

The Spanish Inquisition was permanently established in America, but the Portuguese Inquisition only visited. The Book of Visitation is a record of the Inquisition's only official visit to Pará (today the city of Belém) at the mouth of the Amazon River, in 1763. The Inquisition was supposed to enforce religious purity, and it was extremely alert to any signs of conflicting belief systems, so its records are a good place to look for evidence of transculturation. The Inquisition took particular notice of how people attempted to cure illness. Many of the cures in common use relied on indigenous or African magic that the Catholic Church regarded as witchcraft, and witchcraft was a serious crime punishable by law. Several different cases, involving different witnesses, who testified over several days, are linked by further editorial commentary in what follows.

On the seventh day of October 1763, the Inquisitor Giraldo José de Abranches, Visitor of the Holy Office of the Inquisition to the city of Pará, formally hearing cases at São Boaventura Hospice, took the following testimony from a man who came before him to report superstitious acts of interest the Inquisition. Placing his hand on the Gospels, the man solemnly swore to tell the truth and reveal it to no one else. He said his name was Manoel Francisco da Cunha, forty-three years old, a carpenter by trade, born in Portugal in the parish of São Salvador da Xamalde in the Bishopric of Porto, married to Catarina Francisca Xavier, dwelling near the church of Santo António. He added that he was a Christian of old stock, without taint of Moor or Jew.

SOURCE: José Roberto do Amaral Lapa, ed., *Livro da visitação do Santo Ofício da Inquisição ao Estado do Grão-Pará (1763–1769)* (Petrópolis, Vozes, 1978), pp. 137–38, 158–60, 171–72.

The witness reported that about three and a half months ago, he couldn't be precise about the date, but it was certainly before the Feast of São João, he's sure of that, around nine o'clock in the morning, that the following events transpired. Or at least, that's when they began. The witness owns an African slave named Maria, of the Bujago nation, who was gravely ill, and various sorts of horrid creatures the color of brass had crawled out of her womb, and nobody knew what to do. Fortunately, he learned of another African slave who was able to cure such things, José of the Mandingo nation, property of Manoel de Souza, an unmarried trader with a business on São Vicente Street. The witness obtained Souza's permission for the Mandingo to treat Maria.

As soon as he entered the house of our witness the Mandingo examined one of the strange creatures that had come out of Maria's body, and he said that more were still inside. Then he pronounced mysterious words over her, words that neither Maria nor our witness, nor his wife, who was also present, could understand. Then he went out to the kitchen and the witness saw him boil certain herbs that he had brought with him concealed. But he cannot say more because the Mandingo did not allow him to see clearly. When the water had cooled, the sick slave drank it while, over her, he pronounced words that were not understood.

The Mandingo returned in the afternoon and repeated the treatment, not allowing our witness and his wife to watch. And he did the same thing on the morning and the afternoon of the next day. Always, while the sick slave drank what he gave her, he pronounced words not one of which could be understood.

After the last treatment, he asked our witness for an ear of corn and a hoe, and he took them out to the back garden. There he dug a small hole at the foot of a lemon tree and buried the ear of corn, pronouncing words that sounded something like a prayer. The witness could not hear well because he was not allowed to watch, but from behind the door he then saw the Mandingo uncover the ear of corn to look at it, saying finally that all the creatures who remained inside Maria would then come out.

And so it occurred. Within a few hours a small bag of tissue came out of her body, and the witness opened it to find inside three creatures, each of a different form and color, one like a tiny fox, one like a fuzzy lizard, and one like a miniature alligator.

[*The outcome of these cases went unrecorded. José was unhappy with what he was paid for Maria's spectacular cure, however, and he started grumbling about it, which we know because the grumbling eventually got back to our witness, who denounced José to the Inquisition perhaps preemptively, fearing that otherwise he might be accused of sponsoring witchcraft in his house. Probably that's why he was among the first in line to tattle when the Inquisition began its proceedings in Pará.*]

*   *   *

[*The next week a mulata servant went to the Inquisition to report something that had happened twenty years earlier. It's hard to know for sure whether it was a scam or shamanic spirit work that involved dramatization. It is also not clear why the former servant is making this accusation after twenty years. She must have been settling an old score. Whatever Luduvina and her Indian associates did to Inés Maria de Jesús, the story she told the Inquisition was likely to make them sorry.*]

On the fourteenth day of October 1763, the Inquisitor Giraldo José de Abranches, Visitor of the Holy Office of the Inquisition to the city of Pará, formally hearing cases at São Boaventura Hospice, took the following testimony from Inés Maria de Jesús, mulata, born in Pará, the illegitimate daughter of a white man, Ignácio de Andrade, who practiced law, now deceased, and of Valeria Barreta, Cafuza.* The witness is more or less fifty years old, unmarried, a seamstress and lace maker, resident on São Vicente Street. Placing her hand on the Gospels, she solemnly swore to tell the truth and reveal the following to no one else.

About twenty years earlier, the mulata Inés had worked in the household of a white woman, Mariana Barreto, widow of Luís Pereira who lived near the slaughterhouse. Her story was about her

---

*Mixed African and indigenous.

mistress Mariana. Her mistress had become ill with the flux, so she called for another woman, Luduvina Ferreira, white, a widow over sixty, to come treat her. The witness does not know Luduvina's place of birth, nor does she know how she supports herself, but she lives behind the church of the slaves' patron saint, Nossa Senhora do Rosário.

Luduvina felt Mariana's stomach, but Inés does not remember if she applied any poultices or gave the sick woman anything to drink. At that point another friend of Mariana's, also a white woman, arrived. This was Constança Maciel, a neighbor of Inés on São Vicente Street and widow of Manoel Tomás, a man who made regular voyages up river to trade with the forest tribes. Inés left the gathering and did not see with her own eyes, but Constança later told her that Mariana's friend Luduvina commenced a kind of ceremony, singing over the sick woman in an unknown language that is used by Indian shamans to make magic, and while she sang she shook a rattle made from a gourd pierced by an arrow, with loose seeds inside. Luduvina announced that someone had cast a spell on Mariana, and she went out, giving the rattle to Constança and telling her to shake it continuously during her absence. Luduvina soon returned, said Constança, with a gourd dish, which she placed upside down on the floor. Then she put the tip of the arrow on the bottom of the overturned dish and continued singing and gently agitating the rattle. The dish began to move across the floor by itself. It circulated around the house, and Luduvina with it, until it finally stopped of its own accord under the sick woman's bed. All this is according to what Constança told the mulata Inés, but Inés did see the rattle and the gourd dish under the bed later.

After all this, our witness said that on some night later two Indians entered her mistress's house. She only recognized one named António who lived at the house of the brick maker, Jerónimo Roberto, and worked at the São José brickyard until not long ago. She lately heard that he now lives in the village of Cintra, not far away. These Indians and Luduvina shut themselves in a shed without any light. They had Mariana brought to them and, in complete darkness, moving around the house, they began to play their rattles and to sing words that the witness could not make out. And after they had played and sung for a time, they stopped. And then a loud whistling could be heard from somewhere and the roof tiles trembled, followed by thumping sounds all over the house, as if people were jumping, although nothing could be seen. The witness says that the Indians, or perhaps they were demons, began stamping on the ceiling, too. Then a voice was heard asking the sick woman what she had, and she answered. The voice responded that he could not cure her, but soon a spirit who *could* cure her would arrive. Another whistling sound could be heard, and a rush of air through the tile roof, as if the spirit were departing in a hurry. Then yet another whistling sound and trembling of roof tiles as if the heralded spirit were arriving, and more thumping as of the hands and feet of several people, although nothing could be seen. Another voice was heard asking the sick woman what she had, and she answered, but this spirit did not have the cure, either. The loud coming and going of spirits continued a long time on this occasion, and on other occasions in which Luduvina and the two mentioned Indians carried out their devilish and superstitious activities, according to the witness.

[*Whatever else was going on here, a clearer example of transcultural mixing can hardly be imagined.*]

*   *   *

[*Here is another "cold case," this one fifteen years old. The target this time is the "India Sabina," as the Inquisition record calls her. She is accused of witchcraft in absentia after (long after) failing to cure the wife of her embittered accuser. Her accuser is a planter who lives on the edge of town, and in this story we must imagine the surroundings as scattered plantations of sugarcane and cacao on clearings in the Amazonian rain forest. Native people, many of whom have been separated from their tribal origins, becoming "tapuios," still constituted the majority of the population in this part of eighteenth-century Brazil, the Amazon Basin.*]

On the twenty-first day of October 1763, the Inquisitor Giraldo José de Abranches, Visitor of the Holy Office of the Inquisition to the city of Pará, formally hearing cases at São Boaventura Hospice, took the following testimony from a man with information relevant to the Holy Office, who spoke on behalf of his wife, Caetana Teresa, being as she was too ill to come in person. He gave his name as Domingos Rodrigues, born in the parish of São Bras, forty-three years old, a cultivator of the soil, resident on the edge of town. Placing his hand on the Gospels, he solemnly swore to tell the truth and reveal the following to no one else.

Fifteen years ago, more or less, when his wife was not so ill as now and before she had taken innumerable medicines in a vain attempt to get better, her family had called the India Sabina. Perhaps she could cure Caetana they hoped, because nobody else could. She had the reputation of being able to diagnose and cure mysterious afflictions. She was then unmarried, but today they say she's married, although the witness is sure he doesn't know to whom. She was born out in the forest somewhere and was a slave of Bento Guedes, who is no longer living. The witness thinks she might be found in Cintra.

On the day in question, Caetana's family asked Bento Guedes to lend the services of his slave, and as soon as she entered the room where Caetana lay ill, Sabina sat on the bed and asked her symptoms, then said immediately: "You are under a spell, and the person who put it on you is a tapuia* who is a servant in your house." And calling the servants, all of whom were Indians, Sabina pointed at one of them and said: "That's the one." The accused woman remonstrated, but Sabina would hear nothing. "Don't deny it," she said. The house had earthen floors, and Sabina had the men dig under the sick woman's bed. There they found buried a small bundle of bones, feathers, lizards pierced with thorns, and other talismans. Sabina then indicated other places in the house where similar bundles of talismans were buried under the floor. When the tapuia (who is deceased and whose name the witness does not remember) saw how easily Sabina discovered the hiding

---

*A detribalized Indian like António who worked at the brickyard.

places of the talismans, she confessed that she was in league with the devil. The witness's wife and her mother, who was also present, expressed horror, and they were even more amazed at several things that Sabina did next, such as asking for a basin of holy water to be brought from the church, bathing her hand in it, then reaching with three fingers of that hand down the sick woman's throat and pulling out a live lizard. Still, the only thing that had ever really helped had been the Catholic exorcism that Sabina had also recommended for good measure.

[*The testimony goes on to describe how India Sabina was later called to cure the governor of Pará himself. Asking for a knife, she dug a hole in the plaster wall beside the governor's bed to expose a medicine bundle like those already described. Sabina explained that the bundle had been put into the wall years before and was probably responsible for the death of a previous governor. The governor paid Sabina, but after she left he confided to the teller of this tale that he didn't trust her. Something wasn't right about anyone so knowledgeable about witchcraft. That idea was still on the mind of Domingos Rodrigues and his ailing wife Caetana fifteen years later. As for the hapless servant tapuia whom Sabina identified as the perpetrator, she may have been killed on the spot. The record indicates only that she was "deceased."*]

Analyzing the Sources: What are the motives of each witness? While their motives cannot be known for sure, considering them is the first step in analyzing testimony given to the Inquisition by people who made their denunciations spontaneously. How do the witnesses protect themselves in their testimony?

A GUIDE FOR INEXPERIENCED TRAVELERS

Alonso Carrió de la Vandera

Alonso Carrió de la Vandera was a Spanish colonial official, born around 1715. In 1771, he was offered a commission to inspect the overland postal route between Buenos Aires and Lima. His Guide for Inexperienced

Travellers *is a partly fictionalized account of that inspection. In the text, Carrió de las Vandera addresses his remarks to his assistant, a man partly of indigenous descent, whom he scornfully calls Concolorcorvo ("Crow-colored"), and he curries royal favor by lauding Spanish rule, praising Hispanization, and criticizing the Indians, in stark contrast to Guaman Poma. Here, having arrived in Cuzco, the haughty inspector discourses on the qualities of Indians and defends Spaniards against charges of mistreating them.*

Two centuries ago, Señor Concolorcorvo, there were apparently no fewer than seven million Indians living in Peru. I have not seen the ruins of enough abandoned towns to have housed such a large population, so they must have lived in remote areas of the mountains, hunting and gathering their subsistence. Clearly, then, the women of these bleak highlands were never very fertile. From Lima to Jujuy, a distance of five hundred leagues, one finds very few Spanish women, so that men of all qualities, whether Spanish, blacks, or mestizos, tend to seek Indian women. The children of these unions do not count as Indians.

Indians are not much different from Spaniards in their facial features. Thus, when an Indian serves one of us and is kindly treated, the first task is to teach him cleanliness. He needs to wash his face, comb his hair, cut his nails, put on a clean shirt (even of coarse cotton fabric), and then, if he is a good servant and after a couple of months his master provides shoes and better clothes, he more or less becomes a mestizo. Cleanliness and good treatment aided by the benign climate—and not light skin color—is what allows Indian men and women to change their status, and often their descendants will pass for true mestizos and even for Spaniards. I have seen no writings on the decline of the Indian population and have heard only that Spanish *aguardiente** is the main cause.

SOURCE: adapted from Alonso Carrió de la Vandera, *El lazarillo de ciegos caminantes* (Caracas: Biblioteca Ayacucho, 1985), pp. 176–80.
*Raw rum.

I do not deny that the mines consume a large number of Indians, but this mortality stems not from the labor that they must do with silver and mercury, but rather, from their immoral behavior, from their nighttime revelries, and from other excesses that absolutely resist correction. Contact with mercury or the mercury-laden rock has no more effect than contact with any other sort of crude ore. Let us suppose that every year about two thousand more Indians die doing forced labor in the mines than would have perished had they stayed home. This is really quite a small number compared with the previous population of seven million and cannot satisfactorily account for the decline.

Admittedly, Spaniards occupy agricultural lands for their crops, but these lands are not needed by the Indians and the greater part of them have been made fertile by Spanish efforts to construct irrigation ditches and channel water from distant sources, efforts in which Indian laborers have of course played a part. One could say that the Spanish cultivation of these improved lands has been more beneficial than detrimental to the Indians.

Rather, it is the Indian leaders themselves who are much to blame for the decrease of their people. They are so greedy for lands that, when a tributary Indian dies, the community leader conceals his death and pays his tribute in order to retain control of the land assigned to the deceased tributary. The leader adds the stolen land to his own property or sells it to a Spaniard or mestizo. The result is that the Indians' village communal lands decrease day by day and, finding themselves landless, the villagers leave to work on haciendas or to seek a livelihood in the cities. Their departure is prejudicial because they have no children, fall into vice and into debt, and die at an early age or end up in prison or doing forced labor in a workhouse.

Many other causes could be adduced for the decline of the Indian population, señor Concolorcorvo, but it would be a waste of time. Rather, if you wish to accompany me from Cuzco to Lima, prepare for our departure two days from now.

Analyzing the Sources: What concern does the author share with las Casas and Guaman Poma, despite the enormous difference in his attitude toward the indigenous people?

Chapter 3

A Taste of Independence

Two new sorts of primary sources become important in Latin America at the time of independence, between 1800 and 1825: political documents and travel accounts.

The struggle for independence from Spain and Portugal vastly expanded the production of printed documents in Latin America. Printing presses had not even existed in many places during the centuries of colonial rule. By 1825, presses around the region were spewing newspapers, pamphlets, and flyers that provided news of political events near and far. The enormous majority of these documents (in largely illiterate societies) were created by and for the elite, whether patriot or royalist. Reading them, one is impressed by how much their concerns represent a wider Atlantic world. Simón Bolívar's "Angostura Address," for example, quotes French Enlightenment thinkers and recommends imitation of the British political institutions. On the other hand, political realities specific to Latin America are very present in the speech, which confronts the greatest obstacle to nation building in Venezuela: its exploitative history. The second primary source in this chapter is a much rarer sort, a personal diary, not published until many years after independence. This "Diary of a Comandante of American Independence" was written during quiet interludes between skirmishes. It reveals above all the shifting loyalties of the indigenous people who, aside from the early Hidalgo revolt in New Spain, showed very little inclination to abandon their king and join the patriot cause. While political sources are necessary to an understanding of the independence struggles, the level of detail in them can be overwhelming.

Travel accounts are usually more fun. From the sixteenth to the eighteenth centuries, Spain and Portugal jealously guarded their New World colonies from the prying eyes of outsiders, but in the nineteenth century Latin America's newly independent nations opened themselves to visitors. Travel accounts created by nineteenth-century visitors to the region constitute a fascinating primary source, one uniquely accessible to students. For starters, such accounts were very often written in English. In addition, they were published in large numbers and addressed to a general reading public. And, because travel writing was a branch of popular literature, these accounts were widely disseminated and collected in US and British libraries where, encased in ornate bindings, they still await curious readers who are responsible enough to treat them gently.

Travel accounts help us imagine what it would have been like to visit Latin America almost two hundred years ago. Modes of transportation, the appearance of people and places, social manners and attitudes toward foreigners—all naturally receive considerable attention, often on a day-by-day basis, many accounts being organized and dated as diaries or, in another variant, as periodic letters written to friends or family. (It should be noted, however, that even in these cases publication was an important purpose for writing, rather than an afterthought.) In addition, early nineteenth-century travelers were visiting places that few of their readers had other ways of learning about, and they tried to provide all sorts of potentially useful basic information on geography and economic activities. Many travelers were scientists who used accounts of their travels to report information on everything from botany to geology. The know-it-all attitude adopted by many travelers should give us pause, though. How much did they really know? How good was their Spanish or Portuguese? What was the source of the information that they often proclaimed with such confidence? The answer, of course, varies from traveler to traveler, and sometimes the answer is simply unknowable.

One thing is abundantly clear, however. Nineteenth-century travelers to Latin America normally wrote with a *superior* attitude.

British travelers were coming from one of the world's dominant international powers, after all. That was not true of US travelers before the 1890s, when the United States had not yet become a world power, but US travelers did share certain racial and religious (anti-Catholic) prejudices toward Latin Americans. As a result, English-language travel accounts provide excellent practice at the sort of careful, critical reading mentioned in Chapter 1. That kind of reading against the grain involves trying to understand the bias built into a source and compensating for it as one reads. Only by somehow filtering out blatant prejudice can one glean useful information from nineteenth-century travelers about the countries they visited. And the prejudice that one filters out constitutes useful information in itself. The sixteenth-century chronicler Francisco Cervantes de Salazar wrote about the Nahuas of New Spain in ways that tell us more about Spanish ideas than indigenous realities, and something similar can be said about nineteenth-century travel accounts. Sometimes their most valuable information concerns past attitudes toward Latin America that were common, until fairly recently, in our own culture. Often nineteenth-century travelers viewed Latin American countries through "imperial eyes."

Historians have used nineteenth-century travel accounts to investigate various topics relating to daily life. Travelers observed and commented on matters thought too commonplace or unimportant to elicit descriptions by local writers, such as the basic layout and furnishings of a house. The daily lives of women, to take another example, also get attention in travel accounts, most especially those written by women. This chapter includes excerpts from two famous accounts written by women married to husbands who traveled to Latin America for professional reasons. Travel accounts also provide a vivid look at nineteenth-century slavery in the region. Slavery continued in Brazil and Cuba until the 1880s, while most English-speaking travelers to these countries wrote for audiences who considered slavery exotic and therefore fascinating in a horrible sort of way. As a result, travel accounts like the one written by Henry Koster, excerpted in this chapter, discuss and explain racial attitudes as no Brazilian or Cuban writer was likely to do. We are fortunate to be able to read these descriptions because people of African descent contributed enormously—in

sheer numbers, in productive labor, in cultural richness—to the formation of Latin American societies, and their presence has not been
adequately revealed in previous documents.

PERSONAL NARRATIVE OF A JOURNEY

Alexander von Humboldt

*Prussian scientist and explorer Alexander von Humboldt was among the
earliest and most influential of nineteenth-century travelers to Latin
America. Humboldt's journey, which lasted from 1799 to 1804 and was
made in the company of his friend and fellow scientist Aimé de Bonpland, became the subject of a wide-ranging and detailed travel account
of many volumes. This publishing project occupied Humboldt for
decades, and the following excerpt is placed first in this chapter to
indicate the timing of the trip rather than the publication of his text.
Humboldt's writings recorded scientific observations and statistics that he
collected en route as well as scenes and impressions from this travels. The
excerpt printed here, relating mostly to his stay in Cuba, gives a taste of
his varied interests and observations—from botany to physical geography
and demography. Note that Cuba remained firmly a colony at the time of
Humboldt's visit.*

The aspect of Havana, at the entrance of the port, is one of the gay-
est and most picturesque on the shore of the American tropical
coastline north of the equator. This spot, celebrated by travelers of
all nations, has not the luxurious vegetation that adorns the banks
of the river Guayaquil, nor the wild majesty of the rocky coast of Rio
de Janeiro, two ports of the southern hemisphere. But the graces
which in those climates embellish the scenes of cultivated nature

SOURCE: Alexander von Humboldt, *Personal Narrative of Travels to the
Equinoctial Regions of the New Continent during the Years 1799–1804*, vol. 7,
trans. from the French by Helen Maria Williams (London: Longman,
Rees, Orme, Brown, and Green, 1829), pp. 7–13, 285–87, 436, 466–68.

are here mingled with the majesty of vegetable forms and the organic vigor that characterizes the torrid zone. Amidst a variety of soothing impressions, the European forgets the dangers that menace him in the populous cities of the Caribbean islands. He seeks to take in the different elements of a vast landscape, to contemplate the fortifications that crown the rocks to the east of the port, the inland basin surrounded by villages and farms, the palm trees that rise to a majestic height, and the city, half concealed by a forest of masts belonging to the sailing vessels moored in port. To enter the port of Havana you pass between the two fortresses through a narrow channel three-fifths of a mile long. Thence one enters a basin just over two miles at its widest point and five to six fathoms in depth.

The town of Havana, surrounded by walls, stands on a promontory bounded on the south by the arsenal and on the north and west by fortifications. Beyond the city walls is the military parade ground, which grows smaller, from year to year, with the construction of peripheral neighborhoods called *arrabales* or *barrios extra muros*. The great edifices of Havana—the cathedral, the government house, the naval headquarters, the arsenal, the post office, and the cigar factory—are less remarkable for their beauty than for the solidity of their construction. The streets are for the most part narrow, and most are not paved. As paving stones must be brought from Vera Cruz at great expense, someone conceived the idea of paving the streets of Havana with tree trunks, as is done in marshy places of Germany and Russia. This project was soon abandoned, but at the time of my visit (1800), recently arrived travelers were still surprised to see fine trunks of mahogany sunk in the muddy streets. Indeed, few towns in Spanish America presented a less agreeable, less tidy appearance. People walked in mud up to the knee. The multitude of passenger coaches and carts loaded with cases of sugar and the porters who elbow passersby together rendered walking disagreeable and humiliating. The smell of jerked beef stank in the houses and the narrow, winding streets. It appears that the cleanliness of the streets has lately been improved, and that the houses are now better ventilated. The ill effects of the street layout, however, can be amended only very slowly, just as in the old towns of Europe.

There are two fine paseos where one can stroll in Havana. The first is the Alameda, running from the hospital to the theater, which was tastefully redecorated in 1803 by an Italian artist. The other is the Paseo Extra Muros, outside the city walls, deliciously cool and frequented by carriages after sunset. Near the parade ground is the Botanical Garden, a monument to Christopher Columbus, and something else, a spectacle that provokes both pity and indignation: the market where wretched slaves are displayed for sale.

The landscape in the vicinity of Havana gains its peculiar character from the most majestic of all palm trees, the *palma real,* which Bonpland and I have called the *oreodoxa regia* in our catalog of American palms. The *palma real* has feathered leaves rising perpendicularly towards the sky, curving at the tips. Its tall trunk, swelling slightly in the middle, rises sixty to eighty feet high and looks like two columns, one atop the other. The upper part, of a glossy, tender green, shines in contrast with the lower part, which is rough and whitish. The form of this plant reminded us of the vadgiai palm that covers the rocks of the cataracts of the Orinoco River, pointed leaves swaying over a mist of foam.

Around Havana, as everywhere else, the population growth diminishes the vegetation. The *palma real* on which I delighted to gaze is gradually disappearing now. The marshes which I saw covered with bamboo have been drained for cultivation. Civilization advances, and the soil, stripped of plants, scarcely offers any traces of its former wild abundance. Houses line the roads in Havana's environs, and those that surround the bay are of a light and elegant construction. The owners trace a plan and have the materials brought from the United States, as if ordering a piece of furniture. As long as yellow fever continues to rage in Havana, people will retire to their country properties to breathe purer air. In the coolness of the night, when the boats cross the bay, leaving long, phosphorescent tracks of light behind them in the water, these romantic scenes will continue to furnish charming and peaceful retreats to the inhabitants who seek refuge from the tumult of a populous city.

Bonpland and I decided to split our herbal collection into three lots to avoid the risk of losing what had taken us so much trouble to collect during our journey up to that point. We sent one collection by way of England to Germany, another via Cádiz to France, and the third we left in Havana. Each collection contained nearly the same species. If the cases were taken by pirates, there were instructions to send them to Sir Joseph Banks or to the professors of natural history in the Museum of Paris. We had reason to congratulate ourselves on these prudent measures. Happily, I did not send my manuscripts with the part of the collection bound for Cádiz with our friend and fellow traveler Father Juan González, who left Cuba soon after us. But the vessel in which he embarked sank in a tempest off the coast of Africa and the crew and cargo were all lost. In the wreck we lost duplicates of our herbal collection and all the insects Bonpland had collected in the most difficult circumstances during our South American travels. Then for over two years we did not receive one letter from Europe, and those which arrived in the following three years made no mention of the collections that we had shipped. Imagine my uneasiness at having sent the journal with my astronomical observations and the barometrical measurements of which I had not had the patience to make a copy. After visiting New Granada, Peru, and Mexico I happened to cast my eyes on the table of contents of a scientific journal in the public library in Philadelphia, where I found these words: "M. de Humboldt's manuscripts at his brother's house in Paris, by way of Spain." I could scarcely suppress an exclamation of joy.

The probable population of Cuba at the close of 1825 was as follows: Whites 325,000; Free Colored 130,000; Slaves 260,000. The slave population of Cuba would have diminished with great rapidity since 1820 had it not been for the fraudulent continuance of the slave trade with Africa. If this infamous traffic were to cease entirely through the advance of civilization and the energetic will of the new independent countries of America, the servile population would decline because of the disproportion between the sexes. The proportion of women to men on the island of Cuba is 1 to 1.7, and on sugar plantations, 1 to 4. In addition, slaves would surely continue to gain their freedom. In no part of the world where slavery exists is manumission so frequent as on the island of Cuba, for Spanish legislation (directly the reverse of French and English laws) favors in an extraordinary degree the attainment of freedom. In addition, the position of free blacks in Cuba is much better than it is elsewhere, even among those nations which have for ages flattered themselves as being the most advanced. But what a sorrowful spectacle is presented by civilized, Christian nations disputing which among them, over the span of three centuries, has destroyed the smallest number of Africans by reducing them to slavery!*

Our journey from Cuba to the South American coast near the Sinú River took sixteen days. On the morning of 30 March we rounded Punta Gigantes and made sail for the Boca Chica, the present entrance to the port of Cartagena. From there it was seven or eight miles to the anchorage near the town. On disembarking I learned with great satisfaction that the coastal surveying expedition had not yet put out to sea, and I was able to ascertain from my consultations with members of that expedition the astronomical positions of several towns on the shore which I required for my longitudinal calculations. The consultations also provided information regarding the route of my projected journey to Peru. We learned that the passage from Cartagena to Porto Bello, on the isthmus of Panama, is short and easy. But we were warned that we might have to wait in Panama for a long time for a vessel to take us to Guayaquil, and that in any event the passage from Panama to Guayaquil would be extremely long, because it takes one in a direction contrary to the winds and currents. Therefore, I relinquished with regret my plans to measure the height of the Panamanian mountains that divide the Atlantic from the Pacific Oceans. It would have been difficult to foresee that today, when I write these lines in 1827, people would still be ignorant of their altitude. The persons whom we consulted all agreed that an overland journey from Cartagena to Lima, via Bogotá and Quito in the Andean highlands, would be preferable to a sea voyage and would furnish an immense field for exploration. In addition, Bonpland and I felt the European predilection for *tierra fría*, the cool Andean climate, which gave further weight to these counsels. The distances were known, but we never imagined

---

*This paragraph contains observations that Humboldt published in *The Island of Cuba*, trans. J. S. Thrasher (New York: Derby & Jackson, 1856), pp. 185–88, 211–13, 225.

that it would take us eighteen months to traverse them on mule-back. In compensation, this change in our plan and direction gave me occasion to observe volcanoes, to trace the map of the Magda-lena River, to fix astronomically the location of eighty inland points between Cartagena and Lima, and to collect specimens of several thousand new plant species.

Analyzing the Sources: How would you describe Humboldt's "voice" in this selection? What impression do you believe it would have left in his English-language readers?

DIARY OF A COMANDANTE OF AMERICAN INDEPENDENCE

José Santos Vargas

José Santos Vargas was a drummer boy with patriot forces in Upper Peru who eventually achieved the rank of comandante. His war was a guerrilla war, involving small forces and, often, improvised weapons. These excerpts from his diary provide an unusual look at the difficult situation of indig-enous people caught in the crossfire. Both royalists and patriots used Indian fighters as auxiliaries, armed primarily with slings and clubs and separate from the uniformed white and mestizo troops. Neither treated them with the dignity normally accorded to whites or mestizos. Indigenous people, more than any other group in colonial Latin America, kept to themselves if possible. They wanted to stay out of the conflict, because to help the patriots was to invite royalist reprisal, and vice versa. During the long, confusing years of fighting, many common people—white, black, indig-enous, and mestizo—switched sides more than once, sometimes out of shifting convictions, sometimes simply to save their lives.

SOURCE: José Santos Vargas, *Diario de un Comandante de la independencia americana, 1814–1825.* ed. Gunnar Mendoza I (Mexico City: Siglo Veintiuno, 1982), pp. 119, 125–26, 141–43, 175, 288–90.

26 June 1816. [Patriot officer Pascual] García arrived at Sivingani pretending to be a royalist, accusing the Indians of being insurgents, and asking questions about Comandante Lira and his troops. The Indians immediately gathered and, believing García to be a royalist, they happily declared the following, as with one voice:

"Sir, we have already reported to the authorities of the village, taking them barley, potatoes, meat, and firewood, as much as we were able. We were born and raised under the flag of Spain and have always supported the king's cause. Others may be insurgents, but we are not, no matter who says so. We are finding out where the insurgents are, and they will soon be captured, with our help. Not one will escape. Recently they seem to be on Mount Chajcañota, and we will inform local officials when they make the slightest movement."

"Fine, my children" replied García, "now come and we'll give you proper thanks."

He had about twenty Indians shut inside a house and began to give them his "thanks," with a whip, from fifty to one hundred lashes for each of them, saying that, just as he had tricked them, pretending to be a royalist, they must, in turn, trick the true royalists who would come later, claiming that Comandante Lira was dead.

"Everything the king's men have told you is a lie," García explained. "You think you see the truth but have been blinded by Spanish greed. My job is to open your eyes and awaken you from the lethargy in which we have lived for so long under the yoke of Spanish rule. We must all defend the cause of the Patria, the country where we were born. For the Patria we must sacrifice all other interests and give even our lives. Our triumph is inevitable. Come join our forces, which are now almost sufficient to destroy our enemies. Comandante Alvarez occupies the heights of Mohosa with many men. Comandante Lira has gathered virtually all the Indians of these parts, except for you and the Indians of Collana whom I've been recruiting.

This was the message we spread everywhere, and in vain, because in fact we did not have with us any Indians at all. It felt like trying to reconquer a foreign country.

1 January 1817. On heights near the town of Mohosa we found two hundred enemy soldiers, and Commander Lira had us gather dried manure for a diversion. We made five big heaps of manure that would burn for a long time and, just after midnight, we lit them and left. The enemy saw the light and tried to sneak up and surprise us, but all they surprised were our decoy fires, and we were three leagues away by dawn.

A couple of poor Indians with their llamas were brought to us as prisoners because they'd abandoned their llamas and other possessions at our approach and been found hiding. Lira said they were probably spies and ordered two hundred lashes for each until they talked. At that point, one went running off, crying that they were innocent and were coming to town to buy necessary things for their families, because they had many small children, and that they always hide from soldiers, all soldiers. Some of our own Indians chased down and killed the one who was trying to escape. Thereupon, Lira ordered that the second prisoner be executed. The condemned man looked up and shouted angrily at the heavens, then knelt before Lira, sobbing and saying: Comandante, behold the birds in those trees who know and care nothing of our wars, seeking only to feed themselves and their families. So do we, exactly thus. The man you have killed was my brother, a poor man. You have no reason to harm us. The true Patria should protect and pardon its children, particularly those as innocent as we. Hearing these words, many were moved and prevailed upon Lira to release the luckless wretch, who went away with expressions of gratitude.

9 *January 1817*. This morning the countryside was full of enemy soldiers. They went into the hut of a poor Indian named Fermín Mamani and killed him with their bayonets right there where he was cooking and eating potatoes. Without telling him anything they walked right in and killed him with his mouth full. He didn't even have time to swallow. Then they saw another corn patch and Indian hut nearby and headed straight there, where they found José Flores. Flores told them that he was a tribute-paying member of the nearby indigenous community of Caracollo and a loyal subject of the king. But they took him prisoner to their camp and shot him anyway.

8 *March 1817.* At four in the afternoon, the royalist commander don José Castro Navajas, with fifty reinforcements, tried to throw us back at all cost, but he failed. The Indians of the Patria were exhausted by this time, but they fought with such fervor that the enemy couldn't budge them. Navajas himself dismounted and led an advance until one of our Indians toppled him with a shot from his sling. Navajas struggled to his feet, but another stone hit him in the leg, and he went down for good. One of his men had to come out and drag the commander back to the royalist position by his feet!

The soldiers of the king withdrew to their hill, regrouped, and then about a hundred of them came back at us, shooting. Our Indians went out to meet them, not scared of their bullets any more, and let fly with their slings. The royalists retreated out of range to reload their muskets, attacked again shooting, retreated to reload, and so on. While they raced back and forth our Indians started creeping forward through the bushes and ravines to surprise the enemy. Jumping out, they'd grab the enemies' muskets so the shots went off harmlessly. The enemy soldiers let go of their weapons and ran. Some were clubbed to death or killed with their own bayonets if they didn't run fast enough. Finally they gave up and retreated to their hill.

Somewhat later, a party of 600 royalists was on the road to Oruro under the command of Colonel Quimper. Arriving at the place called Sinispaya, Quimper looked through his spyglass and noticed a small figure on the mountainside above the road. He sent a party of eight men to investigate and they returned to the royalist camp with an Indian shepherd, Mariano López Quispe, nicknamed Lupico, who had been spinning wool and watching his sheep. Colonel Quimper took one look at Lupico, who also carried a sling, saying, "This is a rebel," and ordering his immediate execution. They were about to blindfold the luckless Indian when he said, with a brave heart: Janihua nayaja mulahati nayra iman tañmataqui, which means in his language: "I'm not a mule for you to put blinders on." He looked right at the soldier who shot him. The shot knocked Quispe down, but then he sat up and said, "Okay, you got me, but I know who you are," and shook his fist. So they shot him a couple of more times, and he died. Imagine the valor of this tough Americano that tried to survive his own execution and avenge the misdeed done against him, an innocent man whose only crime was to have been born on the soil of América.

16 March 1817. We spotted the enemy at eight o'clock in the morning on the heights of Cavari. They had their Indians with them, and so did we. To indicate who was who, our Indians wore sprigs of green grass on their hats, and their Indians smeared the crowns of their hats with red clay. That's how we knew when two of theirs crossed over and joined ours. Comandante Lira noticed the newcomers and immediately had them hauled out and tied back to back. The luckless Indians claimed that they had been forced to join the royalists of Cavari, that they were really patriots and our countrymen and had been awaiting a moment to escape and rejoin the soldiers of the Patria, as they had in fact done. And they railed at the royalist commanders and protested their imprisonment. In spite of all their protests, however, Lira listened to them coldly, then ordered that they be taken a few hundred yards away and killed.

19 September 1817. In the action fought on this day, we lost five soldiers and fourteen Indians dead. Of the fourteen Indians, one died in the following manner. He and eleven others were trying to escape down a cliff, and the others had all fallen, when out stepped a well-armed royalist. The royalist took aim at the Indian, kneeling at the cliff edge, but his shot missed.

The Indian rose, saying: "Please, let me go. I'm a man just like you, with a wife and children. I'm here by force, not because I wanted to come attack you. Think how pleasing it would be to God, and how much my whole family and I will remember you in our prayers, if you spare my life. So please let me go."

"Get moving," ordered royalist, grabbing hold of the Indian, "and I'll ask my superior officer to spare your life." The Indian implored the soldier repeatedly to let him go, because he had a large family with many small children, but the soldier only held on to him more tightly. At that point, the Indian saw three more royalist soldiers approaching.

"If you won't have mercy," he said, "then we'll die together," and wrapping his arms around his captor, with a powerful shove, the

Indian dove off the cliff, pulling the royalist with him. Some of our Indians watched all this happen and, sending word to Commander Lira, a bunch of them went to the bottom of the cliff and found both men sorely wounded but still alive. The royalist had no skin left on his face and a broken leg, but our Indian was in even worse shape, having lost the skin on his face and the entire left side of this body. Both were still able to talk, and that his how the Indian related what he had said to his captor before jumping. The wounded royalist begged us in the name of God and the Patria to finish him off, because he knew that he could never recover, and the pain was unbearable. After shouting these things, though, he calmed down and begged our forgiveness, saying that rage had been his undoing.

Hearing all this, Commander Lira said he'd send the soldier to be treated at Palca, and that he should beg God, not us, for forgiveness, but the soldier didn't listen, and now he was saying that he, too, had fought for the Patria, and please, in the name of the Patria, to kill him or at least give him a knife to do it himself. The Indian laughed at him, saying this was his reward for not letting go. Lira told the soldier that they would kill him, as he requested, but that he should wait until they could carry him to Morochata where there was a priest to hear his confession. The soldier angrily asked Lira why, if we believed so much in confession, we didn't have a chaplain with us, and other insulting things. He was getting delirious. So Lira finally gave the order to put him out of his misery, and a few well-aimed club blows quickly did so.

Lira sent the Indian to Morochata but he died on the way. He was from a place called Huacaplaza on the Yani hacienda, Morochata, and his name was Mariano Mamani. Consider the energy and determination of this Americano who, to win a free and independent Patria for his posterity, finding himself unarmed, took an enemy soldier with him when he died. For this reason, Commander Lira carefully explained to all our Indians what Patria meant, why independence from Spain mattered, and exactly how it would benefit our posterity.

10 August 1820. On this day two Indians in the service of the king arrived at a place called Ancocota, in Mohosa, where the local

Indians were celebrating the feast of Santa Rosa. One was Dionisio Condori, who called himself colonel, and the other Mateo Velarde, lieutenant colonel. The participants of the feast were immediately suspicious of them but treated them courteously, with all the ceremony that the Indians use among themselves. Immediately, they began to ply the two newcomers with liquor.

Once the two royalists were feeling the effects of the alcohol, they inquired of their hosts: "Where is everyone else? We saw more people here when we first arrived. Tell everyone to come, because we have the power to pardon them in the name of the king, so that they can get to work and make their tribute payments." The idea, they explained, was to pacify the country and end the uprising against the crown.

The local Indians said that they were willing to ask royal forgiveness, but that the two royalists should wait for a while, that the rest of the community would soon come to receive the pardon, and the newcomers gladly agreed. So all continued to drink and the royalists went on talking in favor of the king and against the cause of Liberty and the Patria. Gradually, the Indians of Ancocota got irritated at the things the royalists were saying. An Indian named Asencio Chipana, who was pretty drunk, got so upset that he went up to them, with tears streaming down his face, and shouted:

"Esteemed officers of the king, aren't you Americanos, or did you come from Europe, from Spain? Have you ever seen the king? You don't know anything about monarchy! I bet you wouldn't even recognize a portrait of the king. As a native of this land, an Americano, I'm a patriot, whereas you talk about the king and go around in his service, mostly because you don't want to live honestly from your own work. If you are Americanos, why have you turned your back on the Patria? You'll see, though. You'll see!"

He sobbed and carried on, mostly because he was so drunk, and the others said: "He's out of his head. Don't pay any attention to him." At that point a large party of Indians arrived with lances, clubs, and slings, and they surrounded the house where this conversation was taking place. Soon there were a hundred and twenty men around the house, and they ordered everyone out except for the two royalist officers, planning to set fire to the house and burn them alive. The two pleaded for a quicker death, and entrusting their souls to God, they knelt down. The others burst into the room, killing the two furiously and without compassion.

> **Analyzing the Sources:** *What specific instances reveal the reaction of indigenous Andeans to the political conflict between patriots and royalists in the wars of independence?*

TRAVELS IN BRAZIL

Henry Koster

Henry Koster, an Englishman raised in Portugal, lived in the northeastern Brazilian province of Pernambuco between 1809 and 1820. His description of the lives of slaves has idealized tints clearly contradicted by much evidence of frequent harsh treatment. Travel accounts from this period sometimes underplay the well-documented harsh treatment received by slaves in Latin America, partly because the travelers received much of their information from the slaveholders. Still, humane treatment such as that described by Koster no doubt existed in places, and keeping in mind its bias, his description helps us envision aspects of life on a plantation. In addition, Koster discusses the lives of free mulattos (particularly the degree to which those of light skin were able to mingle with whites or even pass for whites) and the lives of free "creole" blacks (people of purely African descent, born in Brazil). Free mulattoes and blacks participated in the militia, an important source of social prestige.

All the slaves in Brazil follow the religion of their masters, and, notwithstanding the impure state in which the Christian church exists in that country, such are the beneficent effects of the Christian religion that these, its adopted children, are improved by it to an

SOURCE: adapted from Henry Koster, *Travels in Brazil* (London: Longman, Hurst, Rees, Orme, and Brown, 1817), pp. 2:208–22, 2:237–46, 2:262–67.

infinite degree, and the slave who attends to the strict observance of religious ceremonies invariably proves to be a good servant. The Africans who are imported from Angola are baptized in lots before they leave their own shores, and on their arrival in Brazil they are to learn the doctrines of the Church and the duties of the religion into which they have entered. These bear the mark of the royal crown upon their breasts, which denotes that they have undergone the ceremony of baptism and, likewise, that the king's tax has been paid upon them. The slaves which are imported from other parts of the coast of Africa arrive in Brazil unbaptized, and before the ceremony of making them Christians can be performed upon them they must be taught certain prayers, for the acquirement of which one year is allowed the master before he is obliged to present the slave at the parish church. This law is not always strictly obeyed as to time, but it is never evaded altogether. The religion of the master teaches him that it would be extremely sinful to allow the slave to remain a heathen, and indeed the Portuguese and Brazilians have too much religious feeling to let them neglect any of the ordinances of their church. The slave himself likewise wishes to be made a Christian, for his fellow bondsmen will, in every squabble or trifling disagreement with him, close their string of opprobrious epithets with the name of "pagan." The unbaptized black feels that he is considered as an inferior being, and although he may not be aware of the value which the whites place upon baptism, still he knows that the stigma for which he is upbraided will be removed by it, and therefore he is desirous of being made equal to his companions. The Africans who have been long imported imbibe the Catholic feeling and appear to forget that they were once in the same situation themselves. The slaves are not asked whether they desire baptism or not. Their entrance into the Catholic Church is treated as a thing of course, and indeed they are not considered as members of society, but rather as brute animals, until they can lawfully go to mass, confess their sins, and receive the sacraments.

The slaves, as well as the free persons, have their religious brotherhoods, and the ambition of a slave very generally is to be admitted into one of these and to be made one of the directors of the brotherhood. Even some of the money which the industrious slave is collecting for the purpose of purchasing his freedom will oftentimes be brought out of concealment for the decoration of a saint. The Negroes have one invocation of the Virgin which is peculiarly their own, Our Lady of the Rosary, who is even sometimes painted with a black face and hands. The election of a King of Congo by the individuals who come from that part of Africa, a common practice, seems as though it would give them a bias toward the customs of their native soil, but in Brazil the Kings of Congo worship Our Lady of the Rosary and are dressed in the dress of white men. They and their subjects dance, it is true, after the manner of their country, but to these festivals are admitted African Negroes of other nations, creole blacks, and mulattos, all of whom dance in the same manner, and these dances are now as much the national dances of Brazil as they are of Africa.

The Portuguese language is spoken by all the slaves, and their own dialects are allowed to lie dormant until they are by many of them quite forgotten. No compulsion is resorted to make them embrace the habits of their masters, but their ideas are insensibly led to imitate and adopt them. The masters at the same time imbibe some of the customs of their slaves, and thus the superior and his dependent are brought nearer to each other. I doubt not that the system of baptizing the newly imported Negroes proceeded rather from the bigotry of the Portuguese in former times rather than from any political plan, but it has had the most beneficial effects. The slaves are rendered more tractable. Besides being better men and women, they become more obedient servants, and they are brought under the control of the priesthood, a great engine of power.

The sugar plantations which belong to the Benedictine monks and Carmelite friars are those upon which the labor is conducted with the greatest attention to the system and with the greatest regard to the comfort and ease of the slaves. I can particularly speak of the estates of the Benedictine monks, because my residence at Jaguaribe gave me daily opportunities of hearing about the management of one of their establishments. The slaves of the Jaguaribe St. Bento estate are all creoles and are in number about one hundred. The children are carefully taught their prayers by some of the elder Negroes, and the hymn to the Virgin is sung by all the slaves who can possibly attend, male and female, at seven o'clock every evening. At this hour it is required that every person should be at home. The young children are allowed to amuse themselves as they please during the greatest part of the day. Their only occupation for certain hours is to pick cotton for lamps and to separate the beans which are fit for seed from those which are rotten, and other work of the same description. When they arrive at the age of ten and twelve years, the girls spin thread for making the coarse cotton cloth of the country, and the boys attend to the horses and oxen, driving them to pasture &c. If a child evinces peculiar fitness for any trade, care is taken that his talents should be applied in the manner that he would himself prefer. A few of them are taught music and assist in the church festivals of the convent. Most tasks are completed by three o'clock in the afternoon, which gives industrious slaves an opportunity of working daily on their own provision grounds. The slaves are allowed the Saturday of every week, in addition to Sundays and holidays, to provide for their own subsistence. Those who are diligent fail not to obtain their freedom by self-purchase. The provision grounds are never interfered with by the monks, and when a Negro dies or obtains his freedom, he is permitted to bequeath his plot of land to any of his companions. Elderly slaves are carefully provided with food and clothing.

None of the monks reside on the Jaguaribe estate, but one of them comes from Olinda almost every Sunday and holiday to say mass. Upon the other Benedictine estates there are resident monks. The slaves treat their masters with great familiarity. They only pay respect to the abbot, whom they regard as the representative of St. Bento himself. The conduct of the younger members of the clergy is well known not to be by any means correct. The vows of celibacy are not strictly adhered to. Thus, I have seen upon these plantations many light-colored mulatto slaves, but when the approximation to white blood becomes considerable, a marriage is projected with a person of darker tint.

The Jaguaribe estate is managed by a mulatto slave who married a person of his own color, and she likewise belonged to the convent. Her husband has purchased her freedom and that of her children. He possesses two African slaves, the profits of whose labor are entirely his own, but he is himself obliged to attend to the business of the plantation and to see that the work of his masters is properly executed. This man has offered his own two African slaves to the monks in exchange for his freedom, but they tell him that the Jaguaribe estate could not be properly managed without his assistance, and so he continues in slavery, much against his inclination.

[*In another passage, Koster discusses the situation of free mulattos, who were able to rise socially and free blacks, who were much less able to do so.*]

Sometimes a mulatto enters into holy orders with papers stating that he is a white man but his appearance plainly denoting the contrary. In conversing on one occasion with a man of color who was in my service, I asked him if a certain Captain Major was not a mulatto man. "He was, but he is not now," came the answer. I begged him to explain, so he added: "Can a Captain Major be a mulatto man?" Likewise, I was intimately acquainted with a priest whose complexion and hair plainly denoted his African ancestry. He was a well-educated and intelligent man, I liked him much, and I met with several others of the same description.

The militia contains mulatto regiments in which all the officers and men are of mixed caste. The principal officers are men of property and the colonel, like the commander of any other regiment, is answerable only to the governor of the province. The late colonel of the mulatto regiment, a man by the name of Nogueira, went to Lisbon and returned with the order of Christ, conferred on him by the queen. A chief person of the province is the son of a white man and a woman of color. He has received an excellent education, is of a generous disposition, and entertains most liberal views upon all subjects. He has been made a colonel, and a title of nobility has been conferred upon him. Likewise, the prince regent is the sponsor to one of his children. Many other instances might be mentioned. Some of the wealthy planters of Pernambuco and richest inhabitants of Pernambuco are men of color. The major part of the best artisans is also of mixed blood.

It is said that mulattos make bad masters. This is true, often-times, with persons who were once enslaved and now possess slaves of their own, also with those who have become managers on estates. This change of situation would lead to the same consequences in any race of human beings. I have seen mulattos of free birth who are as kind, as lenient, and as forbearing to their slaves as any white man.

Marriages between white men and women of color are by no means rare, though they are sufficiently so to cause the circumstance to be mentioned when speaking of an individual who has connected himself in this manner. The comment is not made, however, with the intent of lowering him in the estimation of others. Indeed, the remark is only made if the person is a planter of any importance and the woman is of a decidedly dark color, for even a considerable tinge will pass for white. If the white man belongs to the lower orders, the woman is not accounted as being unequal to him in rank unless she is nearly black. Europeans often marry here in this manner, which generally occurs when the woman possesses a considerable dowry. Rich mulatto families are often glad to marry their daughters to these men, although they may be of socially indifferent circumstances, for their daughters consequently will have lighter children. In addition, such men are reputed to be prudent and hard-working, able to amass a large fortune from small beginnings. Whilst I was at Jaguaribe I often saw a handsome young man from the Azores who happened to be with me on one occasion when a military officer from the backlands was staying at my house. The officer asked the young man if he could read and write, and being answered in the negative, said, "Then you will not do," and turning to me, he added: "I have a commission from a friend of mine to bring a good-looking, dependable young Portuguese who can read and write, for the purpose of marrying his daughter."

Still, Brazilians of high birth and property do not like to inter-marry with persons whose mixture of blood is very apparent. A man of this description becomes attached to a woman of color, connects himself with her and takes her to his home, where she is in a short time even visited by married women. She governs his household affairs, acts as and considers herself his wife, and frequently, after the birth of several children, he marries her. In connections of this nature, the parties are more truly attracted to one another than in marriages between persons who belong to families of the first rank, for the latter are entered into from convenience rather than affection. But it often occurs that inclination, necessity, or convenience induce or oblige a man to separate from the woman with whom he has thus been connected. In such cases, he gives her some property and she marries a man of lower rank, who regards her rather as a widow than as a person whose conduct has been incorrect. Instances of infidelity in these women are rare, they become quite attached to the men with whom they cohabit, and they direct the affairs of their houses with as much zeal as if they truly belonged to them.

I now proceed to mention that numerous and valuable race of men, the creole* Negroes, a tree of African growth. Only those who have no pretensions to a mixture of blood call themselves Negroes. They are distinct from their brethren in slavery, owing to their superior situation as free men. They are handsome persons, brave and hardy, obedient to the whites and willing to please. The free creole Negroes have their exclusive militia regiments in which every officer and soldier must be perfectly black. There are two of these regiments in the province of Pernambuco, distinguished from each other by the names Old Henriques and New Henriques. The name is derived from the famous black leader, Henrique Dias, a hero from the war against the Dutch. Some of the most intelligent men with whom I have conversed spoke in enthusiastic terms of Henrique Dias. I have seen one of these regiments accompanying the procession of Our Lady of the Rosary, their patron saint. They were dressed in white uniforms, trimmed with scarlet, and they looked very soldier-like. They were in tolerable discipline and formed a finer body of men than any other soldiers which I had an opportunity of seeing in the country. On gala days, the ranking black officers in their white uniforms pay their respects to the governor, exactly as persons of equal rank belonging to any other caste. Militiamen receive no pay, so that their neat appearance on such occasions bespeaks a certain degree of wealth. Some of the whites rather ridicule the black officers, but not in their presence, and the laughter

---

*Brazilian-born.

that is raised against them is caused perhaps by a lurking wish to prevent this insulted race from displaying the distinctions which the government has wisely conceded to them, but which hurt the European ideas of superiority.

The creole Negroes of Pernambuco are, generally speaking, artisans of all descriptions. They have not yet reached the higher ranks of life as gentlemen, planters, and merchants. Some of them have accumulated considerable sums of money and possess many slaves to whom they teach their own trade or destine for other employment. The best church and image painter of Pernambuco is a black man. He has good manners and quite the air of a man of some importance, though he does not by any means assume too much. Negroes are excluded from the priesthood, however, and from the offices which mulattoes may obtain by passing for white, but which the unequivocal color of the Negro precludes him from aspiring to. In law, all persons not white are classed equally. Owing to their color, Negroes are unable to serve in regiments of the regular army, which at least allows them to escape persecutions which members of other castes suffer because of forced recruitment.

The men whose occupation it is to apprehend runaway slaves are, almost without exception, creole blacks. They are called *capitães do campo*, or "field captains," and several may be found in every rural district. They are men of undaunted courage and are usually followed by two or three dogs trained to seek out runaways and, if necessary, attack them and take them down. The men who bear these commissions can oblige anyone to turn over an apprehended runaway to be returned to his owner.

Analyzing the Sources: Narratives like Koster's once made historians believe that Brazilian slavery was "milder" than that in the United States—a now discredited view. How and why does this selection constitute a best-case scenario? Consider particularly Koster's description of the role of the Catholic Church. Also, how would you characterize Koster's description of Brazilian race relations in the period?

THE ANGOSTURA ADDRESS

Simón Bolívar

Although Simón Bolívar's greatest successes were won on the battlefield, he aspired to be a political philosopher as well as a military commander. In this 1819 speech, he advises the constituent assembly that had gathered in the city of Angostura (today Ciudad Bolívar) to draft a constitution. Bolívar shows his wide reading in European history and his special admiration of England. He emphasizes, however, citing Montesquieu's Spirit of the Laws *(1748), that Venezuela's constitution must suit its circumstances. Bolívar had freed slaves who were willing to join him, and men of African descent figured strongly in Bolívar's army. There had been some racial tension in his forces too surrounding Bolívar's execution of Manuel Piar, a victorious patriot general who accused Bolívar of discriminating against him. Venezuela's new constitution, like all the others in newly independent Latin American countries, would have to reflect the reality of the multiracial coalitions that had rallied around the idea of América for Americanos! Bolívar's Angostura Address seemed interminable when he read it verbatim to the constituent assembly over a period of hours. This is a substantially abridged version.*

Gentlemen:

To inform your deliberations, let us consider the society that exists today, the practical foundations of the Republic of Venezuela.

As América breaks away from the Spanish monarchy, it is disaggregating, much as occurred with the fall of the ancient Roman Empire, when what had been a single empire fell apart into a series of independent nations. There the similarity ends, however. For if the Roman Empire disintegrated into the constituent parts that had already existed prior to the coming of the legions, the same is not possible in América. Our societies hardly conserve a trace of

SOURCE: This abbreviated translation preserves elements of the Louis Bertrand translation in Harold Bierck and Vicente Lecuna, eds., *Selected Writings of Bolívar* (New York: Colonial Press, 1951), pp. 173–97.

what existed here before the Spanish came. Today, we are not Europeans, nor Indians, but rather a species intermediate between the two. Americanos by birthright, Europeans by legal inheritance, we are caught in the middle, having to maintain our position against the original inhabitants of América, on the one side, and against Spanish invaders, on the other. Even the land of our birth is not purely our own, an extraordinarily complicated situation. But there is more. Because our imperial masters held us in a passive state, refusing to allow us self-governance, our quest for liberty is even more difficult than it would otherwise be. Spain denied us the right to exercise control over our own domestic affairs, depriving us of the experience of public life, debate, and administration, limiting the acquisition of exactly those leadership qualities required for the success of political revolutions. We were kept in ignorance and isolated from the world of political ideas.

The people of América are still burdened by the threefold yoke of ignorance, tyranny, and vice. The example of our colonial masters was pernicious and destructive. We have been degraded by the official imposition of deceit and vice and enslaved by our own ignorance. An ignorant people becomes the agent of its own destruction. Ambition and intrigue run amuck among people who are gullible, inexperienced, and lacking in political, economic, and civic knowledge. Ignorant people mistake illusions for realities, licentiousness for liberty, treachery for patriotism, vengeance for justice. Charging forward with misguided confidence, ignorant people who succeed in achieving liberty are likely to stumble, soon, and lose it, because they lack self-control, respect for law, and other virtues necessary for citizenship. Legislators! Your task is arduous because it involves reforming and reeducating a people corrupted by the experience of colonial domination. Liberty is a succulent morsel, according to Rousseau, but difficult to digest. Debilitated by their long servitude, our fellow citizens are not yet up to the challenge of liberty. Their arms and legs benumbed by chains, their sight dimmed by the darkness of dungeons, how can they march firmly toward the temple of Liberty?

Many ancient and modern nations have shaken off oppression, but few, indeed, have known how to maintain their precious Liberty without falling back into their former political vices. Tyranny flows less from governments than from the people themselves. People unaccustomed to self-rule do not feel bound by honor to promote the public good and the national prosperity. They are indifferent to the glorious freedom of living under laws chosen by their own free will. This is an awful truth, but one well documented in world history.

Absolute liberty will work only in a democracy, and what democratic government has been able to long prosper and remain strong? Democracies do not last, whereas monarchies and aristocracies, ruling from above, have been able to hold great empires together for centuries. Is there any government older than that of imperial China? Did not the Roman Empire conqueror the known world? Has not France had fourteen centuries of monarchy? Is there any nation today greater than England, a monarchy as well?

In spite of these bitter reflections, nothing delights me more than the great and noble political advances made by our own Republic. Keeping her sights always high, Venezuela has broken away from Spain and recovered her freedom, her equality, her independence, and her national sovereignty. By establishing a democratic republic, she has rejected monarchy, the prerogatives and privileges of nobility, and similar social distinctions. She has stood for the rights of man and instituted freedom of speech and action, freedom of conscience and the press. These sincerely liberal measures, because of the purity of the intentions that they embody, can never be too much admired. The congress of the first Republic of Venezuela stamped the majesty of the sovereign People indelibly in the national constitution that they authored. The magnitude of their good will strains the imagination.

Dare I venture to criticize the immortal law code that they created? And yet, criticize I must, because there are some emotions that a true patriot cannot keep silent within his chest. Expressions of them must burst forth, impelled by a powerful force, despite all attempts to restrain them. Many illustrious citizens feel as I do, though few have dared to speak out for the adoption of new political principles And so I declare my fervent belief that the next constitution of Venezuela must be quite different from the last.

The federal system established by our existing constitution is worthy, as I have indicated, and yet I am convinced that it cannot work well in Venezuela. To my way of thinking, the prosperity and stability of the North American model that inspired it is almost miraculous, despite the singular qualities of the North American people, not admirable from all points of view, admittedly, and yet steeped in liberty to a degree almost unique in the history of humankind. It is a marvel, I repeat, that they have preserved their inherently cumbersome federal system during the difficult challenges of their recent history. And whatever their experience with federalism, we cannot compare the English and Spanish portions of America because they are utterly different. Would it not be difficult, indeed, to apply the English system of political, civil, and religious liberty in Spain? It is even more difficult to adapt North American laws to Venezuela.

We must attend to *L'Esprit des lois*, where it is written that laws must be suited to the people for whom they are made. Does that treatise not teach us that it would be an enormous coincidence if the laws of one nation happened fit the needs of another nation, and that the laws of each must take into account the physical conditions of the country and the people's way of life? Must not the laws of each nation reflect its religion, character, customs, resources, and trade? The degree of liberty permitted by each constitution must likewise be appropriate to the nation in question. Our own needs, and not the example of Washington, should inform the design of our system of government!

This is a consideration of vital importance. Let us remember that our people are not European, nor are they North American. Rather than being a direct offshoot of Europe, our people are a composite of Africa and América. This mixture began long ago in Spain, with its historical component of African blood and cultural influences, and today, properly speaking, it is impossible to assign us to any previously existing branch of the human family. Most of the indigenous people have been annihilated. Europeans have mixed with them and with the Africans who dwell here. The Africans have mixed with the indigenous and the Europeans. We are all children of the same mother, one could say, with different fathers, come from afar, varying in blood and geographic origin, and so we differ visibly in the color of our skin. This dissimilarity places upon us a crucial obligation.

Following the laws of nature, all citizens of Venezuela should enjoy complete political equality, whatever their color. This kind of equality may not have been consecrated in Athens, nor more recently in France or North America, and yet we must consecrate this principle in Venezuela precisely in order to compensate for the dissimilarities that I describe. Equality, in my opinion, legislators, is the most fundamental basis of our existing system. Those who have studied the matter generally agree that all men are born with equal rights to share the benefits of society. They agree, too, that men are not born with equal aptitude to attain high social rank, because all men should practice virtue, but not all do, all should be courageous, but not all are. Nature creates inequalities in men's strength, character, and temperament. Differences in individual qualities and talents explain the effective social distinctions that can be observed even in societies constituted on the most liberal principles. Laws can compensate for physical and moral differences by creating a fictive political equality, an equality of access to such benefits as education, industry, and the arts. The idea of a state that unites all sorts of people, a state in which diversity increases in proportion to the rise of the population, has been an eminently positive development. The roots of tremendous social discord, jealousy, rivalry, and hatred are eliminated by establishing the principle of political equality.

Unity, unity, unity must ever be our motto! Nothing can save our young Republic from the abyss if we do not meld our population into a cohesive nation. Venezuela has been, is, and should continue to be a republic, a government based on the sovereignty of the people, one that abolishes slavery, preserves civil liberties, maintains the separation of powers, and forever banishes monarchy and special privileges. But what laws will make these principles endure? History should be our guide in this respect. What ancient and modern nations offer viable examples of the political stability that we seek? Among the ancients, Rome, and in modern times,

Great Britain have been the most powerful and free, and both were founded on solid institutions rather than on ostentatious displays of liberty.

Therefore, legislators, I recommend to you the study of British institutions, which promise the greatest benefits to those who adopt them. I do not propose slavish imitation, but rather, only those laws compatible with republicanism. Nothing in our fundamental laws would have to be altered were we to create a legislative branch similar to the British parliament. Our existing constitution followed the North American example in dividing our national congress into lower and upper houses. The first of these, the House of Representatives, has been wisely constituted with all its proper functions and requires no revision. The second of these, the Senate, would in my opinion, be better constituted, following the British example of the House of Lords, as a hereditary, rather than an elective body. In political storms, a hereditary senate would have the power to resist pressures from both above and below, becoming the chief tie that binds and the very soul of our republic, a neutral body not chosen by administrators or by the people. In the interest of self-preservation, a hereditary senate would naturally support the authorities against the masses when these show themselves unaware of their true interests. And yet, a hereditary senate would share the sentiments and the spirit of the nation at large and would not, contrary to what some assume, ignore the interests of the people. In fact, like the Roman senate, the House of Lords has been a mainstay of political and civil liberty.

The first senators would be chosen by congress, and then the government should give careful, immediate attention to the education of their hereditary successors in a special school. The future senators, eventual guardians of the nation, should learn literature, arts and sciences, all the things that enrich the mind of public figure. The creation of a hereditary senate would not be a violation of political equality because it would be an office for which candidates must prepare themselves, an office demanding great knowledge and ability. Furthermore, many of the first senators would naturally be the liberators of Venezuela, who are entitled to enjoy a high rank in the Republic that they have liberated from Spain. A people that does not applaud the elevation of its liberators is unworthy to be free! A hereditary senate would be the cornerstone of the Legislative Branch of our government, which means the cornerstone of the Republic itself.

Let your paternal love be expressed, first of all, in an educational system for the People in general. General enlightenment and sound political morals are the primary pillars of a republican system. Inculcating these qualities in our citizenry is our most urgent need. Let us revive in the world the idea of a people who, not content to be merely free and strong, desire also to be virtuous.

It is my duty, lastly, Legislators, to present you with a faithful picture of my political, civil, and military administration. To do so at this moment, however, would expend your precious time and distract your attention from more urgent matters. Consequently, my cabinet secretaries will report on their respective departments and provide the supporting documentation necessary to form an exact and complete understanding of the state of the Republic. For now, I will emphasize only the most notable measure taken by my government.

Slavery had long covered the face of Venezuela with its barbarous and awful cloak. Venezuelan skies hung heavy with storm clouds and threatened to rain upon us a deluge of fire. Therefore, invoking all that is holy and humane, I called forth redemption to disperse the tempest and break the fetters of the slaves. By that act, the slaves were freed and these embittered step-children of the Venezuela became transformed into a new generation of grateful sons, the proud defenders of their country, eager to strike a blow for Liberty. Surely it is superfluous to describe the justice, the necessity, and the beneficent results of ending slavery, for you know the history of Spartacus and of Haiti. Slavery and freedom are totally contradictory. You have the sovereign power to alter or repeal all of my statutes and decrees, but I plead for the confirmation of absolute freedom for the slaves as strongly as I would plead for my own life and for the life of the Republic.

Many veterans deserve the attention of the government, men who gave up everything to join the struggle, men who willingly experienced the horrible privations and cruelties of war for all our sakes. I have ordered that they be compensated by grants of property taken from the public domain. If I have earned any merit in the people's eyes, I ask you, as their representatives, to reward my humble services by ordering the distribution of national property pursuant to the law which I, in the name of the Republic, have decreed on behalf of the soldiers of Venezuela.

Legislators! Accept with indulgence this profession of my political faith, the utmost yearnings of my heart, the fervent pleas which I make to you on behalf of the people. I pray you, give Venezuela a government able to suppress the anarchy that threatens us, a government imbued with justice, dedicated to the good of the people, a government to usher in the reign of innocence, humanity, and peace, a government that will achieve Equality and Liberty through the inexorable rule of law.

Gentlemen, you may begin your work. I have concluded mine.

BOLÍVAR

Analyzing the Sources: Would you say that Bolívar is idealistic or practical in his ideas about a new Venezuela constitution? Does he believe in the equality of all Venezuelans?

JOURNAL OF A RESIDENCE IN CHILE

Maria Graham

Maria Graham, a writer and illustrator, was born in Scotland in 1785. As the wife of a British naval captain, she accompanied her husband to Chile, and though he soon died, she remained in the country during much of the year 1822, at the very dawn of the country's independence, when it was still ruled by Bernardo O'Higgins, who is remembered today as the country's founding father. After leaving Chile the next year, Maria Graham traveled to Brazil where she was hired by the emperor and empress of that newly independent country to take care of their daughter.

*August 24*th. The dinner was larger than would be thought consistent with good taste, and yet everything was well dressed, though with a good deal of oil and garlic. Fish came among the last things. All the dishes were carved on the table, and it is difficult to resist the pressing invitations of every moment to eat of everything. The greatest kindness is shown by taking things from your own plate and putting it on that of your friend, and no scruple is made of helping yourself to any dish before you with the spoon or knife you have been eating with, or even tasting or eating from the general dish without the intervention of a plate. In the intervals between the courses, bread and butter and olives were presented.

Judging from what I saw today, I should say that the Chilenos are great eaters, especially of sweet things, but that they drink very little. After dinner we took coffee, and, as it was late, everything passed as in an English house except the retiring of most of the family to prayers at the hour of the Ave Maria. In the evening, a few friends and relations of the family arrived, and the young people amused themselves with music and dancing. The elder ones conversed over a chafing dish and had a thick coverlet spread over it and their knees, which answers the double purpose of confining the heat to the legs and preventing the fumes of the charcoal from making the head ache. It is only lately that the ladies of Chile have learned to sit on chairs instead of squatting on the *estradas*.* Now, in lieu of the estrada, there are usually long carpets placed on each side of the room, with two rows of chairs, as close together as the knees of the opposite parties will permit, so that the feet of both meet on the carpet. The graver people place themselves with their backs to the wall, the young ladies opposite, and as the young men drop in to join the *tertulia*, or evening meeting, they place themselves behind the ladies. And all conversation, general or particular, is carried on without ceremony in half whispers.

SOURCE: Maria Callcott, *Journal of a residence in Chile, during the year 1822. And a voyage from Chile to Brazil in 1823* (London, Printed for Longman, Hurst, Rees, Orme, Brown, and Green, and John Murray, 1824), pp. 198–202, 242.
*Low platforms on which women sat to converse and sew.

When a sufficient number of persons is collected, the dancing begins, always with minuets, which, however, little resemble the grave and stately dance we have seen in Europe. Grave, indeed it is, but it is slovenly—no air, no polish, nothing in which the famous Captain Nash would recognize the graceful movements of the rooms full of dancers over which he presided so long and so well at Bath. The minuets are followed by allemandes, quadrilles, and Spanish dances. The latter are exceedingly graceful, and danced as I have seen them here, are like the poetical dances of ancient sculpture and modern painting. But then, the waltz never brought youth and beauty into such close contact with a partner. However, they are used to it, and I was a fool to feel troubled at the sight. After all the dancing was over and the friends had retired, the gates were shut carefully, and the family went to their principal meal, a hot supper. As I never eat at night, I retired to my room, highly pleased with the gentle and kind manners and hospitable frankness of my new friends and too tired to think of anything but sleep.

August 25th. My first object this morning was to examine the disposition of the different apartments of the house. And first I went to the gate by which I entered and looked along the wall on either hand in vain for a window onto the street. The house, like all those to which my eye reached, presented a low white wall with an enormous projecting tiled roof, in the center a great portal with folding gates, and by it a little tower called the *alto* with windows and a balcony at the top, where I have my apartment, and under it, close by the gate, the porter's lodge. This portal admits one into a great paved quadrangle into which various apartments open. Those on either hand appeared to be storerooms. Opposite are the *sala* or drawing room, the principal bedroom, which is also a public sitting room, and one or two smaller public rooms. Behind this band of building there is a second quadrangle laid out in flower pots, shaded with fruit trees, and a pleasant veranda. Here the young people of the family often sit and either receive visits or pursue their domestic occupations. Round this court or *patio* the private apartments of the family are arranged, and behind them there is a smaller court, where the kitchen, offices, and servants' quarters are placed, and through which, as is the case in most houses in Santiago, a plentiful stream of water is always running.

This disposition of the houses, though pleasant enough to the inhabitants, is ugly on the outside, and gives a mean, dull air to the streets, which are wide and well paved, having footpaths paved with slabs of granite and porphyry. And because through most houses a small stream is constantly running, a little more attention from the police might make Santiago the cleanest city in the world. It is not very dirty. When I recollect Rio de Janeiro and Bahia, I am ready to call it absolutely clean.

The house I was in is handsomely, but not elegantly, furnished. Good mirrors, handsome carpets, a piano by Broadwood, and a reasonable collection of chairs, tables, and beds—not exactly the styles of modern Paris or London, but such, I daresay, as were fashionable there a little more than a century ago—look exceedingly well on this side of Cape Horn. It is only the dining room that I feel disposed to quarrel with. It is the darkest, dullest, and meanest apartment in the house. The table is stuck in one corner, so that one end and one side only allow room for a row of high chairs between them and the wall. Therefore, anything like the regular attendance of servants is precluded.

My breakfast is served in my own room according to my own fashion, with tea, eggs, and bread and butter. The family eat nothing at this time of day, but some take a cup of chocolate, others a little broth, and most a *mate*. The ladies all visited me on their way to mass. On this occasion they had left off their usual French style of dress and were in black with the *mantilla* and all that makes a pretty Spaniard, or *chilena*, ten times prettier.

About noon, M. de la Salle, one of the Supreme Director's aides, called with a polite compliment from His Excellency,** welcoming me to Santiago. By this gentleman I sent my letters of introduction to His Excellency's wife, doña Rosa O'Higgins, and it was agreed that I should visit her tomorrow evening as she goes to the theater tonight. Soon after dinner today we went to the plain on the southwest side of town to see the *chinganas* or amusements of the com-

---

**A reference to Bernardo O'Higgins.

mon people. On every feast day they assemble at this place and seem to enjoy themselves very much in lounging, eating sweet puffs fried on the spot in oil, and drinking various liquors, but especially chicha,*** while they listen to a not disagreeable music played on the harp, guitar, tambourine, and triangle, accompanied by women's voices singing of love and patriotism.

> *Analyzing the Sources:* How does Graham's portrait of domestic life in a well-to-do household add to a historical view focused on economics and politics?

LIFE IN MEXICO

Frances Calderón de la Barca

Frances Calderón de la Barca, another Scottish woman, was married to a Spanish diplomat and resided in Mexico City during the years 1839–42. The following passages, extracted from entries that span several months, deal with the sort of dress worn by young mestizo women of the popular class who had enough resources to afford considerable finery—although few indeed would own more than one such dress. Calderón de la Barca first described this sort of dress during a visit to the city of Puebla, so she calls it a Poblana dress, referring to the women of that city.

24 December 1839. The dress of Poblana peasants is pretty, especially on holidays: a white muslin chemise, trimmed with lace round the skirt, neck, and sleeves; a petticoat divided into two colors, the lower part a scarlet and black cloth made in Mexico, and the upper part of yellow satin; with a satin vest of some bright color, covered

---

***The same indigenous corn beer mentioned in Núñez's "Happy Captivity."

SOURCE: adapted from Madame Calderón de la Barca, (Frances Erskine Inglis), *Life in Mexico, during a Residence of Two Years in That Country* (London: Chapman and Hall, 1843), pp. 57, 79, 116–18, 122–23, 200, 210.

with gold or silver, open in front; long earrings, with all sorts of chains and medals and tinkling things worn around the neck; a broad colored sash around the waist; a small colored handkerchief crossing over the neck, fastened in front with a brooch; a *rebozo** thrown over the shoulders; silk stockings, or more commonly, no stockings; and white satin shoes trimmed with silver. This is on holidays. On common occasions, the dress is the same, but the materials are more ordinary.

c. 30 December 1839. A great ball is to be given in the theater to benefit the poor, under the patronage of the most distinguished ladies of Mexico. After much deliberation they have decided that it is to be a costume ball, and I have some thoughts of going in the Poblana dress which I before described to you. As I am told that the Señora _____ wore such a dress at a ball in London when her husband was minister there, I have sent my maid to learn the particulars from her.

1 January 1840. This morning a very handsome dress was forwarded to me with the compliments of a lady whom I do not know, the wife of General _____, with a request that, if I should go to the fancy ball as a Poblana peasant, I wear this costume. It is a Poblana dress, and very superb, with much gold trim and embroidery. I already had another dress prepared, but I think that this is the handsomer of the two.

5 January 1840. Yesterday was Sunday, a great day here for visiting after mass is over. We had a concourse of Spaniards, all of whom seemed anxious to know whether or not I intended to wear a Poblana dress at the fancy ball and seemed wonderfully interested about it. Two young ladies or women of Puebla, introduced by Señor _____, came to proffer their services in giving me all the necessary particulars; dressed the hair of Josefa, a little Mexican girl, to show me how it should be arranged; and told me that everyone was much pleased at the idea of my going in a Poblana dress. I was rather surprised that *everyone* should trouble themselves about it.

---

*A shawl-like garmet.

At twelve o'clock the president, in full uniform, attended by his aides-de-camp, paid me a visit and sat for about half an hour, very amiable as usual. Shortly after came more visits, and just as we had supposed they were all concluded, and we were going to dinner, we were told that the secretary of state, the ministers of war and of the interior, and others, were in the drawing room. And what do you think was the purport of their visit? To adjure me, by all that was most alarming, to discard the idea of making my appearance in a Poblana dress! They assured us that Poblanas were generally *femmes de rien*,** that they wore no stockings, and that the wife of the Spanish minister should by no means assume, even for one evening, such a costume. I brought in my dresses, showed their length and their propriety, but in vain; and, in fact, as to their being in the right there could be no doubt, and nothing but a kind motive could have induced them to take this trouble. So I yielded with a good grace and thanked the cabinet council for their timely warning, though fearing, in this land of procrastination, that it would be difficult to procure another dress for the fancy ball; for you must know that our luggage is still toiling its weary way, on the backs of mules, from Veracruz to the capital.

They had scarcely gone when Señor _____ brought a message from several of the principal ladies here, whom we do not even know, and who had requested that, as a stranger, I should be informed of the reasons which rendered a Poblana dress objectionable in this country, especially on any public occasion like this ball. I was really thankful for my escape.

Just as I was dressing for dinner, a note was brought, marked *reservada* (private), the contents of which appeared to me more odd than pleasant. I have since heard, however, that the writer, don José Arnaiz, is an old man and a sort of privileged character who interferes in everything whether it concerns him or not. I translate it for your benefit: "The dress of a Poblana is that of a woman of no character. The lady of the Spanish minister is a *lady* in every sense of the word. However much she may have compromised herself, she ought neither to go as a Poblana nor in any other character but her own.

**Women of very low social status.

So says to the Señor de Calderón, José Arnaiz, who esteems him as much as possible."

10 January 1840. The fancy ball took place last evening in the theater, and although, owing either to the change of climate or to the dampness of the house, I have been obliged to keep to my room since the day of the bullfight and to decline a pleasant dinner at the English Minister's, I thought it advisable to make my appearance at the dance. Having discarded the costume of the light-headed Poblanas, I adopted that of a virtuous woman of ancient Rome, simple enough to get up in one day: a white skirt, red bodice with blue ribbons, and a lace veil.

We went to the theater about eleven, and found the *entrée*, though crowded with carriages, very quiet and orderly. Inside the boxes were hung with bright silk draperies, and a canopy of the same, drawn up in the form of a tent, covered the whole ballroom. The orchestra was also tolerably good. The boxes were filled with ladies, presenting an endless succession of crepe shawls of every color and variety and a monotony of diamond earrings. Of Swiss peasants, Scottish peasants, and all manner of peasants, there was a goodly assortment, as also of Turks, Highlanders, and men in plain clothes. But being open to the public, it was not a select crowd, and among many well-dressed people, there were also hundreds who, assuming no particular character, had exerted their imaginations to appear merely fanciful . . . and had succeeded.

Upon the whole, I saw few very striking beauties and very little good dancing. There was too much velvet and satin, and the dresses were too loaded with adornments and absurdly short. The diamonds, though superb, were frequently ill-set. There were various unfortunate children bundled up in long satin or velvet dresses, covered with jewels, with artificial flowers in their hair. The room was excessively cold, nor was the underlying odor of the theater entirely obliterated, nor do I think that all the perfumes of Arabia would overpower it. We remained until three in the morning and declined all offers of refreshment, though, after all, a cup of hot chocolate would not have been amiss. There was supper somewhere, but, I believe, attended only by gentlemen.

Holy Week 1840. The whole of Mexico City was filled with picturesque figures. After the higher señoras were to be remarked the
common women, chiefly in clear white, very stiffly starched mus-
lins, some very richly embroidered and the petticoat trimmed with
lace, white satin shoes, and the dress extremely short, which in them
looks very well. A rebozo is thrown over all. Amongst these were
many handsome faces, but in a still lower and more Indian class,
with their gay-colored petticoats, the faces were sometimes beautiful
and the figures more upright and graceful. Women of this class
invariably walk well, whilst many of the higher classes, because of
overly tight shoes and because they are unaccustomed to walking,
seem to feel pain in putting their feet to the ground. The pure Indians, with whom the churches and the whole city is crowded, are as
ugly as can be imagined—a gentle, dirty, and much enduring race.
And none of the foregoing could vie with the handsome Poblana
peasants in their holiday dresses, their petticoats frequently fringed
and embroidered with real gold. We saw several whose dresses could
not have cost less than five hundred dollars. Some were so rich
and magnificent that, remembering the warning of our ministerial
friends, I am inclined to believe them more showy than respectable.

*Analyzing the Sources: What seems to be at stake in the struggle over
whether or not Mrs. Calderón de la Barca, a diplomat's wife, would wear
a Poblana dress to the costume ball?*

Chapter 4

CREATING NATIONAL IDENTITIES

In Latin America, states preceded nations. In other words, countries became independent and were endowed with governing institutions before the diverse inhabitants of each country had acquired a strong national identity. On what basis would they now live together? The patriots of independence had fought, for the most part, under the banner of *América*, defined mostly by their refusal to remain colonies of Spain and Portugal. By the mid-1800s, however, the region had fragmented politically into many separate, independent states, more than a dozen new nations had begun to emerge, and Latin American writers went to work elaborating separate national identities to go with them. What did it mean to be Bolivian or Mexican or Colombian? Writers answered this question by invoking the formative experiences of daily life, such as food, clothing, religion, and language—shared *customs*, in other words. Their writings, called *costumbrismo* from the Spanish word for customs, constitute the principal sources for this chapter.

The diversity of Latin American populations constituted a direct challenge to the creation of new national identities. The inhabitants of new Latin American nations had roots on three continents, and their differing historical experiences—which involved plenty of social conflict—were more likely to create hard (divisive) feelings than warm (unifying) ones. Centuries-long processes of transculturation and race-mixing offered unifying themes, but these themes had to be woven into stories that the people of each nation could "tell themselves about themselves," in a famous phrase. Moreover, in order to be stories that could inspire a sense of common identity across lines of class and race, these stories needed to provide a sense that humble people of African and indigenous descent, the descendents of the conquered and enslaved, shared a history and customs with the descendents of the conquerors and enslavers, a difficult task to say the least. Humble people could absolutely not be left out of the story because they were assumed to be the primary bearers of authentic national culture, the upper classes being more subject to foreign influence.

Costumbrista writers sought to paint distinctive national self-portraits. One collection of costumbrista writing excerpted for this chapter was titled precisely *A Mexican Self-Portrait*. It presented a series of social "types" (the water carrier, the storekeeper, and so on) who, in aggregate, were supposed to make up the nation. Costumbrista sketches could stand alone or be incorporated into fiction or other arenas. They often appeared in newspapers, resembling short stories. The long form of the novel offered many opportunities to deploy costumbrismo. Three selections in this chapter are taken from novels that began to appear in the mid-1800s, becoming foundational building blocks of new national literatures and a crucial gauge of cultural achievement for Latin American elites. The early Brazilian work *Memoirs of a Militia Sergeant* is almost more costumbrismo than novel. *Bolívar's Justice* constitutes a distinctive Latin American genre, the *tradición*, a sort of dramatized popular history, invented by the Peruvian author Ricardo Palma and copied throughout Latin America. Meanwhile, Sarmiento's *Facundo*, the most famous text here, is uncharacterizable: not fiction or exactly nonfiction, part biography, part political diatribe— but full of local color.

To contribute to nation-building, costumbrismo had to evoke warm feelings and a sense of shared identity. Many divides required bridging, notably rural urban divides. *A Mexican Self-Portrait*, for example, is almost entirely about Mexico City. Most of nineteenth-century Latin America's readers and writers lived in cities, so they could most easily identify with urban customs and types. Rural types and customs often appeared exotic beside prevalent European models. Still, rural people were considered the most representative of national authenticity because they lived close to the land and were less "corrupted" by foreign influence. Making city people aware of country cousins was part of the costumbrista project in Latin America. *Facundo* represents the countryside as full of fabulous (and somewhat dangerous) anachronisms of which urban people should be aware.

There were also regional divides, but the most pervasive and threatening divides were those of race and class. Most costumbristas hoped that paternalism could bridge them. *María*'s "happy slaves" represent, in their most blatant form, the nation-building impulse to depict harmonious, paternalistic feelings. Slaves do not resent slavery or chafe at enslavement in *María*'s feel-good alternative universe. In many early Latin American novels divisions of class and race are bridged imaginatively by romantic love. That occurs in the Chilean novel *Martín Rivas*, although not in the excerpt presented here.

In *Bolívar's Justice*, Ricardo Palma uses the wars of independence to suggest another sort of national unification. In Peru, as elsewhere, the wars of independence had been civil wars, creating many hard feelings. These were the great dramas of patriotic history, full of founding fathers and inspirational heroes whose stirring quotations children could memorize in school *if* these bloody episodes could be imaginatively harnessed by nation-building authors. The divisive character of the wars of independence had to fade a bit from people's minds before these struggles could be turned into dramas of unity and social harmony, as Palma did in the 1860s with *Bolívar's Justice*. This tradición by Palma is not very costumbrista, and the *Autobiography* of the Venezuelan caudillo Páez is not costumbrista at all. Both illustrate, however, that invoking past conflict can become a way to celebrate shared values and thus contribute to nation-building.

Materials in this chapter come from some of the leading Latin American authors and literary texts of the day. *Facundo* is arguably the most important Argentine book of all time. *María* was probably the most widely influential novel, not only in Colombia but in all of nineteenth-century Latin America. Palma is still considered one of the region's greats. Creating national identities was important work without which fledgling nation-states could never be strong and stable.

FACUNDO

Domingo Faustino Sarmiento

Domingo Faustino Sarmiento (born 1811) was a liberal intellectual, an adversary of the Argentine caudillo Juan Manuel de Rosas, and finally president of Argentina (1868–74). His biographical/historical/sociological essay Civilization and Barbarism: The Life of Facundo Quiroga and the Geography and Customs of the Argentine Republic *(1845),* Facundo, *for short, became unquestionably one of the most important foundational works of Latin American thought and literature. While not a work of costumbrismo, it certainly does paint a national self-portrait. The following excerpts deal especially with the impact of landscape on society, an idea (highly influential in the nineteenth century) known as "environmental determinism." Sarmiento believed that the vast plains of Argentina left an indelible imprint on the people and helped explain the rule of men like Rosas.*

The limitless, thinly populated plains that stretch more than seven hundred leagues from Buenos Aires to Salta and Mendoza constitute the most notable interior feature of the Argentine Republic. Across these plains, caravans of enormous two-wheeled oxcarts roll freely without encountering the least obstacle, without needing the hand of man to clear the way of trees or thickets. No more than the efforts of the individual and the effects of the natural environment are required to open avenues of communication. Society can do little to improve them.

The leader of one of these caravans needs an iron will, a character bold to the point of recklessness, to defend and dominate his subordinates amid the solitude. At the least sign of insolence, he raises his mighty iron-handled lash and dishes out wounds and contusions. If resistance continues, rather than his pistols, which he seldom deigns to draw, he leaps from his horse, knife in hand, and quickly

SOURCE: adapted from Domingo Faustino Sarmiento, *Facundo: Civilización y barbarie en la República Argentina* (Madrid: Editorial América, 1916), pp. 24–43, 48–51.

reestablishes his authority by the superior skill with which he wields it. Thus, the conditions of Argentine life establish the primacy of brute force, the superiority of the strongest, the authority without limits or responsibility of those who give the orders. On these long journeys, the common people of Argentina acquire the habits of life outside of society, hardened by privations, struggling individually with nature, depending only on their personal capacity and wit against the dangers that surround them continually.

The population that dwells in these extensive regions is composed largely of two different races, Spanish and Indian, that mix together to form an array of intermediate shades. In addition, the black race, which has almost disappeared except in the province of Buenos Aires, has left behind its own intermediate shades of mixture with Spanish and Indian, largely in the cities. With some exceptions, these three races have fused in a rural population distinguished by its lack of industry and love of idleness. This unfortunate situation seems to have resulted mostly from the social incorporation by the Spanish colonizers of native races that have shown themselves incapable of hard, sustained labor even when compelled by force. It was that incapacity, precisely, which led to the fatal importation of African slaves. Nor has the Spanish race proved much more industrious when abandoned to its instincts amid the wilderness of América. Only education and the incentive of social betterment can hope to improve the national population.

It is pathetic and shameful to compare the settlements of German or Scottish immigrants in the province of Buenos Aires with rural settlements of native Argentines. In the former, the houses are painted, their front yards always neat and planted with flowers and shrubbery. The furniture is simple but adequate. The tableware is of copper or tin, but brightly polished. The inhabitants are in constant motion milking cows to make cheese and butter, from which some families have managed to amass fortunes large enough to enable them to move to the city and enjoy the comforts of urban life. In the latter settlements, the rural homes of native Argentines, the situation is unhappily reversed. Unkempt, ragged children scurry in packs like dogs, filth and poverty everywhere. Men lie around on the ground, in the most complete inaction. A small table and a hide-covered box or two may be the only furniture in each miserable hut notable for its general appearance of barbarism and carelessness.

Amid the limitless spaces that we have described stand fourteen cities, scattered here and there: the provincial capitals. Argentine cities have the regular layout of almost all Spanish cities in América. Their streets intersect at right angles and their habitations are widely spaced, excepting only the case of Córdoba, which is denser and more European-looking—an appearance accented by the multitude of domes and bell towers belonging to its numerous and magnificent churches. Cities are the locus of Argentine, Spanish, European civilization. In cities, one finds commerce and industry, justice and education, government and laws, notions of progress, everything, in sum, that characterizes a people of culture and refinement. The man of our cities wears European clothing and leads a civilized life such as that of civilized men anywhere else.

When one sets foot outside the cities of the Argentine Republic, however, everything changes immediately. The man of the countryside wears different clothing and leads a totally different life. Far from desiring to imitate the urban man, the country man rejects European luxuries and scorns refined manners and clothing. Anyone who dares show himself in the country wearing a tailcoat, for example, or mounted in an English saddle, would attract aggressive mockery, and worse, from the people of the countryside. In the countryside society lapses into feudalism or disappears completely. Governance becomes impossible because the police cannot exercise their function and the courts have no way to extend their control over criminals. Domestic life loses its moral compass as curates abandon their solitary chapels and religion lapses. Civilization itself founders, and barbarism becomes the normal state of affairs.

In the absence of all the means of civilization and progress, which can only develop when people are gathered in a numerous society, behold the life of the countryside. Women take care of the house, prepare the food, shear the sheep, milk the cows, make the cheese, and weave the crude fabric from which the clothing is made. All domestic and household labors, virtually all the work of any kind, rests on the shoulders of the woman. At best, the man may plant a bit of corn for his family, but little and rarely, for no kind of bread figures in its daily diet. The children develop their physical strength in play. If male, they begin early to practice use of the lasso on goats and calves, and as soon as they begin to ride horseback, which they do not long after learning to walk, they are off across the countryside. By the time they have become young men, they achieve complete independence and also utter idleness. Their education is at an end, at that point, and they have become *gauchos*.

One must see, in order to believe, the indomitable character that emerges from this education, from this struggle of the isolated individual against nature. One must see the grave expressions of the gauchos, framed by beard and tousled hair like that of an Arab, to appreciate the disdain with which they regard the sedentary city-dweller who may have read many books but has no idea how to take down a wild bull, who has not the faintest notion how to catch and mount a mustang when finding himself on foot, alone, on the open pampa, who has never faced a puma's attack by thrusting one poncho-wrapped hand into the mouth of the lunging animal while driving his knife into its heart with the other hand. Their incessant individual struggles against nature have given Argentines of whatever class a prodigious national arrogance that offends the other people of América, who often accuse them of excessive vanity. I do not deny the charge but do not regret its truth. Woe is to the nation without faith in itself, for it will never accomplish great things!

The conditions of a cattle herder's life on the pampa thus create grave difficulties for any kind of political organization and much more so for the triumph of European civilization with all the liberty, prosperity, and institutional development which that civilization confers. On the other hand, one cannot deny that the pastoral life has its poetic side. If national literatures are able to shine forth in the new societies of América, it will be in the description of their grand natural environment and, above all, in the portrayal of the imposing struggle between European civilization and native barbarism, between intelligence and brute force. That struggle produces scenes and characters animated by an interior drama alien to the spirit of Europe and therefore exceedingly unexpected to anyone educated within the normal circle of European ideas. Among

the resulting customs and social types there are some highly notable ones, destined someday to provide originality and brilliance to
the theater and fiction of our new American nations.

In Argentina, the most conspicuous, the most extraordinary, of
all is the figure of the tracker. To some degree, all gauchos are trackers. On plains so wide open, where paths crisscross, where cattle
graze freely and horses amble in all directions, one must be able to
recognize an animal's hoof prints, distinguish them from a thousand
others, and follow them for miles. One must be able to know whether
the animal is directing its own movements or being led, whether its
pace is rapid or slow, whether it bears a burden or not. These are
normal skills that all plainsmen must possess.

Once, when I was travelling with a guide across the plains, we
came to a crossroads and he studied the ground, as such men so
often do, and said: "Here's a mule I know, an excellent saddle animal
that belongs to don N. Zapata. It was unsaddled yesterday, though,
when it passed by here." The guide was coming from the Sierra de
San Luis, and the mule train that had left the track was returning
from Buenos Aires, hundreds of leagues distant. The man had not
seen the mule in question for a year, and now he recognized its hoof
prints among those of an entire mule train that had passed along a
trail two feet wide. This seemingly incredible, but nonetheless far
from unusual, ability was demonstrated by a common herder, not a
professional tracker.

The tracker by profession is a grave and circumspect personage
whose declarations are accepted without question by local judges.
His knowledge gives him a certain dignity and mystery in the eyes
of others, who treat him with consideration, the poor because they
fear him, the rich because they need him. Imagine that a theft has
occurred during the night. As soon as it is discovered, people hurry
to identify a footprint left by the thief and, upon finding one, they
cover it with something so that the wind does not dissipate it.
They call the tracker, who takes one look at the footprint and then
sets off in the direction it indicates, hardly looking at the ground,
as if his eyes register in high relief a trail imperceptible to everyone
else. He walks down streets, crosses yards, enters a house, and pointing at a man inside it, says quietly: "It's him." The case is considered

closed. It is a rare criminal, indeed, who dares challenge the tracker's verdict. The judge will consider it persuasive proof. To deny it would be unthinkable, absurd. The criminal bows to the testimony of the tracker as if it were the accusing finger of God himself.

I personally had the pleasure of meeting Calíbar, a famous tracker who exercised that profession in a certain province of Argentina for forty years. Today he is nearly eighty years old and, although stooped by age, remains venerable and dignified. Whenever someone mentions his fabulous reputation, he shrugs. "I'm old and worthless now, but there you have the children." These "children" are, of course, his grown sons, who exercise the profession they learned from such a famous master.

The stories they tell about Calíbar! Once, when he was away on a trip to Buenos Aires, someone stole his best dress saddle and bridle. His wife found a footprint and covered it with a wooden bowl. Two months later, Calíbar returned, inspected what remained of the footprint, which was hardly anything, and nothing more was said about the matter—until a year and a half later, that is, when Calíbar came down a street on the edge of town, eyeing the ground, walked into a house, and found his saddle and bridle, now blackened and worn with use. He had finally picked up a trail almost two years old!

In 1830, a man condemned to death escaped from jail, and they called Calíbar. The escaped prisoner, certain that he would be tracked, had taken all the precautions that a fear of execution suggested to his mind—all of them useless! In fact, they may have further contributed to his demise, because Calíbar took them as a challenge to his reputation and outdid himself. The fleeing prisoner took advantage of every opportunity not to leave a trace of his passage. He went for entire blocks on tiptoe, crossed walled gardens, and doubled back repeatedly. Calíbar was right behind him. The prisoner walked a distance in the water of a drainage ditch and leapt out without leaving a footprint on the edge. Useless. Calíbar saw drops of water on the grass. The man climbed into a walled vineyard. Sometime later, Calíbar arrived, inspected the walls, and announced calmly: "He's inside." A squad of soldiers searched the vineyard and found nothing. "He didn't leave," said the tracker, without a second look. And he was right. The next day the fugitive was executed.

In 1831, a group of political prisoners were planning an escape with the help of sympathizers on the outside. When all was in readiness, someone remembered: "What about Calíbar?" The others gasped, suddenly stricken and terrified: "Calíbar!" Fortunately for them, the political prisoners' families were able to persuade Calíbar to feign illness for four days following their escape, and thus they were able to get away without any difficulty.

What an amazing mystery! What can explain the microscopic eyesight of these trackers? How sublime is the creature that God created in his own image!

Analyzing the Sources: What is Sarmiento's attitude toward the native Argentine "types" who appear in this selection? What do cities and the countryside stand for, respectively?

MEMOIRS OF A MILITIA SERGEANT

Manuel Antônio de Almeida

Memoirs of a Militia Sergeant (*originally serialized in a newspaper, 1852–53) by Manuel Antônio de Almeida (born 1831) is one of the earliest significant Brazilian novels. It depicts the city of Rio de Janeiro during the residence there of the Portuguese king, João VI, who traveled to Brazil in 1808 to escape the clutches of Napoleon. The novel contains many passages that describe the social customs of the period it depicts. The author addresses the reading public of his own city and frequently contrasts an 1850s "now" with "the time of the king," two generations earlier.*

Processions

In Rio de Janeiro, the day of a procession has always been a big holiday with nonstop excitement and crowds. Our readers well know

---

Source: Manuel Antônio de Almeida, *Memórias de um sargento de milícias* (Rio de Janeiro: Imprenta Nacional, 1944), pp. 27–33, 102–4, 117–19.

what a big deal processions still are today. Let them imagine, then, what things were like in "the time of the king," when they were an even bigger deal than now. The streets overflowed with people, especially women wearing mantillas. People decorated their houses by dressing their open street windows with truly magnificent silk and damask fabrics in every color. Small musical stages were set up in almost every wide place in the street. What went on is what still does, only more, and more grandly, "because it was done with faith," the old ladies of the time would say. We, on the other hand, might say, "because it was the fashion." Contributing to the lavish displays of religious festivals was in style, back then, as much as the women's big hairdos or the particular cut of their dresses.

There were more processions then, as well, and the groups who put them on competed with each other to make their particular procession the most lavish and luxurious. The processions of Lent stood out for their extraordinary pomp, especially when the king joined them, so that all the courtiers had to join the procession, too. And the most outstanding procession of Lent was the one put on by the goldsmiths' guild. Nobody stayed home on the day of that procession. Whether on the street or perhaps in the house of friends who were fortunate enough to live along the route, everybody found some way not to miss the "Goldsmiths' Procession," as they called it. Some folks were so devoted that, not satisfied to see it only once, they went from one friend's house to another, watched on this street, then ran to the next, and pronounced themselves satisfied only when they had seen the whole procession two or four or even six times.

The big draw of the Goldsmith's Procession, among other things, was an element shared by no other regular procession in Rio, and our readers may think it rather silly, yet it is our obligation to describe things as they were. The element that attracted such enthusiasm was a group of so-called Baianas who led the procession and attracted the eyes of the devout spectators fully as much as did the sacred emblems and the saints' images carried aloft behind them. The group of Baianas was composed of black women wearing the traditional clothing of the Province of Bahia, hence the name. At pauses in the religious chant that accompanied the procession, the Baianas danced a special dance. To tell the truth, they were worth seeing, and surely there was nothing wrong in using them to open a religious procession.

Everybody knows the characteristic dress of black women in Bahia. It is among the prettiest traditional costumes we have seen, and yet we do not advise anyone else to adopt it. A country where all the women wore that costume, especially if it were one of those fortunate countries whose women are pale and lovely, would be a land of temptation and, no doubt, perdition. Here is a description. Baianas wear several skirts and petticoats that reach no lower than the knee, each one adorned with magnificent lace. From the waist up, they wear only a thin and delicate white blouse, likewise adorned with lace at the neck and sleeves. Around the neck, they wear a gold or coral necklace or (the poorest among them) a necklace of colored glass beads. Around their heads they wrap a large piece of stiffly starched white cloth to make a small turban, and on their feet, they wear high-heeled sandals so tiny that only their toes fit inside the shoe leather, leaving the instep and ankle quite bare. And over their shoulder they gracefully drape a black shawl, but without covering their bare arms adorned with circular metal bracelets.

THE DIVINE HOLY SPIRIT

As everyone knows, the feast of the Divine Holy Spirit is among the favorite festivities of the people of Rio de Janeiro. Even today, as the city's populace gradually lets go of old habits, some good and some bad, the *Divino Espírito Santo* still produces considerable excitement, and yet, nothing like what it produced in the old days. The author of the present book can remember seeing the Divino as a child, and already people were saying that this was nothing, that the holiday had been better in years past, just as the old ladies of today say that everything has gone downhill since whenever. Yet there is no arguing about the following. Rather than starting on Palm Sunday, when I was a boy the festivities of the Divino commenced nine days earlier, with *novena* prayers.

Let us describe the Folias, a special and distinctive part of the festival—the street event that heralded it—even though our readers probably have some notion already. During the nine days leading up to the festival itself, a group of boys of about nine to eleven years old made music and danced in the street every day. They wore broad-brimmed straw hats covered with flowers, and each of them carried a drum, a tambourine, or a musical instrument. With them went other musicians who performed as the group moved along. At the front, or sometimes totally surrounding the boys, went a cluster of men wearing the habit of the lay brotherhood that organized the Folias. These "brothers" carried red banners and other religious insignias; when the group stopped so that the boys could sing and dance in front of a house, the men in habits circulated soliciting contributions in support of the festivities.

The focal point of all this was a boy, normally smaller than the rest, who wore a suit of green velvet, and on his chest, an enormous shining emblem of the *Divino Espírito Santo*. This young "Emperor," as he was called, walked slowly, wearing a grave expression, with the other boys forming a hollow square around him in the street. Confess, readers, that this would be an extravagant sight. As soon as music was heard in the street, everyone inside the houses rushed to the windows to see it.

Sorcery

Down by the mangrove swamp on the edge of old Rio stood a miserable thatched hut so dirty on the outside that one dreaded to imagine the inside. It was composed of two rooms and furnished by three stools, a few reed mats piled in a corner, and an enormous wooden box with the multiple functions of bed, dining table, wardrobe, and china cabinet. The house was almost always closed up, lending it a sinister air, and it was inhabited by a man of the most detestable appearance, an old *caboclo*,* his face filthy and repugnant, his body covered with rags. The reader will be surprised, no doubt, to learn that the function of such an inauspicious being was, in the expression of the day, to "bring fortune."

In those days, people put great store in such stuff, and they regarded the practitioners with superstitious respect. Obviously, the

---

*A man partly, if not entirely, of indigenous descent.

astute practitioners turned that respect to their endless advantage. And it was not only the common people who believed in magic spells. It is said that members of Rio's high society paid considerable money in the illicit purchase of magical good fortune.

A respectable man named Leonardo was one who sought out the *caboclo* of the mangrove swamp, the most famous practitioner in Rio. Leonardo subjected himself to countless little procedures, each of which began with a monetary contribution, all without results. He had suffocating smoke blown on him and drank foul-tasting brews. He had learned by heart certain mysterious prayers that he was supposed to repeat many times a day. Almost every night, at the direction of the *caboclo*, he had to place objects or quantities of money in specific places around the city to propitiate certain divinities. Still no results. So Leonardo decided to undergo the final procedure, which was arranged for the stroke of midnight in the house by the mangrove swamp.

At the appointed hour, he arrived to find the disgusting sorcerer standing in the door, refusing him entry until he took off his clothes and allowed himself to be draped with a filthy blanket. The interior of the hut was adorned with magical paraphernalia so ridiculously sinister that we will not take the trouble to describe it in detail. We will mention, however, that among the things whose significance only initiates in the *caboclo*'s magic properly understand, there was a small fire burning in the middle of the room.

When the ceremony began, Leonardo had to kneel in the four corners of the house and recite the incantations that he had memorized, as well as new ones learned on this occasion. Then, as he knelt by the fire, three figures emerged from the other room of the house and, joined by the *caboclo*, began a sinister dance around the kneeling figure.

Analyzing the Sources: How do various elements of the author's description of life in early-nineteenth-century Rio de Janeiro add to an emerging picture of Brazilian national identity?

A MEXICAN SELF-PORTRAIT
Various Authors

The 1855 book Los mexicanos pintados por si mismos *was an unusual project of costumbrismo, an illustrated, comprehensive gallery of Mexican social types contributed by many authors. The types included only a few women, such as the midwife, the seamstress, the socialite—and the* china *(pronounced* chee-na*), described in the following excerpt. Although* chino/ china *means "Chinese" in Spanish, the meaning of* china *here is from an indigenous language and has nothing to do with Asia. The Mexican* china *was an unmarried, independent young woman of the popular class, normally a mestiza. Had Fanny Calderón worn the poblana dress given her in 1840, she would have been dressing as a "china poblana." After the portrait of the* china *comes further description of Mexico City housing in the period.*

This column is going to get certain people's dander up, namely the fashionable, glove-and-corset-wearing set, women who dance schottische and polka-mazurka, who paint their faces and attend the opera. "How audacious," they will say: "How brazen and ungentlemanly! To write about a 'china,' of all things, a lowly plebeian, as if Mexico City had no more worthy subjects for a journalist's pen, such as coquettes or women who read, and even write! Etcetera, etcetera, etcetera . . ." They might as well say: "As if Mexico City had no belles who have achieved a striking resemblance to their French or English or even Russian counterparts." Certainly no Aztec princess would recognize the attire of a coquette. On the other hand, it is true that an Aztec princess might not recognize the china's clothes, either. But let's just say that, when it comes to looking Mexican, the lovely, fresh, and innocent village china beats her social betters by a long

SOURCE: adapted from *Los mexicanos pintados por si mismos: Tipos y costumbres nacionales por varios autores* (Mexico City: Imprenta de M. Murguía, 1854). The excerpts are from "La china" by José María Rivera (pp. 89–98) and "La casera" by Niceto de Zamacois (pp. 230–34).

shot. Therefore, the china is the first type of Mexican woman whom I will present, begging the pardon of coquettes and feminine literati, who obviously constitute a useful contrast against which to portray the eminently *national* china.

So, out of here! Out, I say, all you high-society types, so English, so French! Make way for my china, a true daughter of Mexico! Make way for the pearl of our poor neighborhoods, the soul of our all-night fandangos, the flower of our bronze-skinned masses, a woman who makes my knees go limp, my eyes go starry, my. . . . If you don't like flattering adjectives and poetic comparisons, dear Reader, then you might as well turn the page, because my portrait of the china is going to be full of them.

The particular heroine of this article is named Mariquita. She is only twenty-three years old and has twenty-eight lovers, including the owner of the corner store and the son of the local police inspector. She has black eyes capable of undermining the strongest male resistance, dark, velvety skin, a slender waist, and a totally disarming level of grace and self-confidence. She never gets fainting spells or sick headaches or the other stylish afflictions of her delicate, modern cousins. Mariquita lives in a rented room, and she keeps the door open, because cleanliness is her strong suit, and that applies to her person, her clothing (and not just the outside layer), and her living quarters.

Her room is small, but its floor is spotless. There is a bed in one corner, with modest linens, scrupulously clean. Beside the bed, a wooden chest where she keeps her dresses, her petticoats, her shawl, her sewing basket, and a few romantic novels. Her necklaces may or may not be there, depending on the day of the week, because they are regularly in the pawn shop except for Sundays, when she finds money to rescue them temporarily before pawning them again on Monday or Tuesday. On the walls, her favorite images of the Virgin Mary. Look quickly, and off we go to find the china who has disappeared and will most likely be found where you hear that music coming from, a neighborhood fandango.

It is a wake, as it turns out, and cheerful enough, because the deceased is a tiny newborn, already an angel in heaven by this point, so why not eat and drink and dance to ease our pain here on earth?

LA CHINA was one of the most notable types portrayed in the illustrated *Mexican Self-Portrait* of 1855. Her "Poblana dress" mixed materials and elements from the Old and New Worlds. *Wikimedia Commons.*

The drinking and dancing started two hours ago. Both musicians and dancers have been taking a shot of tequila before each number and have achieved an exemplary level of *public spirits*. The only person not markedly animated, at this point, is the deceased. You have got to see Mariquita dance, especially now that she is squaring off with a man who has just arrived, the neighborhood's most celebrated dancer of our national *jarabes*. The partygoers crowd in a circle around the two dancers, who face each other and maintain a small distance between them. Mariquita's feet begin moving like quicksilver on the pavement, her body follows like a seductive flame from side to side, she glides forward to incite and challenge her partner, almost brushing against him at one moment, then backward, disdaining his advances. She does her best to provoke him to a maximum effort, because she has vowed to conquer him at his best. Her eyes flash with enthusiasm, the nostrils of her lovely nose flair, her chest heaves, her luscious lips open slightly with fatigue, and her skirts fly, hitting some crouching spectators in the face, filling all the men with desire.

One of the male spectators, his *zarape** wrapped around his lower face to disguise his identity, now provokes Mariquita's dance partner with an insulting remark. The dancer ignores it, but a second insult spurs him to pull a knife from his belt and attack his challenger, who, with similar speed, draws his own blade. Mariquita recognizes that the challenger is her *hombre*, as she would say, and she quickly steps between the angry men and tries to separate them, begging the onlookers for help. She would gladly die, at this moment, to protect her man, but the neighborhood night-watchmen have heard the ruckus and appear to stop the fight.

A moment later, Mariquita is furious because they have arrested her hombre, and she gives the night-watchmen a piece of her mind, then begins a relentless campaign to get her beau out of the slammer. Nothing intimidates her, nothing turns her aside, she is a blur of determined action. First she acquires and cooks the food that the prisoner will need in jail and takes it to him there. She appeals to the judge, pesters his scribe, gives the municipal authorities not

---

*An outer garment worn by men, not dissimilar to a woman's rebozo.

a minute's rest, until finally she manages to win the release of her champion. Sad to say, that very night he may repay her with a barrage of kicks and shouts, but Mariquita is used to that and will stay loyal despite it all.

And that is another of the advantages that she has over you modern women. But enough of such invidious comparisons! You can console yourselves, oh, modern painted beauties, with the thought that, while still flourishing in Oaxaca, Durango, and Guadalajara, the true and legitimate china—lovely, steadfast daughter of Mexico, with her characteristic garb—is fast disappearing from the streets and plazas of our cosmopolitan capital city. In a few years, she will be but a memory. Alas!

Everyone knows (and those who did not know before will know now) that the poor and middling inhabitants of Mexico City live in houses each of which is something like a town in itself, divided into many individual rooms and apartments with their own numbering. The most impoverished live on the ground floor around the interior patio. Here one finds the so-called *tortilleras*, barefoot and wearing poor clothing, their thick, straight, black hair unkempt, kneeling to knead the boiled corn that they call, in Nahuatl, *nixtamal* on the tiny stone platform called a *metate*, where they make *tortillas*. The tortilleras occasionally reprimand their filthy, naked children who are engaged, perpetually, in trying to sneak a finished tortilla out of the basket where these are placed. Meanwhile, the husbands of the hardworking tortilleras (generally water carriers or construction workers) lie sprawled serenely on straw mats spread out on the floor, thinking neither of the past nor of the future, which always, for this class of people, amount to the same thing anyway. What need have such people to concern themselves with the future, when they are content with their straw mats, where they sleep fully clothed to avoid the need of a blanket? They do not require a knife or fork because they eat with their fingers, and have no need of a spoon, because a tortilla will do to scoop up soup or beans. What need to think of the future have people without any ambitions, people who do not require such furniture as a wardrobe because every day they wear all the clothes that they possess? The ground-floor apartments around the patio consist in only one room each, and the room in question serves as workshop for tortilla production, kitchen, living room, dining room, and bedroom for two or more couples and their children, along with the inevitable compadre or comadre or two, who all sleep together side by side on the floor.

Next door to the room that we have just described live an old woman and her two daughters who sew for a living. They work night and day just to earn enough to appear in the Sunday paseo on the Alameda in a halfway decent muslin dress. Their room contrasts with the first one because it is kept scrupulously clean and because there is a bed where the old lady sleeps in one corner and a chest containing the family's clothes in another. Atop the chest, is a blanket rolled up in a spotless straw mat which the two daughters spread on the floor at night, so to sleep beside their mother's bed. In a third corner is a platform with coals for cooking and a large earthen container of water, and in the fourth, a small triangular table upon which sits a potted basil plant, and above that, several cheap graven images of the Virgin of Soledad, the Virgin of Guadalupe, and the Holy Trinity. A few simple and inexpensive but dust-free chairs stand about the room, which is generally decorated with good taste.

Let us now ascend to the second storey where the larger apartments, consisting in more than one room, are located. A stone stair leads up from the ground-floor patio to a wide walkway that surrounds it on the second storey, giving access to the apartments of middle-class tenants. These are people whose manners may be just as refined as those of the upper-class, with the difference that these people are hard-working, the hardest working, in truth, in all Mexico City. Here one finds office clerks, skilled artisans, retirees—in sum, decent people of modest means.

In one of these apartments lives a piano teacher who supplements his income by giving house parties every week. His young wife, who much enjoys such diversions, takes charge of the refreshments and makes sure that there will be some young women present, even though the paying guests have the right to bring their own dance partners. The paying guests are generally prosperous artisans or young men who work as retail or office clerks, with an army officer or two generally in attendance as well—overall, a good-humored, well-spoken, well-dressed crowd of excellent dancers. They generally come by themselves, however, which is why the wife invites the young women who live on the ground floor (and sew or take in washing) to attend the dance at no cost. They appear wearing starched petticoats that plump up their rather inexpensive but well-ironed dresses. In their gleaming black hair, the young women wear crudely-made artificial flowers, and in their gloved hands, they carry handkerchiefs so soaked in cheap perfume as to cause dizziness.

> *Analyzing the Sources: Costumbrismo is almost always strongly gendered, this selection in particular. Discuss it in terms of the voice of the narrator and his attitude toward several of his subjects. What role does social class play?*

MARTÍN RIVAS

Alberto Blest Gana

Alberto Blest Gana (1830–1920) was Chile's first important novelist. His Martín Rivas *(1862) is a "national novel" of the sort still read in secondary schools around Latin America. Martín, who represents the rising commercial middle class, loves the haughty daughter of an upper-class family who finally accepts his love. It's a match made in patriotic heaven. We don't see any of it in this excerpt, though. Here, Rafael, a young man whom Martín has met at law school, takes him to the house of a poor widow and her pretty daughters for some more immediate recreation. Here we see Martín and his friends in the company of their social inferiors, the struggling lower middle class. They have servants but definitely have a lot to learn about modern European refinements of manners, such as those possessed by the character Agustín. On the other hand, there's a sort of cultural capital that Agustín does not possess.*

SOURCE: Alberto Blest Gana, *Martín Rivas* (Havana: Casa de las Americas, 1989), pp. 70–78.

The door of the widow's house was closed, despite the fact that she was a having a party, as is the custom among a certain class of people. Rafael pounded on the door until a servant finally arrived to open it. It is unnecessary, and besides, would be an abuse of the reader's generous attention to provide a thorough description of the servant. She looked like any servant in a poor household, her clothes ragged, reeking of the kitchen. There are some descriptions that my pen prefers not to approach, leaving them for the paint brush of a daring artist. To paint a word picture of such an abject figure would be both tedious and disagreeable.

All eyes turned to Martín and Rafael when they entered the room. The loud noise that they had heard from outside ceased immediately. The young men greeted them stiffly, with a hint of mistrust, and the girls whispered in each others' ears after being introduced to them. A sonorous woman's voice interrupted the silence:

"Weren't you ever introduced to nobody before, people? Let's go!"

It was the widow, doña Bernarda, standing in the middle of the room with her hands on her hips, trying to restart the party. The girls smiled and looked at the floor, but the young men responded to her eloquent exhortation.

"She's right," exclaimed one. "Let's dance. *Cuadrillas!*"

"Cuadrillas! Cuadrillas," agreed everyone.

A piano had been brought to the house that morning, because you are not to imagine that the widow and her daughters actually owned such a thing. A friend of the family's now sat down and began to play cuadrillas as various couples formed squares on the dance floor. It was a motley crew of all ages and combinations. There was a mother, around fifty, trying to look younger, and one of her younger daughters, maybe fourteen, trying to look older. At one point mother and daughter faced one another across the square. The girl was pulling down on her short skirt, which she thought made her look too young, when something started to rip.

"Go ahead, tear the waistband, why don't you?" said the girl's mother loudly, to the embarrassment of her dance partner, who had adopted an unrealistic air of sophistication in the presence of the young gentlemen.

Another young man, more than slightly aware of Rafael and Martín, spoke to his partner with theatrical carelessness, as if to show that he did not find the newcomers' presence intimidating. "I insist that you *are* a thief, señorita, because you steal *hearts*," he declared with more conviction than originality. To which she answered with flushed cheeks and hushed tones, "You're very kind, caballero."

Doña Bernarda did her duty as hostess, making the rounds to say something nice to each and every one of her guests. When she saw mother and daughter, she shook her head with amusement and addressed them sequentially:

"There's life in the old girl yet, as they say! Ha, ha, ha! Pay attention to your mother, honey, and you'll go far!"

The last square of dancers remained incomplete. The widow's son Amador had yet to find a partner, having twice been turned down. He recruited a girl even younger than she of the too-short dress.

"I've never danced cuadrillas," she said in a whiny voice.

"Dance, Mariquita! They'll learn you," insisted her mother.

The girl joined the square, which finally began its evolutions to the sounds of the piano. One of its pedals was evidently stuck, however, and as the player struggled to operate it, he squirmed and bounced on the bench so powerfully that its creaks threatened to drown out the music. The few notes that could be heard above the creaking bench disappeared without a trace beneath the loud voices of the dancers, because Mariquita and the fourteen-year-old caused countless problems because of their inexperience and received detailed corrections from three or four adults at once.

"Now turn this way, Mariquita!"

"Ready, curtsey, and allemande left . . . no . . . left . . . I said *left!*"

"Now forward and back, forward and back . . ."

The music had disappeared so completely beneath the hubub that the piano player shouted for people to stop talking, and doña Bernarda hurried to get him a fresh drink. Amador clapped his hands thunderously to signal the next figure of the dance.

The young people, who had hoped to impart a tone of modern elegance and sophistication to the proceedings, lost all hope of that happening. Doña Bernarda, on the other hand, was pleased to see her party so animated. Each time one of the girls created confusion, inviting a swarm of corrections, the hostess put down her glass and applauded the fuss delightedly.

Martín was amazed to see his friend Rafael join in enthusiastically, contributing to the confusion on purpose, sometimes purely in the interest of hilarity, sometimes to steal the pretty partner of another dancer. At that point, Agustín Encina, the son of an elite family, appeared at the party, in a blinding flash of European-style elegance, including a heavy gold watch chain with which he hoped to win the heart of the diffident Adelaida, the most beautiful of the widow's daughters.

"This rather reminds me of the diversions to be had among the *grisettes* of Paris," observed Agustín, who employed French words, correctly or not, at every possible opportunity. "It's a dismal substitute for Paris, though, obviously. There simply is no entertainment in Santiago for young people of sophistication."

The dandy went to pay his respects to the widow, or rather, hostess, who rewarded his good manners by displaying three teeth that remained to represent her once-dazzling smile. Doña Bernarda was preoccupied, however, by an activity dear to her heart, gambling at cards.

In another room, someone was playing a guitar and the same servant who opened the door was serving sweet homemade liquor from a tray in small glasses. Both men and women drank eagerly. Bernarda's son Amador, who was the guitar player, took glasses from the tray and presented one to Martín and one to Rafael.

"Bottoms up," he insisted, and stayed to make sure that happened.

When everyone had taken a drink, everyone took another, and another, and happiness shined on every countenance.

"The cueca, the cueca! Time to dance the cueca!"

Amador sat on a low chair and played a cueca as the audience formed a circle to watch and two dancers stepped to the middle of the room. It was the fourteen-year-old and a man in a police uniform. Rafael whispered to Martín that the policeman was a leading candidate for suitor of the widow's second daughter, Edelmira. The policeman twirled his handkerchief, Amador raised his eyes to the ceiling, and the cueca began with the following lyrics of questionable poetic merit but irrepressable popularity at gatherings such as this one: "I'm in love with two girls at once. / Could leave one, but I'm no dunce!" The spectators clapped the rhythm enthusiastically and hooted their approval of the dancers.

"Give it to her, boy!"

"Unh, unh, ain't that nice?"

"Don't stop! Don't stop!"

The girl was far more familiar with our lusty national dance than with the niceties of cuadrillas. She and her partner circled around each other until, at exactly the right moment, the uniformed dancer dropped to his knees in front of the damsel, and the dance was over.

"Bravo," shouted everyone.

A transformation had come over the group, expressed in double-entendres and innuendos that far transgressed the boundaries of polite social behavior. So much for the stiff efforts that many had made earlier in the evening to demonstrate manners *de buen tono* in the eyes of young gentlemen like Martín, Rafael, or, even more, Agustín Encina, who belonged to one of best families in Santiago. As often happens at gatherings of the people whom we in Chile call *de medio pelo*, drink and popular music rapidly undermined their attempts at proper social behavior. As a result, the charm of their primitive customs is sullied by imitation of a better class that they cannot hope, in the long run, to approximate. The result is a deplorable caricature of proper etiquette. These observations were made by Rafael to Martín as they observed the fray.

"With the girls, it goes a lot faster," explained Rafael, "so forget all you learned about how to approach a debutante at some fancy soirée. Forget suggestive glances. Here you just walk up and tell her you like her. Doesn't mean you'll get a straight answer, but you can tell her straight, she won't mind."

"I don't think I'm cut out for this," said Martín. "And I need to leave."

"Don't leave before you watch this," said Rafael.

He turned to Agustín and told him that he absolutely must dance a cueca with Adelaida to win her heart. With girls like these, you couldn't treat them like society princesses. You had to get down to their level so they would understand, show them you weren't too good to dance a cueca with them.

"Trust me. It's the only way. "

Agustín's ideas were not very lucid at this point. He found Rafael's analysis convincing, overall, with one objection.

"I've never danced a cueca."

Rafael dismissed the objection as irrelevant.

"It doesn't matter. So in France you did the cancan, no?"

"But of course!"

"It's the same difference!"

Rafael handed the guitar to Amador, who began a prelude, and then, as his abundantly warmed-up vocal cords produced a boozy improvised verse ("Oh lovely, ungrateful tyrant, you scoff at my suffering," or words to that effect), Rafael powered Agustín to middle of the room, face to face with the lovely Adelaida. But the poor fellow was too drunk to do well, now, a thing he could hardly have done sober. An initial stumble turned into a lurch and a series of hops that had everyone in the room howling with laughter. Agustín stabilized, but his new movement of the hips was so wrong that the hoots intensified rather than diminishing. And then, at an utterly inappropriate moment, much closer to the beginning of the cueca than to the end, Agustín dropped to his knees in front of the object of his ardent affections. Amazed and embarrassed, Adelaida burst out laughing, turned, and walked away.

> *Analyzing the Sources: What qualities of people at the party are admired by others? How do they become important socially?*

MARÍA

Jorge Isaacs

The Romantic novel María *(1867) by Colombian author Jorge Isaacs (1837–1895) exemplifies a tendency, common in Romantic fiction, to idealize the social relations of the countryside, presenting an image of paternalistic harmony between landowners and their rural laborers—in this case, slaves. Popular dance constituted a standard touchstone of national identities under construction. Like the* jarabe *mentioned in this chapter's selection on Mexico, the* bambuco *described here was understood to be a "national dance," enjoyment of which bridged social classes. The narrator, a young man who has just returned from years of study in Bogotá, the national capital, is inspecting the family's sugar plantations with his father.*

During my absence, my father had made numerous notable improvements to his properties in the hot country of the Valle del Cauca, including a beautiful and costly new sugar mill, new sugarcane fields to supply the mill, new pastures full of horses and cattle, and a luxurious new country residence with outbuildings.

The slaves, as well-dressed and happy as slaves can be, were submissive and affectionate with my father. Among them, I encountered young men with whom I had played in the woods years before, when we were boys, and they gave unmistakable signs of pleasure at seeing me again. There was one sad absence, however: Pedro, my good friend and faithful companion, an older man who had been assigned to accompany and look after me when I was little. He had shed tears on the day of my departure for Bogotá when he lifted me onto the horse that would carry me away, saying, "Little master, I won't ever see you again!" His heart had told him that he would die before I returned, and so it was.

I observed that my father treated the slaves with warmth and kindness while maintaining an attitude appropriate to his authority as their master. He displayed concern for the good conduct of their wives and lovingly caressed their little children.

One afternoon, at sundown, my father, the overseer, and I were returning from the fields to the sugar mill. While the other two men discussed work that had been done, or that still remained undone, my mind was occupied by reminiscences of childhood: the fragrance

Source: Jorge Isaacs, *María* (Buenos Aires: Emecé Editores, 1943), pp. 17–20.

of ripe fruits, the peculiar smell of a stand of trees that had been cut down to expand the fields; the raucous chatter of flocks of small parrots in the *guayaba* orchard; the distant sound of a shepherd's horn echoing though the hills; the jocular noise of slaves returning slowly from their daily labor in the fields, carrying their tools on their shoulders; and the sight of evening colors in the sky, glimpsed here and there between the swaying stands of *guadua* cane. Everything reminded me of the afternoons when my sisters and María and I, having finally gotten my mother's permission to go play, did anything we liked, climbing our favorite guayaba trees to pick the ripe fruit, watching the parrots come and go at their nests by the corral.

We came upon a group of slaves, and my father addressed one of them, a fine-looking young fellow.

"So, Bruno, has everything been arranged for your wedding day after tomorrow?"

"Yes, master," Bruno replied, removing his straw hat and leaning for a moment on the handle of his shovel.

"Who will be the godparents?"

"Señora Dolores and señor Anselmo . . . if you approve, master."

"Fine. Be sure that you and Remigia go to confession first, no? Was the money that I sent enough to buy everything?"

"Yes, master, everything."

"And you don't need anything else?"

"Whatever you wish, master . . ."

"How about the room? Is it a good one?"

"Yes, master."

"I'll bet I know what you want . . . a dance, isn't that right?"

Bruno laughed and smiled broadly, showing the dazzling whiteness of his teeth. He looked at his friends.

"It's only fair, because you've earned it with good behavior," said my father, and he turned to the overseer, adding: "Arrange it. And make sure they enjoy themselves."

"Will Your Mercies be leaving before the wedding?" inquired Bruno.

"No," I answered with a smile, "we will consider ourselves invited, then!"

Early in the morning of the following Saturday, Bruno and Remigia were married. At seven o'clock that evening, as my father and I mounted our horses for the short ride to the wedding dance, we could already hear the music.

When we arrived, Julián, one of the overseer's trusted subordinates among the slaves, a gang boss, appeared to greet us and take our horses. He had on his Sunday best, and from his waist hung the insignia of his office: a long machete with silver trim. The big house of this plantation, where my family had formerly lived, was now occupied only by farm tools, and these had been cleared out of a large room for the dance. Benches had been placed around the walls, and suspended from the ceiling hung a wooden chandelier holding half a dozen flickering lights. The musicians and singers— a combination of slaves, former slaves, and poor neighbors—stood in one of the doors. The instruments were nothing more than two rustic flutes, two shakers, an improvised drum, and a tambourine. But the black singers' high voices rendered the *bambuco* melodies with such mastery, their song contained such a heartfelt combination of moods, from gay to melancholy, and the lyrics were so tender and simple, that this semi-wild music would surely have enchanted the most cultured musical connoisseur.

The men wore jackets and hats, and so my father and I entered the room without taking ours off. The two people dancing at that moment were Bruno and Remigia. Remigia—wearing a skirt with blue ruffles and artificial flowers, a white blouse with black embroidery, and a red necklace and earrings—danced with all the gentle grace that her supple waist suggested. Bruno—his poncho thrown back over his shoulder, ironed white shirt and pants, a new machete at his waist—danced with masculine vigor and admirable skill. Then Julián announced that the next number would be in honor of the master, and the band played the most beautiful *bambuco* in its repertoire. Remigia, encouraged by both her new husband and the gang boss, screwed up her courage and danced for a few moments with my father, but her movements in the dance became less spontaneous and she did not dare to raise her eyes the whole time. After about an hour, we said goodnight.

Analyzing the Sources: What elements contribute to the idealization of rural life in this passage? Why do you think that scenes of people dancing figure so prominently in such idealizations?

AUTOBIOGRAPHY OF GEN. JOSÉ ANTONIO PÁEZ

José Antonio Páez

The Venezuelan caudillo José Antonio Páez (1790–1873) was a rural man of middling social origins who rose to become a leader during the wars of independence and, afterward, the first president of Venezuela. Charging lancers, roll calls of heroes, and paternalistic bonds between Páez and his followers give this passage from his 1869 Autobiography an archaic tone reminiscent of a medieval epic. Páez was an old man recalling events of thirty years earlier, in an elevated style that he could not have composed by himself. In this passage, the old caudillo describes events that occurred between his two presidencies of the 1830s. Although out of office, he remained the real power behind the government at the time. Paradoxically, even this kind of conflictive history, evoking a shared experience and accenting the bravery of old adversaries, could help form national identities.

After the triumph of Independence, the cattle of the Province of Apure had been distributed among the valiant warriors of the army whose lances doomed Spanish despotism there. By distributing the herds, our country repaid their services and gave them a stake in the prosperity of the territory which they had conquered with heroism and defended with unfailing courage. Cornelio Muñoz, intrepid captain of my former guard, had property there; so did Rafael Ortega, my constant companion in hardship and glory, whose

SOURCE: From José Antonio Páez, *Autobiografía* (New York, 1869; reprint ed. of H. R. Elliot, 1946), pp. 2:297–301.

recent death still grieved me at the time of these events; then there were Francisco Guerrero (second in command of the army in Apure), Remigio Lara, Juan Angel Bravo, Facundo and Juan Antonio Mirabal, Doroteo Hurtado, Leon Ferrer, Andrés Palacio, Marcelo Gómez, and others whose names I have recorded already when describing my campaigns in the Orinoco plains. Also among them were Juan Pablo and Francisco Farfán, who had aided me on more than one occasion to succeed in my desperate struggle. These two were true bedouins of the plains: gigantic in stature, with athletic musculature and valor bordering on the ferocious, obedient only to naked force. They had served at first in the ranks of the royalist Yáñez. But when I had offered to give the rank of captain to any plainsman who brought me forty fighters, they enlisted with their followers and rode with me in Apure from that time on. If I had been strict with my troops, I would have had to punish these brothers severely, because they often deserted for a time with their men to go on plundering raids. Later they would reappear.

Just before the Battle of Mucuritas the Farfán brothers disappeared on one of these escapades, and I finally threatened to lance them through if they did not get out of my sight with all their people. That is why they did not share in the glory of Mucuritas. Later I allowed them to return, and I have told elsewhere how valuable the Farfán brothers proved in the capture of Puerto Cabello in 1823. They eventually returned to their herds in Apure, and there they lived peacefully until the year 1836.

In that year they raised the flag of rebellion—according to some, in connivance with other rebels on the coast; according to others, in response to a personal affront—without even a pretext of principles to justify their uprising against the government. The government directed the governor of Apure, Gen. Cornelio Muñoz, to organize a column to march against them, providing him with men, horses, arms, money, and a few troops from other provinces. The president also authorized General Muñoz to extend any sort of clemency compatible with the dignity of the government. He well knew that an insurrection based in Apure could put the whole Republic in danger. For my part, I sent several letters to the rebel leaders, reminding them of their patriotic duty. In reply, they tried to convince me that what they demanded was no more than I had promised to the people of Apure during the war of independence, that in a free Venezuela they would have to pay no taxes.

"Your demands are unjust, quite unjust," I wrote back to them. "In no American republic are taxes lower than in Venezuela. The customs house supplies our treasury. The only internal taxes are those essential for the maintenance of public works in the provinces, which must have schools to educate the young and roads for the betterment of trade. The provinces should supply these needs with their own funds. Refusal to pay taxes for ends so important would mean an eternity of backwardness and misery." The rebels finally accepted the clemency offered by Muñoz in his decree of July 9, and Francisco Farfán wrote me that "ignorance of the situation, the influence of others, and the lack of any adviser who could discern right from wrong had plunged him into an error that grieved him in his heart. He had fallen into it despite his good intentions and persisted in it thoughtlessly." He wrote: "I am aware of all the good Your Excellency has done for me, more than I can repay. But if gratitude would serve as repayment, I could bestow a wealth of it upon you, my friend and comrade, to whom I look up as a son to his father."

What happened next will show whether Farfán's repentance was sincere. Early in 1837 he rebelled again, this time in the Province of Guayana, proclaiming reunification with Colombia, the reform of the Constitution, the reestablishing of special legal privileges for military officers and clergy, the institution of trial by jury, the abolition of all taxes on rural property, a decree of amnesty for various conspirators fleeing justice, and finally the proclamation of General Mariño (the instigator of all of this) as Supreme Chief.

Cornelio Muñoz mobilized against Farfán, but his subordinates failed in their operations. Major Navarrete was defeated on the banks of the Orinoco and Colonel Mirabal was beaten on the plains of the Merecure. The rebels took Achaguas and obliged Muñoz to entrench himself in San Fernando. The president then decreed the formation of an army under my orders, naming Col. Agustin Codazzi chief of staff for the Division of Apure.

Codazzi marched to the aid of Muñoz, besieged by Farfán in San Fernando, and managed to force his way into that beleaguered town. I moved my troops to San Fernando as well and, on arrival, sent Captain Mirabal's infantry and Major Calderin's cavalry to reconnoiter. The enemy had crossed the river and withdrawn about a mile from the city just before my arrival. My men's horses were exhausted, so at nightfall I had the advance parties return so that the entire force would be able to resume the pursuit together. When the moon rose, I had the men take their horses across the river, and we set out at eight the next morning. Reaching the place called Rabanal, I learned that the rebels had passed hours earlier. I saw that it would be impossible to catch them with our whole army, so I took the best-mounted men on ahead, leaving the rest to come along afterward. With sixty fighters, I trotted in pursuit of a rebel force that numbered three times that. At the place called Yuca, about fifteen miles from San Fernando, I heard that they were only slightly ahead of us and, increasing the pace, I caught up with their rear guard a couple of miles from the town of Payara.

We entered the fight with that rear guard (composed of eighty men armed with carbines) and defeated them. As we chased these routed rebels through the town, my small force was divided into two groups. The enemy was waiting in a field to the west of the town: three columns of cavalry with a reserve force of infantry. The group to my right charged ahead impetuously but was repulsed, and the whole enemy army bore down upon them. Seeing this, I rushed to join them with my own group in order to face the onslaught with a compact mass of sixty lancers. In the extraordinary battle which followed, each man defended the ground within the radius he could reach with his lance, leaving an adversary sprawled there or dying there himself. Juan Pablo Farfán came personally to put me out of action, but the robust lance of my servant Rafael Salinas knocked him dead out of the saddle.

The rebels finally gave up the field, and the soldiers of the government were not less ardent in the pursuit than they had been in the heat of combat. We lost a mere two men dead and seven wounded; the rebels lost one hundred and fifty dead, among them a brother and an uncle of the ringleader, Francisco Farfán. Farfán sought his own salvation in the swiftness of his horse, and his followers fled in such disarray that one could not see ten of them together in their flight.

This deed of arms took place on April 26, 1837. I received a thousand congratulations for the victory, but they would have been more pleasant if the glory had not been won at the cost of Venezuelan blood. Such bravery, had it been displayed in the face of a foreign foe, would have moved the grateful nation to erect a battlefield monument to THE LIONS OF PAYARA.

Analyzing the Sources: What elements of this narrative help us understand political conflict in the period? What elements suggest a basis for national pride?

BOLÍVAR'S JUSTICE

Ricardo Palma

Ricardo Palma (1833–1919) was Peru's most important nineteenth-century author, the long-time director of its national library, and a man partially of African descent. Palma cultivated his own genre, which he called "traditions," of brief texts like the following, not exactly history and not exactly short stories, rather a cross between the two. He wrote them for decades during the second half of the 1800s, this particular one in 1877. To understand Bolívar's Justice, *it is crucial to keep in mind that Bolívar's patriot army in Peru was composed mostly of Colombians, a situation that led to inevitable tensions.*

In June of 1824 the patriot army was billeted at various points in the Andean highlands of Ancachs, preparing itself for the campaign that, in August of that year, resulted in the battle of Junín and, four

SOURCE: Ricardo Palma, "Justicia de Bolívar," in *Bolívar en las tradiciones peruanas* (Madrid: Compañía ibero-americana de publicaciones, 1930), pp. 9–17.

months later, in the splendid triumph of Ayacucho. Bolívar was residing at Caraz, and had with him his general staff, Neocochea's calvalry, La Mar's Peruvians, and the several battalions—Bogotá, Caracas, Pichincha, and Voltíjeros—that were later to distinguish themselves under the command of José María Córdoba. Another division, formed by the Vargas, Rifles, and Vencedores battalions, was stationed in the city of Huaraz.

The patriot officers were prone to gallant adventures, fearless and undefeated on the battlefields of both Mars and Venus. Just as they had enlisted to struggle heroically against the seasoned and numerous royalist army, when not actually fighting the enemy, they assaulted the impulsive daughters of Eve with no less energy and fervor. The officers of this largely Colombian army thus gave motive for anxious excitement among young women, considerable heartache among the mothers of those who were not married, and unmitigated sorrow among the husbands of those who were. Those infernal military peacocks could not pass a single halfway attractive young thing without saying, in the words that Córdoba later uttered so famously on the battlefield of Ayacucho: "Advance to victory!" The familiarities that they allowed themselves in Huaraz were enough to upset the least prickly and least suspicious husband. How easily those young liberators crossed the line!

The door of every house in town stood open to them, and there was no use in trying to shut them out, because they were adept at besieging any citadel and always found some way to gain entrance. Moreover, nobody dared to shut them out. They were in style, one could say, and during this phase of the struggle for our national independence, nobody wanted to appear a lukewarm patriot. Finally, it would have been the height of ingratitude to turn up one's nose at men who had come from the distant banks of the Cauca and Apure Rivers to share the hardships and glories of our struggle to break free of Spain.

The division billeted in Huaraz had a real brass band, and after evening roll call, the officers, who, as we have indicated, loved to party, were in the habit of taking the music to some house in town—whichever one they so desired—for a bit of impromptu dancing, to which the mistress of the house invited other women of the neighborhood.

A certain lady, whom we will call Señora de Munar, the widow of a wealthy Spanish inhabitant of Huaraz, had a house not far from the town's main plaza and lived there with two daughters and two nieces, all of whom could be considered extremely marriageable because they were pretty, rich, well-bred, and belonged to the established aristocracy of the locality. In the expression of the day, these girls had "salt, pepper, oregano, and cumin," which is to say, everything that men from Spain looked for in a woman from América.

Now, this Señora de Munar, doubtless out of loyalty to her deceased Spanish husband, was a zealous royalist, but one night when the young Colombian officers appeared at her house with their musicians and manifest intentions of arranging a dance, she could find no way to exclude them from her aristocratic drawing room.

As for the girls, it is well known that their hearts leap at the prospect of a dance. The señora swallowed hard and remained silent at each bit of flirtatious flattery that the officers directed to one of the damsels. Occasionally she pinched the arm of a niece whom she saw melting with indecorous delight. Periodically, she admonished under her breath the excessive attention paid by a daughter to the young liberators' gallantries. But that was all.

It was already after midnight when one of the young ladies— one whose charms had aroused the imagination of a captain of the Vargas Battalion—began to feel herself indisposed and withdrew to her room. The smitten young libertine, believing that he could successfully evade the vigilance of the girl's mother, went in search of the nesting place to which his turtledove had retired. The dove resisted the insistent demands of this don Juan, which were probably crossing the line, indeed, when from behind a hand snatched the sword that hung from his waist and plunged it into his body.

The person who thus punished actions that were about to dishonor her family was the elderly Señora de Munar.

The captain ran into the drawing room covering the wound with his hands. His comrades, among whom he was well beloved, thundered with anger, and, after surrounding the house with soldiers and rounding up all the "suspects" in skirts, they carried the dying man back to their barracks.

The news of the uproar reached Bolívar just after lunch in Caraz. Immediately he mounted his horse and rode to Huaraz, arriving there within a very few hours.

That very day he issued the following communiqué to the entire army:

"His Excellency the Liberator has learned with indignation that the glorious flag of Colombia carried by the Vargas Battalion has been disgraced by those who ought to be the most zealous custodians of its honor and splendor, and in consequence, as an exemplary punishment for this offense, he decrees the following:

"First, the Vargas Battalion will henceforth occupy last place in the army's formation, and its battle flag will not be returned to it until a victory over the enemy erases the infamy which has befallen the battalion.

"Second, the body of the offender will be buried without military honors, and the sword that Colombia gave him to defend liberty and morality will be broken in front of the assembled troops."

Such an order is worthy of the great Bolívar. And such was required to maintain the prestige of the cause of Independence and restore military discipline.

Sucre, Córdoba, Lara, and all the other Colombian commanders insisted that Bolívar strike the provision that disgraced the entire Vargas Battalion because of a fault committed by a single officer. The Liberator denied their request for three days, at the end of which time he conceded to it. The moral lesson had been taught, and maintaining the first provision of his order now mattered little.

The Vargas Battalion cleaned the stain of Huaraz by means of the valor it displayed in the actions of Matará and Ayacucho.

After the funeral of the Colombian captain, Bolívar went to Señora Munar's house and said to her:

"I salute you, señora, with all the respect due to a worthy matron who, despite her womanly weakness, found the strength to save her honor and the honor of her family."

From that moment on, Señora de Munar stopped being a royalist, and she answered with enthusiasm:

"Viva el Libertador! Viva la Patria!"*

Analyzing the Sources: Because of their particular history, Peruvians found the Wars of Independence problematic as inspirational national history. Where is this evident in the preceding selection?

---

*Long live the Liberator! Long live our Country!

Chapter 5

THE PERILS OF PROGRESS

By the 1880s, Latin American writers had a new job to do. Somehow, they had to come to terms with the idea of Progress. Progress meant change—the abandonment of traditional ways and the embrace of material, social, and ideological transformation. The changes that defined Progress were embodied, above all, in European examples. To be like England or France or the United States, in whatever way, meant Progress. Most Latin American readers and writers found the idea of Progress desirable and inevitable, but also, a bit unsettling. These transformations were not automatic, after all. They required resources, and they produced both winners and losers. While Latin American governments (almost all in the hands of liberal Europhiles) promoted Progress, some conservative traditionalists (especially humble people of the countryside) resisted it. But theirs was a losing battle.

Ready or not, the material transformations that went by the name of Progress had begun to arrive from Europe at a prodigious rate. Telegraphic cables spanned the oceans and provided almost instant communications across them. Manufactured goods from European (and, to a lesser extent, US) industries were imported by the ton in the capacious holds of steamships that were vastly quicker and more reliable than sailing vessels. The countryside of Latin America underwent dramatic changes as landowners, stimulated by the arrival of the railroad, ramped up production of agricultural export products to fill ships' holds for the return trip. The region's major cities—its capital cities, above all—took on a new look, as colonial-style Spanish architecture gave way to the ornate facades inspired by Italian examples, and wide avenues were opened following the example of Paris. New European immigrants—many of them, too, Italian—were attracted to work on the land but usually ended up in major cities such as Buenos Aires, Montevideo, Rio de Janeiro, or São Paulo. Upper-class Latin Americans traveled frequently to Europe and often cited European thinkers as intellectual reference points. The lure and influence of Europe is everywhere in Latin American writings of the late nineteenth century.

So what were the perils of Progress? Furnishings and artworks imported from Europe defined luxury and good taste, as emphatically exemplified in the novel *The Stock Market* (1891). And yet the new ideas and new commercial abundance seemed to invite crass materialism and class conflict. Furthermore, the commercial abundance was very unevenly distributed. In the cities, the mansions of those who profited much from booming trans-Atlantic trade inspired the envy and sometimes the hatred of those left behind economically. In the countryside, Progress benefited large landowners, but it often impoverished rural workers by depriving them of traditional forms of subsistence. The mythic gaucho no longer roved freely over a boundless landscape, butchering semiwild cattle whenever he chose. Instead, he became a rural proletarian who sheared sheep for countless hours under the watchful eye of an overseer to provide wool for the international market, as in the novel *No Direction* (1885). Social tensions increased in many parts of rural Latin America. Slaves who had gained their freedom and moved to the poor neighborhoods of burgeoning cities sometimes rubbed elbows with newly arrived European immigrants, as in the novel *The Beehive* (1890), but their situation was not promising, and the immigrants themselves sometimes seemed threatening to middle-class people.

The greatest symbol of Progress was also its primary "vehicle" (pun intended, of course): the train. Railroads connected sleepy backwater regions to capital cities and oceanic ports and, via steamship, to European (and, to a lesser extent, US) ports on the other side of the ocean. Railroads not only facilitated contact with the European and US centers of Progress but were almost always constructed, owned, and operated by foreigners. Writers consistently celebrated the railroad, as in the 1880s newspaper chronicle *The*

Inauguration of the Railway from Mexico City to Texcoco, but the "iron horse" could evoke some ambivalent responses as well. Could technological innovation be, in some ways, a faddish obsession, an empty and thoughtless sort of imitation? The short story "Evolution" (1884) subtly invited its readers to ask themselves that question. And what about the perils of those terrifying fifteen-mile-an-hour velocities that led to a train wreck in *Birds without a Nest* (1889)? Of course, this is perhaps the least destructive train wreck ever described, and perhaps that is the answer. The perils of Progress seemed, for the time being, far outweighed by the advantages.

Still, some cast a nostalgic glance backward. Isidoro de María of Uruguay corresponded with Ricardo Palma and adopted a similar style for his own "traditions and memories" of *Old Montevideo*. Altamirano too is nostalgic for a simpler past in *The Blue-Eyed Bandit*. This was a minority attitude among the literate few, however.

THE INAUGURATION OF THE RAILWAY FROM MEXICO CITY TO TEXCOCO

Ignacio Manuel Altamirano

In the 1880s, Ignacio Manuel Altamirano (1834–1893) was the grand old man of Mexican letters, the man whom younger writers called "maestro." Altamirano had been a fighting Liberal like Benito Juárez, part of the great midcentury movement called La Reforma. Like Juárez, Altamirano was a man of the strongly indigenous south who looked somewhat out of place when he mingled with the light-skinned elite of Mexico City. In the early 1880s, Altamirano wrote a number of chronicles for Mexico City newspapers, including the following celebration of the railroad connecting Mexico City with nearby Texcoco.

———————

SOURCE: adapted from Ignacio Manuel Altamirano, *Paisajes y leyendas: Tradiciones y costumbres de México* (Mexico City: Editorial Porrúa, 1974), pp. 219–23.

The railway from Mexico City to Texcoco was inaugurated on the fifteenth of last August, practically in silence.

In silence, I say, because advance notice was slight, only modest announcements in a few newspapers. There were not a great number of invited guests, nor did the reporters who covered the event endlessly announce the identities and descriptions of those in attendance, more or less the same list who have been attending all such events for years. The number of cakes and bottles consumed during the inaugural journey remains undisclosed. Nor have the newspapers divulged the more-or-less witty remarks made, and by whom, in order to pass the time during the trip—the only interesting thing that the reporters generally write in their little notebooks, because it is valuable for the public to know what such people are saying on such occasions.

On the other hand, if the bustling and sweet-smelling metropolis of Mexico City did not celebrate the train's departure with the music of bells and trumpet flourishes, the train's arrival in poor, obscure Texcoco was indeed motive for a celebration in the streets around the newly erected railroad station, a great celebration that attracted enormous crowds of people from Texcoco and numerous hamlets in its environs.

The celebration showed a hint, a faint hint, of Texcoco's vitality in bygone times. Today poor and languishing, Texcoco was once a great city, a rival of Tenochtitlan that occasionally defeated the Aztec capital on the battlefield. When Texcoco finally succumbed to Aztec overlordship, it did not become a tributary, but rather, a respected ally, governed by its own laws.* Despite its proximity, just across the lake from Tenochtitlán, indigenous Texcoco always retained its competitive spirit and separatist tendencies vis-à-vis Tenochtitlan.

Of course, the Texcoco of today is not truly a direct descendant of the indigenous Texcoco of old. Today's Texcoco is a hybrid in all ways—in its construction and appearance, in the customs of its people, in the people themselves, mostly mestizos or descendants of Spaniards. Like Mexico City, Texcoco's inhabitants have changed so

*Both Sahagún and Díaz del Castillo told how the Lord of Texcoco accompanied Moctezuma when he greeted Cortés.

much over the centuries that one could say the current inhabitants have nothing in common with the people who dwelled there before the conquest. All that has remained is the name and location beside the lake, things that the Spanish could not destroy, whether as rigorous conquerors or zealous missionaries, things that the natives who fled enslavement and destitution could not carry with them.

In justice, however, we must confess that the downtrodden state of towns and cities like Texcoco that were known, in ancient times, for their prosperity and opulence cannot be explained totally by the sword of Spanish conquest nor by the additional neglect of Spanish colonial rule. No, the incessant cannon of our post-independence civil wars played a part, as well, by making material progress impossible for decades.

And yet, on the fifteenth of August, the impoverished descendent of the once-proud lady of the lake put on party clothing, adorned herself with festive garlands of flowers, and set the bells of her half-ruined churches madly ringing. Texcoco seemed to stir from her three centuries of torpor and sit up in spite of her anemia. Her pale, sad countenance broke into a smile when she heard the voice of the locomotive, the voice of hope, coming at last to this silent region to instill spirit and vigor. The movement of the locomotive will shake things awake and restore the vitality of the native people of this place, scattered and crushed by three centuries of conquest, despotism, and civil war.

It was as if Texcoco received an infusion of youth with the approach of the locomotive. Her circulation seemed to improve, and the blood flowed into her pale and sunken cheeks, giving them a healthier color. A flash of joy and hope shone in her sunken and fever-swollen eyes. She adorned her jet-black hair with blossoms and sat by the shore of her poetic lake to await the chugging messenger of her bliss. It had been so, so long since she had tasted such happiness, cherished such hope, felt herself buoyed by such a consoling vision.

The waters of the lake have always linked Texcoco to Mexico City, it is true, but those sullen and swampy waters, rather than a fraternal bond, became a confining chain after the Spanish conquest.

No longer a sister city, Texcoco became the mere servant of Mexico City (the arrogant mistress of the Spanish king and then, after independence, disdainful chief housekeeper of the Republic).

Texcoco continued to send Mexico City boatloads of fruit, flowers, and other articles of value, but in return she received only waste, fever, and death. The lake, so vast and calm, became little more than a cesspool for the effluents of unhealthy and licentious Mexico City. Now, for the first time in centuries, Texcoco was to be linked to the capital of the Republic by a mode of transport that was not a humiliating open sewer.

The railroad tracks had arrived!

Moreover, the two ribbons of steel that began at the eastern edge of Mexico City and extended eastward to Texcoco were destined to continue east, to Puebla, and beyond, until reaching the waves of the Gulf of Mexico. The ribbons of steel were like a gold ring symbolizing a marriage, a marriage uniting the high valley of Mexico with European civilization on the other side of those waves and with the prosperous future that Mexico deserves.

The arrival of the railroad was Texcoco's first intimation of what the future holds in store. This is what moved the city's people to rejoice upon hearing the whistle of the locomotive that brought the first train from Mexico City. Interestingly, the entrepreneurs who are carrying out the construction of the rail line are Spanish. If the first arrival of the Spanish in Texcoco brought missionaries of Christianity, this second Spanish mission brings a gospel of Science and nineteenth-century Civilization.

The people of today's Texcoco hurried to the town's new railway station to give their enthusiastic greeting to the new envoys of Civilization. They spread flowers on the tracks in front of the locomotive and offered it their appreciative applause. They delivered several heartfelt speeches in expression of their gratitude to a representative of the Spanish company. Someone even read a poem that he had composed to commemorate the inauguration of railroad. It was nothing like the sublime songs of Nezahualcoyotl from the old glory days of Anáhuac, but it showed that the ancient poetic inclination of these lands is alive and well.

Analyzing the Sources: Does Altamirano seem to have any mixed emotions about the coming of Progress to Texcoco? If so, where may they be found?

THE BLUE-EYED BANDIT

Ignacio Manuel Altamirano

Even as he welcomed the railroad, Altamirano pined for the simple virtues of an imagined past. Altamirano's novel The Blue-Eyed Bandit *reverses the familiar racist hierarchy of the nineteenth century, making its bad characters light skinned and the good ones dark skinned. The novel is set in the early 1860s, when bandit gangs ran amok in the Mexican countryside. The following passage is too straightforward to require much explanation. Nicolás, an honest, hardworking indigenous man, loves Manuela, one of the two young women in this scene, but Manuela despises him because (we eventually learn) she prefers a blue-eyed bandit chief. She and her bandit meet a bad end, of course. And the other young woman, Pilar, a virtuous mestiza, gets Nicolás in the happy ending.*

On the edge of town, near the river, stood a humble but nonetheless lovely little house, with its walled garden of lemon, orange, and banana trees. In the internal patio of that house, a small family—composed of an elderly señora and two young women, both quite beautiful but contrasting in appearance—sat to enjoy the cool breeze.

One was about twenty years old and fair, with that pallid whiteness one sees occasionally in the tropical lowlands of Mexico, her eyes dark and vivacious, her lips red and laughing, her head held high. This young woman had a proud and disdainful look that came, no doubt, from her slightly aquiline nose, from the frequent

SOURCE: Ignacio Manuel Altamirano, *El zarco*, trans. Chasteen (Mexico City: Editorial Porrua, 1992), pp. 5–11, trans. by John Charles Chasteen.

fluttering of her velvety eyelashes, and from a smile more mocking than benevolent. She sat on a rustic bench and entertained herself by braiding red calendulas and white roses into her black, silky tresses. One might mistake her for an aristocratic maiden shunning the prying eyes of the court, disguised and hidden away in that tropical garden, perhaps with the intention of meeting her suitor for a romantic tryst.

The other young woman was about eighteen, and her complexion was darker. Her skin had the delicate tone of a true daughter of Mexico: not purely Spanish in physical type, but not quite Indian, either. Her large, dark eyes, her mouth that smiled sadly at her companion's mocking comments, her bowed head, and her delicate body together expressed a melancholy so intense that one could discern immediately a character diametrically opposed to the character of the first young woman. Slowly and listlessly, the dark beauty braided common orange and lemon blossoms into her hair. She had collected them from the orange and lemon trees so abundant in the town, and she had hurt her hands in doing so, for which her companion kidded her mercilessly.

"Look, Mamá," said the fair young woman to the elderly señora who sat a bit further off, sewing in a wicker chair. "Look at this silly thing who's been at it all afternoon and gotten nowhere. She hurt her hands trying to get the highest, freshest blooms on the trees, and now she can't braid them into her hair. What she wants is to get married . . . and soon!"

"Who, me?" asked the dark young woman, timidly raising her eyes as if embarrassed by the very idea.

"Yes, you!" replied the other. "Don't pretend not to. You dream about getting married. That's all you talk about all day long. And you choose orange blossoms because they have that association. Not me. I'm not ready to get married yet, so I wear the flowers I like best. Anyway, a wreath of orange blossoms is for a corpse. That's what they put on girls who die unmarried."

"Maybe I like them because that's how they'll bury me," said the dark young woman.

"Girls, don't talk that way!" scolded the older woman. "With times the way they are, and the two of you talking like that, how can a person keep her spirits up? You, Manuela," she said, turning to the proud, fair one, "let Pilar wear the flowers she wants, and you wear the ones you want. You *both* look pretty . . . and nobody sees you anyway," she concluded with a sigh.

"It *is* a shame, *such* a shame," agreed Manuela with obvious feeling. "Now, if we could go out to a dance, even spend some time at the window . . . that might make a difference."

"Fine times these are," complained the señora bitterly, "for attending dances or spending time at a window. What would we do with a party since, God save us, we have to live hidden away so that those horrid bandits won't know we exist! I can't wait for my brother to come from Mexico City and take us away from here, even if we have to walk. Who can live in this place anymore? One of these days something is going to frighten me to death. The life we lead today in Yautepec, Lord knows, is no way to live. In the morning, a fright if the church bell rings and we hurry to hide in the church or the neighbor's house. In the afternoon, we've hardly had lunch, and more fright if we hear the church bell or see people running. At night, we are startled by every step, every bump, every sound of horses in the street. And if we hear a shot or a shout, we don't sleep a wink all night. It is impossible to live this way. All people talk about are robberies and murders. They've grabbed so and so and taken him into the hills, and sure enough his body appears. There is a swarm of vultures over here or there. The priest has gone to hear the confession of so and so, whom the bandits left for dead. Tonight that bandit Salomé Plasencia will be coming into town— or maybe it's Zarco or Palo Seco, instead—and we should all go hide. Then here come the government troops and their tying people up and executing them, too. Tell me, is this any way to live? It is infernal torment . . . and my heart can't take it!"

Thus, weeping copious tears, the old woman concluded her description of life in Yautepec, a description that was only too accurate and perhaps even not quite as bad as reality. Manuela, who had blushed vividly at the mention of Zarco's name, reacted with sympathy when she heard her mother complain of heart trouble.

"Mamá, you hadn't told me your heart was bothering you. Does it hurt, really? Do you feel ill?" Manuela asked, approaching her mother with obvious concern.

"No, daughter, not sick. I'm fine. I'm just saying that this life afflicts me, saddens me, makes me feel desperate, and it really will make me sick if things go on this way. No, I haven't been sick, thank God. That's one bit of good fortune we've enjoyed, amid all the bad we've have to endure since your father died. But I'll worry myself sick about you, in this town, with all the neighbors saying: Doña Antonia, better hide Manuela or even send her to Cuernavaca or Mexico City. She's in danger here, being so pretty, if the bandits find out about her. They've got spies here who could let them know, and they'd swoop into town one night and carry her away. That's what everyone tells me, Jesús be with me! The priest himself has said it. The mayor has said it. All our relatives have said it. There's not a blessed soul in this whole town who doesn't say it every day. And here I am hopeless, with no idea what to do . . . alone . . . with no way to make a living except for our garden, which is all that keeps us here, with no other ally except my brother, who now ignores my letters, I've sent so many. Do you see, daughter, why I say my heart can't take it? If my brother weren't promising to come get us, we'd have just one way to save ourselves . . ."

"What's that, mamá," asked Manuela with a start.

"Getting you married, my dear one," responded her mother with infinite tenderness.

"Me married? With whom?

"What do you mean, with whom?" said the old woman in a tone of gentle reproach. "You well know that Nicolás is in love with you, that he would be the happiest creature in the world if you consented to marry him. Poor thing, it's two years now since he's been coming to visit us every single day, rain or shine, despite all hazards, despite the way you snub him, so often and so unjustly, hoping only that your heart will finally soften and accept his love . . ."

"So here is that topic again, no, mamá?" interrupted Manuela, who had reacted energetically with open disgust as soon her mother mentioned Nicolás. "I should have known from the first where you were headed. You always talk about Nicolás, always propose I marry him, as the only way to remedy our situation, as if nothing else were possible!"

"But *what* else, girl?"

"We could go to Mexico City with uncle, or we could just keep on living as we have, hiding at any sign of trouble."

"But your uncle doesn't ever come! And three women can't very well travel to Mexico City by themselves, now, can they? And entrusting ourselves to anybody is dangerous now, with the roads so infested with bandits who'd probably find out in advance and lie in wait for us."

"Wouldn't it be just as risky to travel with uncle?"

"Maybe, but he's family and would do his best to protect us. He'd probably hire armed men for an escort or come with a contingent of government troops from Cuernavaca or Mexico City. And we'd know he'd keep his lips sealed about our plans, too. He'd probably plan for us to travel by night through Totolapam or Tepoztlán. Anyway, we'd be safer. But he doesn't come, you see? And he's stopped answering my letters. He must know what's going on around here, and I'll bet his wife and children refuse to let him take risks. Still, he's our only hope . . ."

"Well," replied Manuela, who refused to concede the point, "even if that's the way things are, Mamá, what would we gain by my marrying Nicolás?"

"Oh, daughter! You would be a married woman, under the protection of a worthy man, that's what we would gain."

"But that worthy man, as you call him, is just the blacksmith of the Atlihuayan estate. If the owner of that estate, a powerful señor, has gone to Mexico City because he is powerless against the bandits, what is the blacksmith going to be able to do against them? He's nothing but a poor artisan, Mamá," protested Manuela, her lower lip jutting out in disdain.

"He may be a poor artisan, but Nicolás is brave and every inch a man. The bandits have never dared to attack him on the road. His assistants and friends hold him in high regard. On the Atlihuayan estate, you would be safe from bandits, and if you don't want to stay around here at all, Nicolás has saved a lot of money, you know, since he's been head blacksmith. The master tradesman who taught him and left him in charge is a foreigner who now lives in Mexico City, you know. He is very fond of Nicolás, and I'll bet we could stay at his house until things get better around here."

"No, mamá. Never!" interrupted Manuela. "My mind is made up. I'll never marry that horrible Indian. I can't stand to lay eyes on him. He repulses me and I just can't abide his presence. I'd prefer anything to being with him. I'd prefer to be with the bandits!"

"With the bandits?" cried her mother, throwing down her sewing. "May I never live to see such travesty! I'd sooner die!" To Pilar, the dark young woman who had listened throughout in silence, the old lady said: "You, who are only my goddaughter, would surely never cause me such sorrow. 'Horrible Indian?' This princess thinks she deserves some ideal lover." And to Manuela: "How did you become so conceited? You are a poor girl, even if God did give you that white face and those eyes that get you compliments from all the storeowners in town. That 'horrible Indian,' as you call him, is a young man of high principles, a poor orphan from Tepoztlán who learned to read and write before becoming a blacksmith. He is already in charge of the forge at an age when most are barely journeymen, with an excellent reputation and the respect even of rich men. He *earned* what little he has with honest labor and the sweat of his brow. That is always a fine achievement, most especially these days and around here. There isn't anyone else to compare with him. Am I right, Pilar?"

"Yes, godmother," answered the modest young woman, "you are completely right. Nicolás is a very good man, a hard worker, who loves Manuela very much. He would give her everything she asks for and be a wonderful husband. I'm always telling her so. And he doesn't look horrible to me . . ."

"Of course not! He's not white, not Spanish, and not one to wear fancy clothing or cut a fine figure at dances and parties, that's all. He's quiet and reserved, and that doesn't seem a defect to me."

"Nor to me," added Pilar.

"Well, Pilar," said Manuela, "if you like him so much, why don't *you* marry him?"

"Me?" gasped Pilar, turning pale and then blushing to the point of tears. "Why do you say that? He loves you, not me." And at that instant a soft knock sounded at the door.

"Go open the door for him, Pilar," said the señora. "It's Nicolás."

Analyzing the Sources: What seems to be the moral of this story (the novel as a whole) if one reads it as an allegory in which the characters represent elements of Mexican society more generally?

EVOLUTION

Joaquim Maria Machado de Assis

Joaquim Maria Machado de Assis is generally considered the greatest Brazilian author ever. A descendant of slaves, he was born free (1839–1908) into a Brazil whose plantations were still powered by slave labor. While naturally critical of slavery, Machado de Assis wrote mostly elegant fictions for the entertainment of the white Brazilian upper class, whose lives and manners he depicted in a manner well exemplified by the following 1884 short story. Machado's themes tended to be more psychological than social, but both interests can be detected in "Evolution."

Benedito was forty-five years old when I met him. I will not say when that was, because everything in this story is going to be oddly incomplete.

At the time, Benedito had relatively little gray hair, and he submitted what he had to a chemical process so efficacious that the gray hairs could not be distinguished from the rest—except when he got out of bed in the morning, but no one saw him when he got out of bed. Everything else was natural—legs, arms, head, eyes,

SOURCE: Joaquim Maria Machado de Assis, "Evolução," in *Relíquias de casa velha* (Rio de Janeiro: Civilização Brasileira, 1977), pp. 114–120, slightly abridged.

clothing, shoes, watch chain, and walking cane. Even the diamond stick pin that he wore on his tie was authentic and natural. It had cost him a considerable amount of money, and I myself saw him purchase it in the shop that belongs to . . . I was about to let slip the jeweler's name. Let's just say that the shop was on fashionable Ouvidor Street.

In moral terms, Benedito was himself, the same then as now. One's character does not change, and Benedito's was generally good, or at least, mild. In intellectual terms, he was scarcely original. We can compare him to a busy inn where ideas of all sorts encounter one another and sit down to eat with the innkeeper and his family. Occasionally, there might be someone obnoxious, or even two declared enemies, present at the table, and yet no one quarrels because the innkeeper imposes mutual respect among his guests. This is how Benedito managed to reconcile his vague atheism with his founding of a couple of religious brotherhoods somewhere in Rio, possibly Gávea, Tijuca, or Engenho Velho. He put on and took off his atheism and devotion like a pair of silk socks. I never saw his socks, by the way, but he told his friends everything.

We met during a journey from Rio to Vassouras. We had gotten off the train and boarded a coach to take us into town from the railroad station outside it. We exchanged a few words and were soon chatting freely, with the quick familiarity inspired by travel, even before becoming formally acquainted.

Naturally, our first topic was the progress that the railroad was bringing to Brazil. Benedito reminisced about the time when travelers had to sit astride a donkey all day. Each of us then told stories, mentioned names, and ended up agreeing that railroads were vital to the progress of our country. Those who have never made a long journey simply cannot appreciate how such solid, serious banalities alleviate the tedium of the road. One's spirit is refreshed, one's muscles, relaxed, one's circulation, improved by a serviceable banality. It leaves one at peace with God and Man.

"Our children will not live to see a railway network span the entire country," he said.

"I'm afraid not. Do you have any children?"

"None."

"Neither do I. No, we'll not have such a network, not even in fifty years. And yet, it is our greatest necessity. I like to compare Brazil to a baby that is crawling on the floor. It will only begin to walk upright when it has many, many railroads."

"A nice image!" exclaimed Benedito, his eyes sparkling.

"I don't care much if it's nice, as long as it's accurate."

"Nice *and* accurate," he replied amiably. "Yes, sir, you are right. Brazil is still crawling on the floor. It will only begin to walk upright when it has many, many railroads."

We arrived in Vassouras. I went to the house of the local judge, an old friend of mine, while Benedito spent only one night before continuing to his destination in the countryside nearby. A week later I made the return trip to Rio, by myself, and a week after that, he too was back in Rio.

We met at the theater and talked for a long time, exchanging news, and Benedito ended up inviting me to lunch the next day. I went, and he gave me a meal fit for a king, followed by good cigars and an animated dialogue. I noticed that Benedito's conversation had been more interesting during our journey together, when it refreshed the spirit and left us at peace with God and Man. But perhaps the interest of his conversation was merely overshadowed by the meal, which was really magnificent and left little space for philosophizing. Between the coffee and the cognac, he said to me, leaning on an elbow and gazing at the lit end of his cigar:

"On my return from Vassouras, I saw how right you are with your idea about how Brazil is still merely crawling."

"Hmmm?"

"Yes, sir, it's just as you said in the coach we shared. We will only begin to walk upright when we have many railroads. You can't imagine how true that it is."

And he made a number of observations about the difficulties of life in the countryside, its isolation and backwardness, while conceding people's good intentions and their desire for progress. Unfortunately, the current government had not responded to the needs of Brazil and seemed intentionally to keep it behind the other countries of South America. But we must realize that principles are everything and men are nothing. A people is not made for its government, but rather, a government for its people, and *abyssus abyssum invocate*, which means in Latin that one disaster leads to another. Then he got up to show me other rooms in his house, all furnished and decorated in good taste. He showed me his collections of coins, stamps, old books, paintings, and weapons. He had both swords and foils but confessed that he was no fencer. Among the paintings I saw a beautiful portrait of a woman and asked who she was. Benedito smiled.

"I won't ask any further," I said, smiling as well.

"No, no use in denying it," he offered hurriedly. "It is a young woman whom I liked very much. Pretty, no? You can't imagine how pretty. Her lips were ruby red, and she had roses in her cheeks. Her eyes were black as night. And her teeth! Her teeth were like pearls . . . exactly like them."

Next we entered his study. It was ample, elegant, slightly inconsequential, perhaps, but lacked nothing. It had two shelves of books in fine bindings, a globe, and two maps of Brazil. The desk was of ebony, a beautiful piece of work. The Laemmert statistical almanac of Brazil lay casually open atop it, beside a glass inkstand—"rock crystal," he said, explaining the inkstand as he explained everything else. In the next room there was an organ. He played the organ and liked music very much. He spoke of it enthusiastically, mentioning particular operas, outstanding passages, and informed me that, as a child he had begun to learn to play the flute. He gave it up before long—which was a pity, he concluded, because it is such a lovely instrument. He showed me a few more rooms. We went into the garden, which was splendid, so ably did Nature aid Art and Art crown Nature. He had roses of all sorts and from all over, for example. "There is no denying that it's the queen of flowers," he said.

I left his house dazzled. We met afterward a few times on the street, at the theater, at the house of mutual friends, and I had the opportunity to get to like him. Four months later, I traveled to Europe on a business matter that kept me away for a year. He was busy trying to get elected to the Chamber of Deputies. I was the one who had suggested that idea, without any real political intention, but merely as a pleasantry, roughly as if I were complimenting him on the cut of his vest. He took the idea seriously and became a candidate. One day I was crossing a street in Paris and bumped into Benedito.

"What are you doing here?" I exclaimed.

"I lost the election," he said, "so I've come to travel in Europe." He stayed with me, and we travelled together from then on. He confessed that losing the election had not discouraged his parliamentary ambitions. To the contrary, it had encouraged those ambitions, and he spoke to me of a master plan.

"I'd like to see you become a government minister," I told him.

Mention of a ministry took him by surprise, and he beamed but then quickly dissembled.

"Not likely," he said, "but when I become a minister, you may be sure that my chief care will be industry. We've had enough parties and politics. We need to develop the vital forces and enormous resources of our country. Do you remember what *the two of us said* in the coach to Vassouras? Brazil is still crawling, it will only walk upright when it has railroads."

"You are right," I agreed, a little startled. "Why else did I come to Europe? Because of a railroad. I've made all the necessary arrangements in London."

"Really?"

"Absolutely."

I showed him the paperwork, which he examined in amazement. Because I had collected notes, statistics, leaflets, reports, copies of contracts, all sorts of information on industrial matters, and showed it all to him, Benedito announced that he, too, was going to start such a collection. And I did see him visiting banks, commercial associations, and government ministries, collecting a lot of paper that he piled into briefcases. But the ardor with which he did so, while intense, did not last long. It was borrowed, one could say. Benedito collected something else much more enthusiastically: political slogans, parliamentary phraseology. His head was full of these, a vast arsenal. He delighted in their apparently inestimable value, and he repeated them frequently in his conversations with me, for practice. Many were of English origin, and these were his favorites, bringing with them the prestige of the House of Commons. He savored them so much that I do not know if he would accept liberty itself without the slogans that went along with it. I rather doubt it. I rather think that, if he had to choose, he would opt for those pithy, easy slogans, none requiring reflection, some of them beautiful, some high-flown, all of them axiomatically true, conveniently filling up the spaces between other words, leaving listeners at peace with God and Man.

We returned to Brazil together, but I got off the ship in Pernambuco while he continued to Rio. I later returned to London and did not get back to Rio for another year. By that time, Benedito had been elected to the Chamber of Deputies. I paid him a visit and found him preparing his maiden speech. He showed me notes, passages taken from official reports, books on political economy, some with pages marked by strips of paper labeled Exchange Rate, Property Tax, Grain Issue in England, John Stuart Mill's Opinion, Adolph Theirs' Error Regarding Railroads, and so on. He was earnest, detailed, and emphatic. He spoke to me about these things as if he had just discovered them, explaining everything from the beginning. He was determined to show the knowledgeable men of the Chamber that he, too, was knowledgeable. He asked about my own project, and I told him where it stood.

"I hope to inaugurate the first section of track within two years."

"And what about the English investors?"

"What do you mean?"

"Are they satisfied?"

"Very much so. You can't imagine."

I related a few technical particulars. He listened distractedly—whether because my narrative was extremely complicated or for some other reason. When I finished, he said that he was pleased to see me promoting industry because that is what this country really needed, and by way of illustration, he did me the favor of reading me the opening passage of the speech which he was to deliver within a few days.

"It's still a rough draft," he said, "but the main ideas are in place." And he began to read:

"Amid the growing agitation of the public spirit, amid the partisan clamor that drowns out the voice of legitimate public interest, allow me to make heard the following plea that comes to us, gentlemen, from the Nation itself. It is time for us to devote our attention exclusively—and take note of that word, *exclusively*—to the material improvement of our country. I know what the reply may be. You will say that a nation has not only a stomach for digesting, but also a head for thinking and a heart for feeling. I respond that all this is worth little or nothing if the nation does not also have legs for walking. And here let me repeat what I said to a friend of mine, a few years ago, during a journey through the interior of Brazil. Brazil is like a baby crawling on the floor. It will only walk upright when it has many railroads. . . ."

> *Analyzing the Sources: What is the "evolution" in this story? What comment does the story make about the nineteenth century's devotion to Progress?*

NO DIRECTION

Eugenio Cambaceres

Argentine author Eugenio Cambaceres (1843–1888) wrote in the Naturalist style associated with the French novelist Émile Zola. As a literary style Naturalism contrasted with the Romanticism of novels like María. *While Romantic novels often idealized the social relations of the countryside, Naturalist novels tended to view them (and most other things) starkly. For example, the following scene of rural workers—the opening of Cambaceres's best-known novel,* No Direction *(1885)—differs enormously in tone from the view of "happy slaves" in the previous chapter's excerpt of* María *and from the earlier, also Romantic, view of rural Argentina presented by Sarmiento.*

The sheep stood in parallel lines leading to a table piled with wool that several men were busy binding into bundles.

The men placed the bundles in the wide pan of the scale that hung by a rawhide cord from the rafters of the building and then tossed the weighed fleece to one side, where others heaped it onto what looked like a mountainside of melting snow.

SOURCE: Eugenio Cambaceres, *Sin rumbo* (Buenos Aires: Editorial Minerva, 1924), pp. 11–13.

The sheep, their feet brutally hobbled, leaned against one another and turned their heads toward the open door, their eyes half-closed with fear and exhaustion, panting breathlessly.

Around the walls of the room, men and women worked bent over, in clusters.

Theirs was a motley array of clothing typical of the countryside, all of it filthy: the *alpargata* footwear with soles of coiled fiber, the primitive rawhide *bota de potro*; the French-style beret and baggy *bombacha* trousers of the modern gaucho, the *vincha* headband and *chiripá* loincloth of the more impoverished or old-fashioned kind; the women's uniformly ragged gingham dresses.*

Amid the reigning silence, interrupted now and again by bleats of pain from the sheep and coarse jokes from the sheep shearers, the shears made a high-pitched plink like the plucked strings of a violin. The shears dove quickly through the thick fleece, snipping, surfacing here, disappearing there, like panicky creatures in search of a hiding place, occasionally catching the flesh of the sheep between their blades in haste, so that long strips of skin came off with the wool, leaving wide, bloody wounds on the animals' flanks.

The hot north wind huffed and puffed at the structure's three wide entrances.

"Medication!" shouted a voice.

It belonged to a stocky, muscular, bronze-skinned young man with high cheekbones and small, fierce, deep-set eyes.

One of those human types whom one encounters on the plains, stubborn as a mule, sly as a fox, savage as a tiger.

The old cigarette-smoking Basque who served as provisional veterinarian had approached with his can of tar (the "medication") and was about to apply it with a small brush to the freshly opened wound when another man, standing beside him, spoke in a rude and angry tone:

"Where did you learn to sheer sheep, kid?" he asked the stocky young man.

"Oh, get off my back, would you, old man?"

---

*Articles of gaucho garb are difficult to describe and impossible to translate. The point of the passage is the mixture of old and new.

"You're just aching to get your tail whipped, kid."

"Not even if you were my father," replied the boy, and, whistling a rustic ditty through his teeth, he pulled a hand-rolled cigarette from behind his ear, lit it as calmly as could be, and crossed his legs casually over the recumbent animal whom he had just wounded, all the while watching his challenger out of the corner of his eye.

The scorn and repressed laughter with which the others celebrated the boy's cutting remark brought a flush of blood to his challenger's face.

"You insolent—" he bellowed, beside himself with rage, and the sound of a blow accompanied the sound of his voice.

The young gaucho's reaction was automatic. His hand dropped to his belt and he lunged erect brandishing his knife.

The barrel of a revolver stopped him cold.

With the impotent fury of a wild animal that bites at a rod thrust through the bars of his cage, the boy suddenly ceased his aggressive attitude, lowered his gaze, sheathed his knife, and let his arms drop to his sides.

"What do you hit me for, boss?" he asked softly with false humility, but his trembling, bloodless lips betrayed his bitterness and frustration.

"So you'll learn to behave yourself and act like a man. . . ."

And, addressing the man who kept track of each shearer's work, he said: "Villalba, pay this fellow for what he's done today, and I don't ever want to lay eyes on him again."

He added, for the benefit of the other workers:

"If anybody else has a commentary, you can go ahead and make right now. The door is big enough for everybody."

The wind entered with a whirl, hanging a thick curtain of dust in the air. There was no sound but that of the shears diving through animals' thick fleece and snipping with a high-pitched plink like the plucked strings of a violin.

Analyzing the Sources: Who, in this passage, descends from the free-roving gauchos of an earlier period described by Sarmiento?

OLD MONTEVIDEO

Isidoro de María

Isidoro de María (1815–1906) was not one of the young writers enamored of Progress. Instead, his interest was in remembering the distinctive past that Progress was erasing as it transformed major Latin American cities beginning in the 1880s. Like Ricardo Palma, the Uruguayan de María was a sort of historian, literary rather than academic in style. In 1888 he published the second volume of his Old Montevideo, Traditions and Memories, *which contains a famous description of* candombes, *the festivities of Montevideo's population of African descent. These festivities, with their African nations electing ceremonial kings at Epiphany, are a familiar part of the African diaspora. The black population of Montevideo had declined from something like a quarter to only a few percent during the 1800s, making it one more vanishing memory of the city to be preserved. In this sketch, de María focuses on a stretch of seashore where the city's black community went to socialize during a period when many were still enslaved.*

The seashore on the south side of Montevideo was the place where the city's residents went to stroll, and there too—or rather, at the end of the paseo down by the old south battery—the blacks still organized their tangos* in the open air fifty or sixty years ago, in my youth. Their dances then were completely different from those of the white race. If whites danced to the sound of harps, pianos, violins, guitars, and wind instruments, blacks danced to sound of drums and other percussion instruments. If we had our fandangos and figure dances, they had their *candombes*. The tangos were held every Sunday, and all the blacks danced, men

---

SOURCE: Isidoro de María, *Montevideo antiguo: Tradiciones y recuerdos* (Montevideo: Biblioteca Artigas, 1957), pp. 1:274–75, 279–82.

*At the time, any dance attended by black people.

young and old, as well as women, with permission gained, of course, "by your leave, master or mistress," unless they were free and didn't need permission. The only children of Africa who did not attend were those whose masters worked them without a moment's rest.

Each African nation had its place along the shore, pounded smooth by bare heels and sprinkled with a thin layer of sand. First there were the Congos, next the Mozambiques, followed by the Benguelas, Minas, Cabindas, and Angolas, each nation forming a circle on its own dance ground, with drums large and small, thumb pianos in gourd resonators, and tin rattles with pebbles or seeds inside, that go *chinchirin chindá chichí, chinchirin chindá chichí.* And they sang *calunga cangué . . . eee, elumbá* and clapped in rhythm, and the dancers' bodies wiggled from head to foot.

All Montevideo turned out to watch the blacks put on their Sunday tangos. We children loved to see our old black "uncles" and "aunties," who served us good-naturedly every day, dancing candombes, not to mention all the little black children bobbing along, having the most wonderful time. Our mother laughed along with us, and even our father half-smiled as he put a coin in the plate held in front of him by a buxom maid with a bright smile. Seeing Father do this, all the children cried at once, "Buy us sweets!" There was no saying "no," of course, and we selected sweets from the trays that lined the paseo, each tended by an old auntie announcing her wares in a shrill voice: "*Alfajores . . .* delicious *alfajores* for the children!"

It was wholesome entertainment for everyone, and the Africans enjoyed themselves most of all. They even seemed to forget, during the festivities, the sad condition of enslavement in which they had lived since greedy slave traders tore them away from their native land. Sunday tangos by the seashore lasted until the sun went down. Then the strolling families turned their steps toward home, and so did the dancers, although not without first having a little gulp of something to soothe throats parched by so much *eee lumbá, eee lumbá.*

Even better, but only once a year, were the black festivities of Epiphany, 6 January, "the day of kings."

"Let's go see the King of Congo," said our mother, and we children leapt for joy. And of course, our father wouldn't miss it, either. And so off we went, so did everybody else, to see the "throne rooms" of the various African nations that elected their ceremonial kings and queens at Epiphany. Each nation put a lot of effort into decorating its throne room, most of which were located on the south side of the city, near where they put on Sunday tangos. And, oh my, did the old uncles and aunties dress up to attend the court of the King of Congo or Cabinda or Mozambique! Good hearted mistresses contributed clothing and jewelry (but no wigs, as the reader will comprehend) to adorn each African nation's queen and her attendant princesses and chambermaids. The old uncles appeared stiffly attired in castoff ties and tailcoats and top hats, more than slightly the worse for wear, perhaps, but strictly in accordance with etiquette.

The king himself—look, it's old uncle José Vidal!—sat upon his throne dressed in military uniform with gold trim, epaulettes on his shoulders, his chest covered with medals. His queen, auntie María del Rosario—she's the best pastry cook in Montevideo!—sat beside him on her own throne, looking equally regal, with her knitted shawl and her gold necklace glinting on her ebony skin. People of all descriptions bustled in and out of the throne room, where it was hard to stay for long owing to the heat and stuffiness, if you get my drift. And very soon, it was all over, goodbye scepter and diadem, hello bucket and broom!

Before the queens and kings returned to work, however, they processed en masse to city's main church where one of the lateral altars was devoted to the black Saint Baltazar, one of the three kings or wise men who followed the star to Bethlehem. From there the regal procession went to pay its respects to the governor and other municipal dignitaries, who always received the ceremonial royalty of Montevideo's African nations with the courtesy due visiting heads of state. So when they finally emerged to become cooks and street sweepers once again, our old uncles and aunties were at least in a predictably good mood!

Analyzing the Sources: How does this author's nostalgic popular history play into the dominant neocolonial emphasis on Progress?

BIRDS WITHOUT A NEST

Clorinda Matto de Turner

Clorinda Matto de Turner's Birds without a Nest *(1889) was among the first Latin American novels to focus on the plight of the indigenous people. Born in 1852, Matto de Turner exemplified liberal anticlericalism by making a corrupt Catholic priest the novel's villain. Her protagonists are progressive-minded whites from Lima who have come to the indigenous high Andes with a foreign-owned mining enterprise. Only a passive role remains for the novel's indigenous characters in need of rescuing. In this scene, the enlightened capitalist don Fernando Marín boards a train with his wife, his daughter, and a poor godchild whom they are taking to Lima to enjoy the benefits of Civilization.*

An elegant railroad car drawn by a locomotive christened (with a bottle of champagne and everything) Mineshaft was ready to pull out at the sound of the train whistle.

Meanwhile, the first-class passengers examined the merchandise for sale along both sides of the tracks, where Indian women offered gloves of vicuña wool, peach preserves, butter, cheese, and fried pork skins, products of the excellent livestock of the mountainous interior, or *sierra*, of Peru.

Don Fernando helped his wife Lucía and the two girls into their red-plush upholstered seats, then settled luxuriously into his own. He pulled out his tobacco, rolled a smoke in silence, and, after lighting it, put away the box of matches, took a few puffs, and left the cigarette between his lips as he untied the packet of books that

SOURCE: Clorinda Matto de Turner, *Aves sin nido* (Cuzco, Universidad Nacional del Cuzco, 1948), pp. 239–43, 249–51.

they had brought to read on the journey. After a few more puffs he said to his wife:

"Which of these would you like to read, Lucía my dear?"

"Give me Salaverry's *Poetry*," she responded with a smile of satisfaction.

"Fine. In that case, I will enjoy Palma's *Traditions* with their delightful Peruvian flavor," said don Fernando as he handed the requested volume to his wife.

Then he crossed his legs and leaned back just as the train began to roll, soon reaching the dizzying speed of fifteen miles an hour, swallowing distances, leaving flocks, pastures, and Indian huts all behind. Lucía curiously looked over the passengers in the other seats, who were beginning to seek ways to amuse themselves. A thin, dark, bearded army officer, seated next to a couple of country fellows who traded in cochineal and sugar, proposed a diversion:

"Shall we kill some time with a hand of cards?"

"Not a bad idea, captain, but where on earth will we get playing cards?" replied one of the country fellows who was all bundled up in vicuña wool.

Whereupon the captain produced a deck of cards from his pocket, saying: "A soldier who doesn't drink, woo the ladies, or play cards . . . should be a friar."

A friar who was seated nearby took the comment personally and glared at them. The cardplayers ignored him and improvised a table for their game. The friar opened a book, and three women seated near don Fernando's daughters, Margarita and Rosalía, began to talk to them and offer them peeled slices of apple. Half an hour later, women and girls were curled up asleep and the friar, too, was snoring, so deep in the sleep of the just that the excited shouts of the cardplayers made not the slightest impression on him.

The door at the end of the car opened and in came a corpulent fellow about thirty years old, his complexion ruddy from contact with the frigid Andean air, his moustache neatly trimmed, a large mole on his right ear. He wore a grey uniform including a cap with a black visor, and he carried a ticket puncher in his hand.

"Your ticket, reverend?" he said, stepping close and raising his voice enough to wake the friar, who opened his eyes and sleepily drew his yellow ticket from his book and handed it to the conductor without opening his mouth.

The conductor punched the ticket and returned it, turning next to the cardplayers. The two country fellows held out their tickets, and the officer produced a document that the conductor returned (with a murmur of displeasure: "these guys and their *papers*") after examining the signatures at the bottom.

Then he turned to don Fernando, and while he was punching their tickets Lucía inquired:

"Could you please tell me how far we have travelled to this point?"

"Four hours, señora . . . which is to say sixteen leagues, and we must go another sixteen to reach our destination," responded the conductor and continued down the aisle.

"What a prodigious journey, no? And without a single care or bother we'll shortly be in Lima," said don Fernando to his wife, shutting his book.

"Prodigious indeed, my dear. Look, Fernando, how precious these two look asleep . . . as peaceful as little angels!"

"Yes, they're angels, Peruvian angels, we could say, with all that native color in their cheeks."

Margarita raised her arching eyelashes and looked fixedly up at her godmother as an iron-and-wood railroad bridge came into view ahead, spanning a shallow river in a picturesque manner. And in the middle of the bridge was a small herd of cattle that the engineer had only just noticed.

The locomotive's whistle shrilled repeatedly, and the cattle fled in terror, but not as fast as the oncoming train. The passengers feared their certain death and cried out in terror, but there was nothing they could do. With the shattering velocity of a lightning bolt, the train ran over the fleeing animals, crushing their bones under its wheels, which went off the rails. Mister Smith, the valiant engineer, was prepared to sacrifice his own life to save those of the passengers who had entrusted him with their safety, and he attempted to puncture the boilers with a revolver shot in order to slow the progress of the train, unsuccessfully. Meanwhile a brakeman had decoupled the first-class car, and now it also, left the rails, and left the bridge, too, the only car to do so. It came to rest intact in the moist sand of the river bank.

The first person to leap to the ground was Mister Smith, shouting loudly in broken Spanish: "Everyone stay putting!" The windows of the train, all of which had lost their glass in the accident, sprouted the heads of curious passengers. Fortunately, there had been only a few minor injuries.

"Mister Smith, that was nearly the end of us!" said don Fernando to the engineer, who was an acquaintance of his. "Now when will we ever get to Lima?"

"Oh, señor Marín, what twisting of fate! But don't worry, the train will be tomorrow in Lima," replied the engineer as he supervised the necessary repairs. And with the energy that distinguishes his race, he set up a system of pulleys which, at the end of two hours' steady work, had extracted the derailed car from the sand of the riverbank and returned it to the rails, ready to continue the journey.

Analyzing the Sources: According to the impression left by this selection, who is responsible for the advance of Progress in Peru and who are the beneficiaries?

THE STOCK MARKET

Julián Martel

Julián Martel was a Buenos Aires journalist, born in 1867 to an impoverished branch of one of the city's traditional elite families. His novel The Stock Market *(1891) is set on the eve of the 1890 financial crisis that shook Argentina, ending a period of rampant real-estate speculation. The novel won immediate acclaim, but Martel did not have time, in his short life, to write another. The following excerpt describes the luxurious life of a lawyer, Doctor Glow, who is deeply involved in the speculative bubble that is about to burst. Non-Spanish surnames like Glow's were (and are) frequent in Buenos Aires, especially among the upper classes.*

"Is my wife home yet?"

"No, sir. She has not returned."

"She went out with the children?"

"Yes, sir."

Standing at attention as he spoke, the doorman bowed respectfully in honor of the arrival of the master of the house, who began slowly to ascend the broad marble stairway of the high atrium illuminated by three large bronze and crystal gas fixtures. The numerous gas jets within each fixture emitted torrents of light that bounced off the walls and the domed ceiling painted in oil with a thousand arabesques so intricate and beautiful that any of the unknown artisans who created that dreamlike palace called the Alhambra would gladly have signed his name there.

As Doctor Glow* put his foot on the last gleaming step, he paused, his hand resting on a handsome alabaster jar, enormous and heavy, decorated with one of those Japanese plants of wide, dark, capriciously shaped leaves, so well suited to the refined taste of our encyclopedic century. Well satisfied, he looked around him, and his lips curled again in the same contented smile that they had worn earlier in the day when he entered the stock market. He reflected that this mansion, a veritable palace, situated on Avenida Alvear in the heart of the most aristocratic neighborhood of Buenos Aires, belonged to him and to him alone. He had lived there no more than two weeks, and the impression that the mansion made upon him was still fresh. It was the sensation experienced by a man accustomed to a life of modest comfort who suddenly found himself raised to unexpected heights of luxury and opulence.

He gazed at the splendid vestibule with its costly adornments, its seats with French leatherwork, its elegant, mirrored coatrack, its table crafted of a variety of exotic woods upon which reposed two thick volumes of the works of Shakespeare (the Hetzel edition), and, of course, the floor—a mosaic of a thousand colors, like a car-

---

Source: adapted from Julián Martel, *La bolsa* (Buenos Aires: Ediciones Estrada, 1946), pp. 71–6, 151–52, 156–57.

*As "doctors of law," lawyers frequently use that title in Spanish.

pet spread out to be trodden upon by the white slipper of a sultan's lady.

Doctor Glow's voice echoed in the spacious vestibule.

"It is imperative that the two candelabras be placed by the foot of the stairs tomorrow without fail."

"Of course, sir."

The doorman, with his wide sideburns, his black jacket and red tie, stood as if frozen stiff at the foot of the stairs.

The doctor turned, pushed aside the Moorish tapestry that covered a doorway and entered a darkened room. Reflected light from the vestibule glinted faintly off mirrors and adornments on its walls.

"Juan!"

"Sir?"

"Come up."

The doorman's boots sounded on the stairs.

"Have the gaslights lit throughout the house."

After giving that order, Glow sat heavily in the first arm chair that his hand located in the darkness. He soon sensed the arrival of shadowy forms, heard the clatter of a stepladder and the sound of a match being struck, and suddenly . . .

A world of bright marvels bloomed out of the darkness! The servant at the top of the ladder was lighting the gas jets of the large central chandelier, one by one. From below, he resembled a tailcoated god able to call forth a glittering universe.

With a priceless expression, Doctor Glow looked around him at the one-piece Obusson carpet, at the footstools covered with hand-painted satin, at the walls smoothly encased in pale pink silk, at the thick draperies that hung majestically from high on those walls, at the ceiling decorated with the most elegantly-painted Cupids imaginable, at the sumptuous furnishings upholstered with fabrics representing warlike scenes of antiquity, at the bronze statues on their richly adorned pedestals, at the bric-a-brac scattered across the table-tops, including objets d'art in capriciously shaped glass cases, at the sculpted stands that supported open books or paintings, and at the large mirrors in their gold-filigreed frames, each with its potted flowers, a floral offering to whatever beautiful woman might chance to contemplate her own image in the beveled glass. Beyond all this, he observed another salon still shrouded in shadows that gave it a vaporous and fantastical air.

"Now turn on the lights in the next room."

The servant, carrying the stepladder that he opened to ascend to each gas fixture, went from one room to another, lighting them all, the various sitting rooms, the dining room, the library, even the bedrooms, while, following behind him, Doctor Glow never tired of admiring the accumulated splendors of his truly regal residence, as dazzling as a scene from the *Arabian Nights*.

When the palatial mansion stood bathed in the sparkling light that cascaded from each chandelier, when all its floors were illuminated and artificial day had been imposed on patios and gardens, then Doctor Glow wandered through it all, intoxicated by pleasure and vanity, pausing in front of each piece of furniture, gazing ecstatically at each painting, finding his image in each mirror. Meanwhile, through the half-open doors one could constantly glimpse his hovering employees—now it was the curious blonde countenance of the chambermaid, now the clean-shaven physiognomy of the English coachman, now the white cap of a kitchen scullion, now the sideburns and inverted v-shaped eyebrows of the doorman.

Through the window glass Glow looked down on winding garden paths and the gigantic sculpted grotto with its splashing fountains that a gardener had just put into motion. He delighted in the bower whose wooden latticework would soon be covered with the honeysuckle vines that had already begun to grow up around it protectively, brandishing their shield-shaped leaves against the attack of some formidable imaginary enemy. A series of iron posts, evenly spaced, held aloft globes of frosted glass. Sentinels erected to impede the advance of darkness, they bathed the flowerbeds in a soft resplendence. Beyond were a few palms swaying in the evening breeze, patches of pitch black, glints of pale green and electric blue, and finally, the street on the other side of the gold-plated iron fence. Glow could see the figures of pedestrians who stopped in astonishment at the sight of the silent mansion bedecked and illuminated as if for a party. One of the figures had eyes that glowed like a cat's, observed the doctor, perhaps one of those ravenous beings who lurk around the palaces of the rich after dark, a knife in their belts, a protest in their hearts, instigated by hunger, advised by envy. Doctor Glow turned away from the window in disgust.

Beneath a radiant and cheerful sun and an immaculate blue sky, the high society of Buenos Aires is out for a ride, a triumphal march toward the park at Palermo. What a spectacle they constitute as they ride along the high ground overlooking the river at La Recoleta in a dazzling procession of horses and coaches. The ordinary city folk who are out to breathe a little fresh air, to enjoy the shade of the trees, to gaze at the swans and ducks of various colors on the various small lakes, to admire the artificial grotto with silver threads of water streaming down its cement flanks, and perhaps to try the excitement of the roller coaster—the ordinary folk stop, amazed, to contemplate the avalanche of fancy carriages on the Avenida Alvear. They like to hear the rumble of wheels and the clatter of horses' hooves on the pavement and to see the rays of the sun glint on the gleaming carriage bodies and the bright uniforms of the coachmen who sit as calmly and stiffly as English lords out for a drive in Hyde Park, the sun sparkling on their top hats and silver buttons.

Poor ordinary city folk! Poor clerks and modest employees of every variety! Do not feast your eyes on the lovely ladies who pass before you like an enchanting vision. They are not for you. You would have to have a carriage, an expensive tailor (whether or not you could afford him), and appear frequently at the theater and in fashionable salons before any of these women would deign to smile or look at you. You would have to be seen at the stock market, at the club, be involved in investments, play *lansquenet* and *baccarat*. Look how lovely they are, and how they go past without even seeing you! In open carriages they pass, some lying capriciously amid a delicate swirl of lace and velvet, in the shelter of their parasols, some lolling on satin cushions, lost in amorous thoughts.

There goes Doctor Glow—whose tricks have just won him another million on the stock market—seated beside his wife and children, who put their precious little heads out the window of the family's fancy new coach, which Glow is taking out for the first time today in celebration of his recent financial triumph.

There they all go, in a whirlwind of traffic: majestic coaches belonging to distinguished families like Glow's; poor rental conveyances occupied by public women and their clients; small vehicles inhabited by ambitious law clerks whose reckless dealings may land them in jail; and spirited horses ridden by the gallant young men who pursue the lovely ladies, gallant young men who enjoy a family fortune the origin of which they do not even understand, believing that manna falls from heaven equally and effortlessly for all.

There goes, in sum, an entire society, to the sound of cracking whips, the whiny music of an organ grinder playing some popular dance tune somewhere out of sight, and in the background, the dull roar of the rollercoaster like an approaching storm. There goes an entire society, raised up by greed and speculation, celebrating the most scandalous orgy of luxury and ostentation that Buenos Aires has ever seen or will ever see gain, a vision of the apocalypse!

Analyzing the Sources: What is Martel saying about the function of the wealth generated by rural workers such as those portrayed in Cambaceres's selection? What seems to be the probable outcome of the situation that he describes?

THE BEEHIVE

Aluísio Azevedo

Literary Naturalists wrote most often about cities rather than the countryside, and they focused most especially on the lower classes, often going out, notebook in hand, to observe the urban poor in their "natural habitat." Brazilian author Aluísio Azevedo (1857–1913) created a national sensation with his 1890 Naturalist novel O Cortiço. Cortiços (literally "beehives") were compounds where hundreds of poor workers inhabited lines of contiguous small houses built around a courtyard. Often, laundresses did their washing and hung the clothes to dry in the courtyard, as in the case of Azevedo's fictional cortiço São Romão, located in Rio de Janeiro.

It was five o'clock in the morning, and the "beehive" called São Romão was waking up, opening not its eyes, but rather, its myriad doors and windows. The profusion of damp clothing, left hanging by the laundresses from the day before, lent its dampness to the air, and with it, the acrid odor of cheap laundry soap. Between the lines of dwellings stretched the stone pavement, generally cloudy and grey with its coating of dried soap suds, especially bleached and bluish around the washtubs.

Sleepy heads poked out of doorways. One heard enormous yawns, a clearing of throats, a clinking of coffee cups in saucers. The smell of hot coffee smothered all competing smells. "Good mornings" crossed between open windows, and conversations interrupted the night before took up where they had left off. Kids romped outside already, and from within the dwellings came the muffled cries of babes in arms. The rising hubbub contained laughter, the sound of crowing roosters, clucking hens, quacking ducks, and somewhere, angry voices arguing. A few women brought parrot cages out and hung them on the exterior wall. Like their owners, the parrots greeted each other raucously, shaking their feathers in the morning light.

Soon a buzzing agglomeration of men and women had gathered around the outside water faucets. One after another, they bent down and washed their faces in the threads of water that flowed from the low faucets. A puddle gradually formed under each faucet, so that the women had to tuck their skirts up between their thighs to keep them dry. They exposed their tanned upper arms and necks as they held their hair atop their heads so as not to wet it. The men did not worry about that. To the contrary, they stuck their heads right under the faucets, rubbing their faces and blowing their noses in their hands. The doors of the latrines opened and closed incessantly. No one stayed inside long, and people emerged still buttoning trousers and skirts. The children did not wait for the latrine and did their business in the high grass behind the houses.

SOURCE: adapted from Aluísio Azevedo, *O cortiço* (Rio de Janeiro: Livraria Garnier, 1925), pp. 49–54.

Gradually the buzz grew louder and thicker, individual voices could no longer be distinguished, and people conversed in shouts. The store had opened and women began to buy things there, coming and going like a line of ants. The bread seller arrived carrying a large basket on his head and a small folding table under his arm. He set up the table in the middle of the patio and awaited customers, who soon swarmed around him, children above all. The customers who had been served ran back to their houses clutching a warm loaf. A milk cow walked from door to door, her cowbell clinking sadly, followed by a muzzled calf and by the milkman carrying cans for the milk that she produced on the spot.

The buzz in São Romão was peaking as the pasta factory began to operate down the block, adding the monotonous puffing of its steam engine to the cacophony. Around the faucets, an enormous bunch of cans—especially large kerosene cans—had collected, and the splashing sound became a steady gurgle as people filled them with water. The laundresses were beginning their work, filling washtubs, hanging up clothes that had been left to soak overnight. Some began to sing. A garbageman entered the gate with his cart, furiously cursing the donkey that pulled it. Vendors of various sorts continued to come and go for a long time. Many sold meat, but none vegetables, because the "beehive" had many garden plots. Peddlers offered glassware and kitchenware and baubles of all descriptions, and each had his own distinctive way of announcing what he had for sale.

The first woman to start washing was Leandra, a Portuguese immigrant with a loud voice, powerful arms, and haunches like a draft animal. No one knew if Leandra was a widow or separated from her husband. Her entire family, including a twenty-five-year-old daughter with children of her own, lived in São Romão. Leandra's younger daughter, who was seventeen years old, was fiercely proud of her virginity and had so far managed to slip like an eel through the fingers of the men who pursued her with no intention of marrying. She was good at starching and ironing and especially skilled at fashioning men's undergarments.

The washtub next to Leandra's was used by Augusta, who was Brazilian, white, and married to Alexandre, a forty-year-old mulatto policeman with a big mustache, quite full of himself when he went to work in spotless white trousers and boots. They had several small children, one of whom lived with a godmother elsewhere in the city, a high-priced French prostitute who had her own house. Next came Leocadia, a short Portuguese woman, not so young, but in good shape, whom the other women scorned as promiscuous. Her husband was a blacksmith. After her, came Paula, an old woman partly of indigenous descent, whom her neighbors regarded as half-mad but whom they also respected for her power to cure a fever or a rash using spells and incantations. Otherwise, they found her ugly, melancholic, and ill-tempered, with pointed teeth like a dog's. Her long, straight hair remained jet-black despite her age. They called her "the Witch." Next on the line of washtubs were old Marciana and her daughter Florinda. Marciana, a mulatta, was a solemn woman of exaggerated cleanliness, who scrubbed her floors so often that they seemed perpetually wet. As soon as a bad mood struck her, she began to dust and sweep, and intense anger made her run for a bucket of water to dump furiously on the living-room floor. Her daughter was fifteen years old with a warm brown complexion, sensual lips, lovely teeth, and a monkey's lustful eyes. Florinda's body cried out for a man, but she had managed to maintain her virginity at all cost so far, despite the repeated efforts of the landlord to seduce her by adding a bit extra to her daily purchases at his store. Then there was old Isabel—or *dona* Isabel as the other women called her deferentially—a person of formerly more elevated social status, now as poor as the rest and eaten up with bitterness. She had been married to a store owner who had gone bankrupt and committed suicide, leaving her with a frail and sickly daughter whom Isabel had sacrificed everything to educate, even paying for French lessons. Old Isabel had the gaunt face of a devout old Portuguese, and her onceplump cheeks now hung limply from the corners of her mouth like empty sacks. Her eyes were always puffy as if she had been crying. When she dressed to go out, it was always in the same old black silk dress and red shawl, and all that remained of her former grandeur was a tiny gold snuff box, from which the old lady took an occasional pinch with an inconsolable sigh.

Pombinha, Isabel's daughter, was pretty, pale and blonde, but fragile and a bit high-strung, with the manners of a well-bred girl of good family. Her mother did not permit her to wash or iron, and indeed, the doctor had expressly prohibited it. She had a fiancé employed by a merchant house, well liked by his boss and by the other employees, a young man with a bright future who had adored Pombinha since she was little, but Isabel did not want them to marry yet, because, even though Pombinha was nearly eighteen, she had never menstruated. So everyone waited anxiously for the marriage, which promised to restore the family's lost social position. Meanwhile, Pombinha was the pride and joy of São Romão. When its inhabitants needed a letter written, it was she who wrote it. She was the one who normally made up the laundry lists and kept the accounts for the laundresses. It was she who read the newspaper aloud for the residents of the "beehive," who treated her with great respect and gave her presents, allowing her to live a little better than most. She always wore nice shoes, colored stockings, a well-ironed dress, and, when she went out of São Romão, a bit of jewelry. People who saw her at church on Sundays would never think that she lived in such a place.

The last washtub in the line was manned by Albino, a scrawny and effeminate fellow the color of cooked asparagus. He spent all his time among women, and they treated him more or less like one of them, saying things in his presence that they would never say in front of another man, even telling him about their love lives and infidelities. Albino was a peacemaker, arbitrating disputes among the laundresses and married couples. He even used to go collect payment for his colleagues, simply as a favor, until one day when a group of students for some reason paid him with a beating. After that, he hardly ever left São Romão, except during carnival, when he went out dressed as ballerina. He passionately loved to do that and saved money all year to buy a new costume. Other than at carnival, nobody ever saw Albino, whether on Sunday or during the week, whether working or resting, without an apron over his neatly pressed white trousers, a clean shirt, and a scarf around his neck. He did not smoke or drink, and his hands were always cool and moist.

One by one, all of the washtubs were occupied and all the men of São Romão went out to their daily labors. Among the last was a group of street peddlers, leaving to make their daily rounds, carrying boxes of cheap merchandise, and quarreling and cursing at one another in Italian.

Analyzing the Sources: What can be learned about Latin America's late-nineteenth-century immigrants from this carefully reconstructed slice of life? Matters of sexuality are frankly discussed. What does this add to the other selections in this chapter?

Chapter 6

REACTIONS AGAINST NEOCOLONIALISM

Even before Latin America's neocolonial order crumbled around 1930, the region's writers had begun to react against it. Their reaction took the form of new resentments against powerful outsiders and a new interest in what set Latin American countries apart culturally.

The War of 1898, fought by the United States against Spain, helped precipitate the reaction. The war began when the United States intervened in Cuba, still a Spanish colony at the time, to support Cuban insurgents in their war for independence. But the outcome—US occupation of Cuba, followed by continuing US intervention there and elsewhere in the Caribbean—led to anti-US feeling throughout the region. And, somewhat ironically, the trouncing that Spanish forces received in the war made many Latin Americans more sympathetic to Spain, as well. Therefore, the anti-US reaction often took on a Hispanist coloring that emphasized and positively valued the cultural legacy of Spain. In this mood, a number of influential Latin American writers contrasted "Latin civilization" and even the "Latin race" (associated with all countries that spoke languages descended from Latin) against an "Anglo-Saxon race" and civilization, embodied by England and the United States. Probably the most influential of these writers was José Enrique Rodó of Uruguay, for whom Latin culture represented spiritual values that should be cultivated while Anglo-Saxon culture represented an excessive materialism that should be resisted. Meanwhile, Colombian José María Vargas Vila denied that US expansionism represented "civilization" of any kind, but rather, arrogance and aggression. *Facing the Barbarians*, his 1902 warning to Latin America as a whole, was subtitled *The Yanqui—Behold the Enemy.*

A few Latin American authors began to reject the pessimism of "scientific racist" thinking that both devalued non-European blood-lines and also insisted that race mixture—long viewed as a basic element of Latin American demographic realities—led to biological instability and overall degeneration. While baseless in fact, scientific racism was the most up-to-date European thinking in the early 1900s, the prevailing conventional wisdom in the Western world, and rather than reject it wholesale (a tall order for people steeped and educated in European thought), Latin American thinkers reinterpreted it. Their reinterpretations insisted that people of African, indigenous American, and especially *mixed* descent (*mestizos* in Spanish, *mestiços* in Portuguese) constituted viable, valuable national populations. Euclides da Cunha's description of the *sertanejo* backlander of northeastern Brazil provides an excellent example. While still framing his argument in terms of scientific racism, da Cunha narrates the heroic resistance of the sertanejo religious community of Canudos, which defied the Brazilian army's repeated attempts to destroy it in 1897. The fourth expedition finally obliterated Canudos in a bloodbath that da Cunha witnessed personally. The sertanejos of Canudos might be backward religious fanatics, goes the powerful feeling that runs through da Cunha's prose, and they might not be white, but these are people one can be proud to call Brazilian.

Meanwhile, in Buenos Aires, another sign of national authenticity was coming to the fore—the tango. Tango music and dancing was urban popular culture, an Afro-Argentine music and dance genre of considerable funkiness around 1900. The black roots of the tango are hard to recognize in current styles of the dance, but they were no secret for Argentine readers in the early twentieth century, when Vicente Rossi wrote his study *Black Stuff*, excerpted for this chapter. Rossi obviously delights in the tango's sudden, powerful international fame, which was initiated by a tango vogue that took hold in Paris just before World War I. For the first time, or so it seemed to Rossi, a Latin American cultural product had attracted the admiration and imitation of Europe, reversing the general neocolonial orientation.

Other Latin American authors turned to "tradition" as an anti-dote to Progress based on European models. Like *costumbrista* writers of an earlier day, the traditionalists of around 1900 were in search of national authenticity. Folklorists were busy exploring villages and the countryside, and what they found and called "tradition" was basically the rural popular culture of the mid-1800s, before the onset of Progress. No more idyllic traditionalist description of life in a Mexican village could be found than the one that appears in Francisco Gamboa's Naturalist novel *Santa* of 1903. An idyllic description of anything at all was rare in Naturalist fiction, and rarer still, in that bleak literary school, was Gamboa's fervent religiosity. So, while writing in a novelistic style that had originated in France, Gamboa gave his version of Naturalism a traditionalist Mexican twist.

In the 1920s, a number of major Latin American "regionalist novels" depicted distinctive landscapes and lifeways. José Eustasio Rivera's *The Vortex* (1924) memorably evoked rubber tappers in the Amazonian rain forest and their foreign exploiters. *Don Segundo Sombra* (1926), by Ricardo Güiraldes, told of a wise old gaucho who taught the landowner's son how to be a man. And *Doña Bárbara* (1929), by Rómulo Gallegos, celebrated the culture and natural splendors of the Venezuelan llanos. Though little read today, these novels were enormously admired in the middle twentieth century. *Doña Bárbara*, particularly, became one of the best-known Latin American novels ever, even more through cinematic and television versions than in print.

ARIEL

José Enrique Rodó

Uruguay's José Enrique Rodó was born in 1872. His book-length essay Ariel *(1900), based on characters from Shakespeare, was read and respected throughout Spanish America. Rodó counterposed the spritely figure of Ariel, who personified the Latin American spirit, against the materialistic figure of Caliban, representing the United States. The elite young men of Latin America should resist imitation of the United States and cultivate*

*their own, more spiritually inclined culture, argued Rodó. The following
excerpts from* Ariel *introduce the wise Prospero, Rodó's imaginary spokesman and provide an example of the sort of parables Prospero uses to teach
his young elite disciples.*

The venerable old master whom they called Prospero, alluding to the
wise wizard in Shakespeare's *The Tempest*, was bidding farewell to
his young disciples at the end of a year of study, gathering them about
him for one last time.

He had taken them into his large library, decorated with an elegance that did honor to the noble presence of Prospero's most faithful companions, books. The most prominent object in Prospero's
library, its inspiration and guiding spirit, was an exquisite bronze
statue of the fantastical Ariel who appears in *The Tempest*. Prospero
normally sat beside the statue and for that reason the students called
him by the name of Ariel's master in the Shakespearean drama. But
there may have been more profound reasons, as well, for their choice
of names, something about the master's character and teachings.

Ariel, the winged spirit of the air, represents nobility and refinement in Shakespearean symbolism. Ariel signifies lofty and disin-
terested motivations, a graceful and vivacious intelligence, cultural
spirituality, and the dominion of reason and sensitivity over irra-
tionality and base impulse. Ariel represents all that human beings
should aspire to become, the aspirational endpoint of their evolution, in which the vestiges of brute, instinctual sensuality, symbol-
ized by Caliban, are purged, chiseled away by persistent effort.

The fine statue showed Ariel in the moment when, freed by Prospero's magic, the winged spirit is about to soar into the sky and disappear in a flash of light. Wings spread, his billowing bronze tunic
gilded by the caress of reflected light, his ample forehead upraised,
his lips slightly parted in a serene smile, everything about the figure of
Ariel indicated his graceful, impending leap into flight. And, although

---

SOURCE: José Enrique Rodó, *Ariel* (Madrid, n.p., 1919), pp. 19–21,
41–43.

conferring a sculptural firmness upon his winged subject, the inspiration of the artist had managed to retain Ariel's seraphic appearance, his idealism and loyalty.

Prospero gently caressed the forehead of the statue, meditating. Then he gestured for the group of young men to gather around and, with his firm voice—a magisterial voice, able to lay out ideas with great clarity, able to insinuate itself into the depths of the human spirit, penetrating like a ray of light, shaping all it touched like a chisel striking marble, a paint brush daubing canvas, or a wave rippling the sand—with his firm voice, he addressed his attentive and affectionate listeners as follows.

[*The ensuing parable taken from Prospero's final lesson illustrates Rodó's emphasis on the proper attitudes of social superiors toward the common people (summed up by the French phrase* noblesse oblige) *and on their need to hold spiritual values aloof from the hurly-burly of life. Here the master speaks.*]

I find an apt symbol of the human soul in this story retrieved from a dusty corner of my memory.

Once upon a time, in some vague and indeterminate part of the Orient where careless stories nest, there lived a kingly patriarch. The patriarch's kingdom dwelt in innocence and happiness, and he later came to be called, in the memory of men, the Hospitable King. The king's goodness and piety were antidotes to all sorts of unhappiness. Everyone sought his hospitality, which provided bread to feed the hungry and kind words to soothe the souls of the tormented. The king's kind heart was sensitive to every vibration in the hearts of others. His palace stood open to all his people. All was liberty and animation within its halls, and no guards ever barred the door. The open porticos of the palace sheltered groups of common shepherds who gathered there to listen to rustic music. Old men chatted there in the afternoons, and there, on mats of woven reeds, groups of fresh-faced women spread the boughs and flowers that constituted the only tithe ever required by the king. Merchants of Ophir and peddlers of Damascus could be seen coming and going through the wide doorways at all hours, and they vied to display their jewels, perfumes, and fabrics before the king's eyes. Those who had come on pilgrimages from afar rested their exhausted bodies beside his throne. At dawn, bands of cheerful children came to the king's bedside to see his silver beard and announce the arrival of the sun. After the midday meal, birds were invited to clear the king's table of crumbs.

His infinite generosity extended to humans and nonhumans alike. As in the myth of Orpheus or the legend of Saint Francis of Assisi, winds, plants, and birds seemed to respond to the call of human friendship in that oasis of hospitality. The tiny seeds that happened to lodge and germinate in cracks of the masonry or pavement were allowed to grow and blossom there. No cruel hand wrenched them out. No pitiless foot crushed them to a pulp. Curious vines of ivy grew into the open windows of the palace seeking the interior chambers of the king. Winds rested, when they entered the royal precinct, and lavished upon it their cargoes of sweet aromas and pleasant harmonies. Waves that crested on the nearby seashore lunged toward the palace longingly, as though trying to embrace it, if only to refresh it with a few drops of froth. The atmosphere of liberty, the enormous and reciprocal confidence that all felt toward one another, filled the palace with a pervasive and never-ceasing celebration. . . .

But very deep inside the palace of the Hospitable King, totally hidden from the view of the vulgar throng, accessible only by secret passageways, lay a mysterious room that no one except the king was permitted to enter. Not a single echo of the outside world penetrated the thick walls of this chamber, where a religious silence held sway. The tenuous, filtered light entered languidly through thick, colored glass, illuminating the room with a soft, even glow. A more profound peace never reigned in any woodland solitude or undersea grotto. . . .

There the legendary king could liberate himself from the bonds of reality. There he could dream. There he became introspective and his thoughts could be gently burnished like pebbles tumbling in the foam. There the white wings of Psiquis could be spread open on his noble forehead. And when Death finally came to remind the king that he was, in fact, only another temporary guest in the palace that he called his own, the secret room was closed and silent forever more. No one ever set foot there again, because none of the king's former subjects was so irreverent as to profane the king's space of private dreams, the inner redoubt of his soul.

I liken the king's palace in this story to the interior life of each of you. It should be open, with the healthiest sort of liberality, to the currents of the world. At the same time, however, it should possess an inner sanctum that the rowdy guests never see or even know about, an inner sanctum that belongs to serenity and reason alone.

Analyzing the Sources: Relate the author's style, of which you have a good sample here, to his overall argument described in the headnote. If Rodó meant to inspire the more spiritual "Latin race" to resist crass Anglo-Saxon materialism, who exactly was he addressing, and what was their relationship to the majority of indigenous peoples and to those of African descent?

FACING THE BARBARIANS

José María Vargas Vila

José María Vargas Vila, born in Colombia in 1860, was an iconoclast whose penchant for "speaking truth to power" often got him in trouble. His tract Facing the Barbarians: The Yanqui, Behold the Enemy *(1902) appeared in the wake of a string of US territorial acquisitions that began with the 1898 war against Spain, followed by further interventions in Central America. A sort of cross between prose and poetry, the book uses both "the Barbarians" and "the Eagle" as symbolic stand-ins for the United States. The elevated tone of the book is characteristic of the period, as is Vargas Vila's somewhat confusing application of the term* raza, *"race," to designate something more cultural than physical.*

Everything, it seems, bends down beneath the formidable wing. The cloudiness of the horizon augments the horror of this tragic hour.

Livid sky, bloody raptor.

The imperial Eagle reigns supreme, omnipotent amid the desolation. Its wings block out the sun of Justice. The World trembles in the talons of the butcher bird. History records nothing more dreadful than this moment.

Today, nothing stands up against the Anglo-Saxon in our América Latina.

The winged horses of conquest drag their fiery chariot unimpeded. Four monstrous archangels blow their trumpets toward the four points of the compass announcing the apocalypse of Right, the total devastation of the weak, the definitive triumph of raw might. Opportunistic hordes overrun everything, pillage everything, and the hounds that lapped the blood of Jezebel howl in the shadows beside the unburied, dismembered corpses of entire Peoples.

The ship of human Equality is sinking fast.

América Latina trembles at this bloody, brutal Victory. Vile plunder and barbarous Insolence parade proudly forth, and behind them, the people of the World follow, silent and astonished. Thus did Gaul follow behind victorious Caesar. Thus were the defeated Numidians shackled to the chariots of Rome. The World has been enslaved by Fear, stupefied by the audacity of the Eagle. As if sudden and rudely awakened, the World trembles with horror. It has been criminally subjugated by naked Force, and it bows to the Barbarians on bended knee.

Behold how the victorious conquerors frolic on the smoking battlefield. Contemplate this Odyssey of pillage:

To the cry of "Liberty," the Barbarians hurled themselves on Cuba, the Philippines, and Puerto Rico and made them captives. They announced honorable intentions, appropriate to the sons of George Washington, but they behaved instead like offspring of the

SOURCE: adapted from José María Vargas Vila, *Ante los bárbaros (los Estados Unidos y la guerra): El yanki, he ahí el enemigo* (Barcelona: Maucci, 1917), pp. 45, 48, 62–65, 90, 114–15.

filibuster William Walker. They descended on their small neighbors like the foot of an elephant, crushing the heart out of them.

The Cuban Republic, the Dominican Republic, the Nicaraguan Republic, the Panamanian Republic, and the Philippine Republic all died drowned in their own blood, suffocated by the helping hand of the friendly republicans of the North.

Cuba became a protectorate, conquest in disguise. The Philippine Islands succumbed in battle, outright conquest. Puerto Rico became a US possession, conquest by acquiescence. Santo Domingo and Panama suffered intervention, shameless conquest.

Conquest always and everywhere. And the name of this despicable crime has been changed to Victory.

And writers and thinkers and journalists of our América Latina go along. Fooled by wishful thinking, many accept the distant mirage of noble pretext and actually applaud the Eagle's perfidious sham idealism. Dazzled by Victory, they are converts to the cult of naked Force.

And so, incredibly, they try to persuade us of the Barbarians' generosity and hold up the *Great Republic* of the North as a model for our countries, as if she were our friend, our sister!

A fatal error! Fatal! This error will doom us and lead to further CONQUEST.

Why not tell the truth to the people of our América, show them the truth behind the Eagle, the truth about the barbarian race and people?

An arrogant and voracious race, hungry for our territory, fixed on conquest. A numerous people, cruel, insolent, and disdainful towards us, hatefully convinced of their own superiority.

Why not depict this country the way it really is, this overweening mongrel country that threatens us?

Bolívar, at death's door, already half enveloped in the mists of immortality, pronounced the word that offers the key to our salvation. UNION! UNION! UNION! Thus spoke the dying hero.

Let there be union embracing Mexico and Central America, a great confederation uniting these with Venezuela, Colombia, and Ecuador, bringing Peru together with Bolivia, and Chile with Argen-

tina, Uruguay, and Paraguay. Union for our entire continent, according to Bolívar's great and radiant vision!

A permanent Council should be established to unify all the countries populated by our race, a Council residing in Buenos Aires to
counteract the so-called Pan American Conferences organized periodically by the Invader Nation of the North.

Let us join together to defend ourselves against Invasion and
Extortion, against Europe and North America.

Let us admit the invasion of Progress, but stop the progress of
Invasion.

Let us constantly tighten our diplomatic and commercial relations with other countries of Latin race, including Spain and Italy.

Let us attract Spanish and Italian immigration by all possible
means. Such immigration to our countries will mix with and improve
the quality of our indigenous lower classes, rendering them more
conscientious, more laborious, better able to exercise the rights and
fulfill the duties of citizenship.

For almost thirty years I have been warning the people of our
América against THE YANKEE PERIL. And, amid the deafening
clamor, their ears have not heard me. Their eyes, clouded by the
fog of slavery, have not seen the danger.

In my ostracism and misfortune, stranded on foreign shores,
wherever the winds of exile blew me, I have carried my message of
warning. I have announced the peril and denounced the enemy and
have never fallen silent.

Wherever I have set foot, I have shouted my message from the
bow of my arriving vessel to the people of our América Hispana:

The Barbarians are coming!

And no one listened to me.

And now the Barbarians have arrived.

*Analyzing the Sources: How does Vargas Vila reverse the signs, positive
and negative, that were applied to same events by US leaders such as
Theodore Roosevelt?*

THE BACKLANDS

Euclides da Cunha

The Backlands (1902), by Euclides da Cunha (1866–1909) is one of the most influential books in Brazilian history. Along with most other educated men of his day, da Cunha believed that racial amalgamation led to biological instability and degeneration. And yet the Canudos community's incredible resistance against the Brazilian army, which he witnessed personally, convinced him of the inherent power of the particular race mixture characteristic of the backlands of northeastern Brazil. In the following selections, da Cunha first describes the sertanejo, or backlander, as a racial type, and then narrates the army's brutal final assault on Canudos, where tens of thousands lost their lives.

Indian blood naturally predominated in the backlands populations that formed along the middle reaches of the great São Francisco River. After their initial mixture, these populations then evolved in isolation from the rest of Brazil, conserving the traditions of the past during three centuries, right down to our own day. Whoever travels through those backlands today will observe a notable homogeneity among the people who populate them. The physical characteristics of sertanejo populations vary only slightly, displaying a stable racial type that contrasts at a glance from the highly variable racial mixtures of our Atlantic coastal region. On the coast there is no single, modal type, and one encounters all shades of skin color according to the particular ancestry of each individual, whereas the backland populations seem produced from a single mold, exhibiting an athletic build, straight or wavy hair, and a narrow range of complexions indicating a well-amalgamated combination of European, Indian, and African ancestry. The sertanejos likewise share the same mental and moral makeup, the same vices and the same virtues. This unifor-

---

SOURCE: adapted from Euclides da Cunha, *Os sertões* (Rio de Janeiro: Laemmert, 1903), pp. 588–91, 593–94, 615–16.

mity is truly impressive and indicates that the northern backlander has undeniably become a stable and fully formed ethnic and racial type.

Here some parenthetical considerations are in order. A mixture of highly divergent races is, in the majority of cases, prejudicial. Extreme miscegenation leads to developmental regression, and the *mestiço** lacks both the physical vitality of his non-European ancestors and the intellectual vigor of the European ones. Racially mixed populations may exhibit a certain brilliance of mind, but they are almost always erratic and unstable. We do not possess unity of race, and it is possible that we shall never possess it. The backlands population offers reason for optimism, however: more stable, more robust physically and therefore more capable of superior moral and mental development. Let us conclude this unappealing parenthetical digression, however, and proceed to a direct consideration of the unique figure presented by our backward fellow countryman, the sertanejo.

The sertanejo's gait is gangly, sinuous, swaying, and loose-jointed. His slouching posture aggravates the effect and gives him a beaten-down air of humility. When standing, he invariably slumps against a nearby wall or doorway. When on horseback, if he stops to exchange a couple of words with someone he knows, he slips his weight into the stirrup on a single side and reclines against the saddle. When walking, even when walking rapidly, he does not advance firmly in a straight line, but rather, meanders in a manner reminiscent of backland trails. And whenever he stops on foot for any reason, to roll and light a cigarette, for example, he immediately drops—and drops is precisely the word—into a squatting position and sits on his heels, where he can remain for long periods perfectly balanced on his two big toes, with a charming but also slightly ridiculous ease.

The sertanejo has a characteristic air of fatigue expressed in his invincible sluggishness, his perennial lack of muscular vitality, his lazy speech, his awkward gestures, his unsteady gait, his constant

---

*Portuguese *mestiço* is mostly equivalent to Spanish *mestizo*, although *mestiço* refers to any race mixture, whereas *mestizo* generally refers only to Spanish and indigenous mixtures. Da Cunha's discussion of degeneration in race mixture goes on for pages. Only the key points are represented here [translator's note].

tendency to immobility, even in the languid cadence of the songs he habitually sings.

But this air of fatigue is entirely misleading, and nothing is more surprising than seeing it suddenly vanish. The sertanejo's apparently rickety organism undergoes a complete transmutation in an instant whenever anything requires that he unleash his slumbering energies. The man is transfigured. Swiftly, he straightens up and his movements and profile take on entirely new contours. His head, now firmly erect atop his powerful shoulders, flashes with a fearless and piercing gaze. A charge of energy courses through his nervous system, galvanizing his formerly relaxed body, and from the awkward rustic figure of the backlands emerges a potent bronze titan endowed with extraordinary force and agility.

In his normally indolent posture on horseback, the sertanejo rides along behind his herd of cattle, swaying gently in the saddle almost as if he were lying in the hammock where he spends most of his time at home. But let some steer stray into the tangled scrub some distance up the trail, the horseman suddenly digs his spurs into the flanks of his mount, and off they go, like a shot. Nothing can stop the sertanejo in hot pursuit. Gullies, ravines, dry riverbeds lined by thick and thorny brush do not even slow him down. Anywhere a frightened steer can go, a mounted sertanejo can follow. Leaning forward, glued to his horse's back, his legs clamped to the animal's sides, rider and horse become one, a powerful centaur. Now they burst into a clearing, now they plunge once more into the undergrowth, galloping at full speed. Now the rider twists his body to dodge low boughs, now he leaps off his mount with acrobatic ease to avoid collision with a tree trunk that would otherwise send him sprawling, but, holding firmly to his horse's mane the whole time, he returns to the saddle with single bound, and all this at an undiminished gallop.

No sooner has the unruly steer been retrieved, however, than the sertanejo slouches once again in the saddle, and sways along with the inert appearance of a semi-invalid.

*   *   *

At dawn on the first of October 1897, the artillery began to prepare for the army's final assault on the rebellious settlement of

Canudos. The artillery barrage consisted of converging fire from a semicircle of cannon on the high ground surrounding the cluster of poor huts that remained. The barrage lasted merely forty-eight minutes, but the effect was annihilating. The aim of the guns had been carefully calibrated the night before and they simply could not miss the immobile target. The army was determined to teach the impenitent rebels a fulminating, implacable lesson with a final bayonet charge. So, to eliminate any obstacles to the advancing soldiers, the artillery pulverized and leveled everything on the ground over which the assault would pass.

The tortured stretch of territory was visibly transformed under the withering fire. Roofs caved in, crushing the people huddled in tiny rooms underneath them, walls of mud-daub construction exploded in a rain of splinters and clods, and here and there amid the cluster of crumbling dwellings, tongues of flame licked out, isolated at first, then quickly joining together in a major conflagration. Above the flames, explosive artillery shells arched across the overcast sky of that luminous morning, and not one failed to deliver its deadly payload. They exploded in the ruins of the church, in the town square, on the roofs of the houses, or sometimes passed through the roofs and exploded inside. They exploded in the twisting alleyways blowing rubbish everywhere. The guns ranged back and forth across what remained of Canudos, demolishing it house by house.

No screams were heard, meanwhile, no one was seen fleeing, nothing. And when the last shot was fired, when thunderous noise finally ceased altogether, the quiet of the stricken settlement gave the impression that the population had somehow inexplicably fled. There was a brief silence, then a bugle sounded atop Favela Hill, and the assault began.

By prior arrangement, the waiting troops sprang forward from three points to converge on the ruined church. Most were invisible as they advanced through the alleyways or along the bottom of the dry streambed. Only one battalion, the Fourth Infantry, was visible to the other combatants, who watched it march forward in quick step and close formation, bayonets at the ready, all the way to the entrance of the town square. It was the first time that an army unit had managed to get there intact.

The Fourth Infantry entered the square in heroic style. But within a few steps the formation started to break apart, instantly off balance. Some soldiers dropped to the ground, as if to take up sheltered firing positions behind the wreckage of the ruined church. Some could be seen scattering backwards, others, charging forward. Dispersed groups milled about in confusion. And then, in the air that still hung silent over Canudos, rose a dull rumble as if from an underground explosion.

The sertanejos were coming to life, suddenly and surprisingly, as always, barring the way to the aggressor with theatrical glory. The Fourth Infantry, which was now absorbing the full fire of the ambush, was brought to a halt, and so were the Twenty-Ninth and Thirty-Ninth Infantry, just arriving. All prearranged maneuvers were now abandoned. Rather than converging on the church, the various battalions fragmented as the troops sought shelter in narrow alleyways.

For almost an hour, the army units that watched from the hilltops around the settlement could detect nothing more happening in the square below, other than the mounting din of distant shouting and rifle fire, a muddled uproar punctuated only by constant, successive, muffled, and anguished bugle calls. The two attacking brigades simply vanished, completely swallowed up by the jumble of splintered houses around the square. Nor did the sertanejos appear, as one might have expected, running toward the square. Assaulted from three directions, the sertanejos were hypothetically to be driven together toward the massed formations of bayonets that were supposed to be waiting for them. But the army's plan had failed totally, and that failure spelled defeat. Encountering unexpected resistence, the troops had stopped and entrenched themselves defensively in a manner entirely contrary to their assigned mission. And now, spilling out of the maze of huts and smoking rubble around the square, the sertanejos descended invisibly on the soldiers who were pinned down there.

Shortly before nine o'clock, the beleaguered army units were encouraged by an illusion of victory. Several reserve battalions reached the square, and one of their members managed to unfurl a Brazilian flag and spread it out on a remaining wall of the ruined church by tucking its corners into the cracks. Dozens of bugles sounded a tribute, and thousands of throats joined them, shouting "Long Live the Republic!"

Surprised, the sertanejos ceased firing, and the square was filled for the first time with jubilant troops. Many spectators, including three generals who had been watching from a safe distance, poured down the slope to join them in square. Hats and swords waved in the air as the joyful soldiers abandoned their positions in a delirious tumult and ran to embrace one another in celebration.

The cruel struggle had finally ended, or so it seemed.

Then, just as the generals began to fight their way through the noisy throng, they were startled to hear bullets began to whine loudly just above their heads. The battle was on again, and the square was suddenly swept clean once more.

And, returning in disarray to their sheltered positions, slipping down along the high banks of the dry streambed, crouching and running for cover wherever they could find it in the grip of sudden terror, bitterly disappointed, feeling singularly cheated by the disappearance of the victory that had appeared so imminent, mocked again by the sertanejos in the very moment when they had thought them vanquished at last, the would-be victors began to understand that the final battle was not going to be over until it had devoured them all, one by one. Their six thousand modern rifles, their six thousand sabers would not be enough. The blows of twelve thousand arms, the stamp of twelve thousand boot heels, untold numbers of shrapnel-producing shells, all the executions, all the destruction by fire, thirst, and starvation, all the ten months of fighting with its pulverization of the settlement during a hundred days of continuous cannonading under the impassive, clear blue skies of Canudos, all the devastation of its churches, with their altars thrown down and their holy images reduced to ashes—all this had been to no avail. To no avail had they attempted to extinguish the ardent religious vision, consoling and powerful, that had called the settlement into existence.

Other measures would be required to deal with an enemy so impervious to the most violent and destructive forces of nature. Fortunately, the army had foreseen the need for such measures and provided itself with dozens of dynamite bombs. Dynamite filled the need precisely. Somehow, the sertanejos had inverted the usual psychology of warfare. Their reverses only stiffened their resolve. Hunger made them stronger. Defeat made them as hard as rocks.

It made perfect sense. The army's final assault had struck solid rock, the bedrock of our nationality and our race.** Dynamite, therefore, was precisely the thing. Its use was appropriate and necessary. It was a consecration.

The firing ceased, and an anguished silence descended on the firing line as the dynamite was deployed. Then, a convulsive earth tremor shook the settlement and radiated out toward the overlooking hills with their encampments and artillery batteries. Seismic shocks rippled across the ground as the last standing fragments of church walls, like rows of jagged teeth, finally tottered and fell, as roof after roof was blown into the air, creating a low-hanging cumulus cloud of dust. Terrified shrieks were heard in the brief intervals between the thunderous explosions that rocked the earth. Now, it seemed, the end had indeed come as the very last bit of Canudos was blasted apart.

Outside of the zone of destruction, the troops waited for the flaming thundercloud to subside in order to renew their definitive assault.

But they would have to wait still longer. Rather than advancing, they found themselves reeling back as, incredibly, incomprehensibly, the smoldering rubble began to spit bullets at them once more. The would-be attackers had to dive for shelter. Barely did they glimpse, amid the smoke and flames, the movement of a few figures, women carrying children or pulling them along by the hand deeper into the collapsed rubble, figures fleeing randomly or writhing on the ground, their clothes on fire. And other figures, coming at them through the

---

**Readers who have followed my logic and evidence concerning our national genesis, and thus recognize our unfortunate current lack of racial unity, will appreciate the significance of my having identified a remarkably stable ethnic subtype in the sertanejo population. It is only natural that, once I accepted the bold and inspiring conjecture that we in Brazil are destined to achieve racial unity eventually, I should have identified the sturdy backlander as the physical nucleus of our future development, the veritable bedrock of our race [author's note].

smoke, leaping over flames, making no attempt now to hide, standing up on the few remaining rooftops: the last defenders of Canudos.
Their faces and naked torsos singed and smudged, boldly, suicidally,
on they came . . .

*Analyzing the Sources: Da Cunha worked within the overall paradigm
of the racist thinking of his time, yet he tried to reinterpret the implica-
tions of scientific racism for the development of the Brazilian nation.
What was the gist of his reinterpretation?*

SANTA

Federico Gamboa

*Santa (1903), by Federico Gamboa (1864–1939), is yet another Naturalist
novel. Their interest in the urban underclass led many Naturalist authors
to write about prostitutes. In Latin America, the most important such
novel is Gamboa's Santa, which has been made into a movie four times in
Mexico. Gamboa was a Conservative traditionalist who ran for president,
at one point, for the Catholic Party. Gamboa's traditionalism can be gauged
in the following excerpt that describes Santa's idyllic life as a village girl
before she was seduced and fell into a life of prostitution in Mexico City.
This passage, with its rosy overtones of costumbrismo, contrasts with
Santa's later life of urban decadence.*

Santa tried to drive the memories away by waving her hands in
front of her, the way that back in her good times as a decent girl
she had occasionally waved away the bees upon approaching their
hive or fended off the most amorous doves when visiting the dovecote. But her memories did not go away. To the contrary, as if pro-
voked by the snores of the drunk beside her, they rioted all around

SOURCE: Federico Gamboa, *Santa: A Novel of Mexico City*, ed. and trans.
John Charles Chasteen (Chapel Hill: University of North Carolina Press,
2010), pp. 25–31.

her, flitting in and out like fairy workers busily trying to reconstruct the temple of her innocence and the stronghold of her ado-
lescence, both desolate and in ruins, but they only managed to
make a knot in her throat, fill her eyes with tears, and wound her
heart, a heart still much more virginal than her splendid young
prostitute's body.

And that is why the sad, dark room was suddenly inundated with
the light of her memories.

There it is . . . the little white house, hidden away on one of the
narrow, unpaved lanes of her village, lanes flanked on both sides by
thick foliage, flowers, and ivy that scales the high walls constructed
here of brick and mortar, there of gently crumbling adobes. One
enters—through a rustic wooden gate that presents no resistance
to the slightest push—into a yard adorned only by the overarching
sky and six orange trees, their boughs bending under their load
of golden fruit or covered with white flowers that swoon with the
power of their own fragrance. There is the well, deep, dark, echoing faintly with tiny mysterious sounds like a fairy cave, its water
crystalline to the eye and icy to the taste, the nooks and crannies of
its ancient stone rim colonized by daisies, its pulley whining terri-
bly whenever the bucket descends into the depths. On one side of
the smoky kitchen, with its wide-mouthed little chimney, is the bee
hive, and on the other, higher up, the dovecote, although the doves
prefer to spend their time in the branches of the nearby woods or
the ruined tower of the chapel of San Antonio, also nearby. In back,
a fat pig lies wallowing lazily in the mud, tethered by a leg; hens
and their chicks scratch the dirt, looking up at the sky with a single
eye, from time to time, by tilting their heads almost horizontally to
the ground; and a large yellow and black dog, Coyote by name,
dozes tranquilly in the thick shade of the orange trees. On the covered walkway that runs along the side of the house, to the left of the
entrance, are various rustic chairs and stools, and there, too, hang
the cages of various songbirds that fill the air with their harmonies
and arpeggios each day from the first glimmer of light. On the wall,
bull's horns serve as hooks from which to hang the bridle and other
riding tack of the family's only horse, taken out each day to pasture
along with cows and calves belonging to the owner of the local store.

Tied to the posts that support each extreme of the covered walkway are two fighting cocks, one of them jet-black and the other sporting yellow feathers on its wings and around its neck, both crowing and flapping their challenges to each other when not sharpening their beaks on the ground always wet, sooner or later, with drinking water from the rusty sardine can placed beside each bird, overturned in the course of some abortive practice attack.

Inside the house, only four rooms:

First, the living room, which is also the dining room, to judge by the square table in the center of it and the massive water jug along the wall under shelves crowded with plates and dishes, cups, and glasses of the most ordinary sort of materials. Along the other walls, wicker chairs. In a corner, a somewhat worm-eaten triangular piece of mahogany furniture that displays—along with a conch shell, a ceramic piggy bank (though shaped like an apple), and a pair of vases with silk flowers—the family's most treasured possession: a sculpture of middling quality representing the Santo Niño dressed in sequins and fringed silk, his right hand raised in blessing, seated on something one cannot quite see, and imprisoned in a large niche of leaded glass. On the floor, straw mats of various sizes; and hanging from a large nail beside the window, a guitar whose lack of dust and full set of strings testify to regular use.

Next, the bedroom of mother and daughter, who sleep in the same bed, a bed without springs or headboard, but spacious and spotless and defended by three things on the wall above it: a monochrome lithograph of the Virgin of Soledad fixed with four tacks; a colored one of the Virgin of Guadalupe in a frame that was once gilded; and a yellowed palm leaf that is replaced every Palm Sunday, whose Christian virtue protects the humble home from lightning strikes. During the day, the bed is the domain of a cat that passes the hours there, curled up in a ball.

Then, the bedroom of the two grown brothers—the breadwinners of the family, Esteban and Fabián—with two ordinary cots, a seed bin, two large trunks covered with half-cured cowhide, a piece of furniture always hung with recently and not-so-recently worn clothes, and on the walls, arranged with a certain care, an infinite number of small colored images, celebrity portraits including dancers, circus performers, and professional beauties, that come in packages of La Mascota Cigarettes. Leaning in a corner, the shotgun, with a powder horn and a bag of shot small enough to use for hunting in the woods and large enough to defend the house with, or to patrol the village with, on the nights when the brothers were assigned to do so with other young men of the village.

At the end of the house, the kitchen, with its interior cooking area and small brazier closer to the door, between two rough stone *metates*, on which mother and daughter grind corn to make tortillas.

Everywhere there is pure air, the perfume of the roses that peep over the walls, the sound of wind rustling the leaves in the trees and water spilling softly over the village's two mill dams. During the day, the hum of insects in the sun; during the night, fireflies lit up by love, pursuing each other until, meeting, they go dark. Behind the house, myriad maguey plants, with their unvarying shade of green; on both sides, gardens and orchards; across the way, the property of their parish priest, Padre Guerra; and a few paces away, the chapel, tiny and poor, but furnished with saints who comfort the farmers in their grief and, occasionally, grant their wishes. A bit further on, the cemetery, open and silent, without marble statuary or poetic inscriptions, but offering a comfortable, protected spot for eternal slumber with its carnations and heliotropes that greedily cover the gravestones, the names of the disappeared, and the dates of their disappearances. And there is the bank of the small river, flanking the village square, shaded by ancient ash trees, the bridge hewn from a single enormous trunk, the three wash stands of crude tile where village women do laundry, and starting at the edge of the two mill ponds and their big dam, the road paved with fat, deeply seated stones that leads to the lava flow called the Pedregal.

Here, Santa is a young girl, and later, a young beauty. The little house belongs to her, the pampered daughter of old Agustina, at whose warm side she sleeps night after night. She is the idol of her brothers Esteban and Fabián, who watch over and protect her, the pride of the village, the ambition of its young men, the envy of its young women, healthy, happy, and pure. What innocence in her spirit! What loveliness in her nubile body! But why have her hips grown broad and her flesh grown so silky soft? Why have her bosoms,

oh, so much more marked than they were—and not so long ago—
grown these rosebuds, and why do they tremble and ache with the
curious explorations of her own fingers? Why does Father Guerra
not allow her to describe these worries to him in the confessional,
but instead, counsel her only not to look at her own breasts?

"You don't worry like that about the flowers, do you? You don't
examine them every day to see how much they've grown, do you?
Well, be like them, grow and become more beautiful without even
realizing it. Be fragrant without knowing it. And so that you won't
lose your virginal beauty and purity, pray, confide in me, adore your
mother, take care of your brothers . . . and *live*, breathe deeply, laugh
by yourself, and above all, love your guardian angel, the only male
who will never deceive you."

The dawn of Santa's young adulthood simply prolonged her
childhood, without troubles graver than the death of a favorite hen
or a plant that she tended and watered, such as the carnation that
she found withered one morning after a hard frost, its stem broken
and its petals strewn—hemorrhaged like strange drops of blood—on
the ground. Aside from these small sorrows and others like them,
hers was an existence without dark clouds, as she grew and developed, becoming more beautiful, adoring her mother, taking care of
her brothers, and breathing deeply, but not laughing by herself,
because the birds, envious no doubt, laughed with her, as did the
orange trees and the river and—why not admit it?—even the bell in
the little chapel, that laughed with her when announcing mass at
6:30 on Sunday mornings, the mass attended with equal devotion
by the villagers and by the rich families from the capital who came
to summer at San Angel, and attended, too, by various officials and
personages of local importance such as the pharmacist, who sometimes entertained the villagers in the evenings by employing who-
knows-what mysterious arts to set several large bottles aglow with
purple, red, and yellow lights. . . .

How lovely to awaken on workdays before the early rising sun! In
a moment, the impotent silence of night, which is soothing in its
way, would be interrupted by the crow of a rooster to which other
roosters would respond, and then others and still others, ever farther
away, in locations impossible to know exactly, and Santa would half

open her eyes but see only her mother, toward whom she had moved, timidly, ever closer in the darkness. Half asleep, she felt herself caressed and sensed her mother's warm breath under the sheets:

"Go back to sleep, *hija*," the soft voice says. "Go to sleep. It's still dark!" It takes a while for sleep to return, and in the meantime she cannot really hear or see straight, and everything is confused, impalpable, except for a physical well-being so intense that it totally immobilizes her. She perceives that above, on the roof, the doves are fanning their tails and cooing, that the pig is grunting outside, and that in the next room Esteban and Fabián are out of bed, pouring water in the washbasin. They cough and strike matches to light a cigarette or the stove for breakfast. Santa is going back to sleep now, losing a sense of the passage of time between noises that she hears, and she barely registers the entrance of her brothers into the bedroom, on tiptoes so as not awaken her, for which she smiles in somnolent gratitude. They have come to say goodbye, to receive the daily blessing that will protect them and give them, the family breadwinners, strength to continue as workers at the Contreras textile mill miles away from their house. The brothers remove their hats, kneel, and bow their heads very low so that their mother will not need to sit up and can stay under the blanket, and, following the ancient custom, they reverently implore:

"Your hand, mother . . ."

Agustina's outstretched hand blesses each of them, and feeling blindly, she pulls them to her together and embraces them together, confusing the two heads that she loves equally, and the two big men softly kiss the old hand that makes the sign of the cross in the air. They leave, on tiptoe again, and in the yard Coyote barks at them jubilantly. They close the front gate, and in the silence that covers the sleeping village, the sound of their footsteps, loud at first, disappears little by little, like the rhythm of a distant pendulum. Santa's mother sighs and raises her voice as though to be better heard by the Almighty:

"Lord, take care of my sons!"

Rays of pallid light begin to poke their way in the cracks around doors and windows, the noises get louder, and the bells of dawn begin to ring at the old Carmelite convent, and ding dong, ding dong, their music flies down the roads, by houses, orchards, and newly sown fields. Agustina rises and tucks the blanket carefully around Santa, who, reconquered by slumber, sleeps for another hour and dreams that life is good and that happiness exists.

Overflowing with health and tranquility, Santa rises and sings in the early morning as she cleans the cages of her birds, draws chilly water from the well, and washes her face, neck, arms, and hands with soapsuds that caress her skin as they slowly slide off it, making her smile with contentment. Her young blood races through her veins, colors her cheeks, and fills her red lips, as if kissing them gluttonously. Soon she is dressed for the day and has fed the chickens and doves, who crowd around her and follow her gently like devoted subjects. The pig, grunting with satisfaction, has buried his snout in the little pile of corn that she carried to him in her apron, and Coyote has greeted her, bounding and barking. The store owner's young helper has come to take their old horse out to pasture with the animals belonging to his master, don Samuel: melancholic cows, recently milked, their calves ravenous, turbulent, and protesting. Cows and calves depart down the lane in a slow procession, sticking their faces into the leaves and flowers on the walls, examining the maguey plants, even swirling into the always-open cemetery, where graves thick with green offer them a delicious breakfast.

"Santa! I'm leaving, get the chestnut horse out here!" shouts the boy from the lane, without looking at her or at the cattle, who continue their lazy march, because he is so intensely occupied untangling his sling with teeth and fingernails. Santa shoos the chestnut through the gate, unencumbered by saddle or bridal, and says to the boy:

"Careful, Cosme! Don't gallop him or get him too hot. . . . Want some milk?"

"Just give me some and you'll see! Don't you have any honey from your bees? It makes stale bread taste wonderful," says Cosme, as he takes a length of cord from around his waist to improvise a lead for the horse.

Santa goes to the house and returns with a glass of frothy milk in one hand and, in the other, a slice of bread spread with honey that hangs off its edges in transparent threads that never reach the ground. Cosme drains the glass of milk, runs his tongue around his lips, seizes the honeyed crust of bread, and throws himself on to the chestnut, squeezing its flanks with his bare heels. The old horse responds with a canter despite its years, and the boy, prodigiously balanced atop the bounding animal, twists his upper body back toward Santa as he takes a bite of the bread.

"Don't get mad, Santa. I'm only going fast now because the cows are getting away from me. As soon as I catch up . . ."

The rest of his sentence is inaudible as he disappears around a bend in the lane, the horse now at a full gallop, Cosme leaning far forward the way circus riders do in the ring.

It is not yet seven o'clock, and yet the sun leaning over the mountain ridge turns the treetops golden, peers here and there into the houses, and casts absurdly long shadows of everything that it finds, making a rose bush seem antediluvian, an ordinary dog appear a hulking dinosaur, and a tree trunk, many leagues in length. With the glinted reflections of the river and the floral aroma exuded by all nature—even leaving aside the ripple of water, the singing of birds, and the rustle of the wind in the trees—there is something impalpable that floats on the air and rises like a wordless prayer that the earth, eternally wounded, thinks and utters upon awaking each morning, a profound prayer of thanksgiving for having escaped, for one more night, the cataclysm that hangs over it and that will finally, treacherously come to mutilate it and annihilate its sacred, infinite, maternal fecundity. . . . Full of these impressions, Santa lifts her eyes to the heavens, her nostrils flaring, and stands motionless, almost ecstatic, herself an unconscious part of the earth's wordless prayer of thanksgiving.

Analyzing the Sources: How does this selection relate to the idea of Progress? Remember that Santa's eventual life as a high-society prostitute is characterized by the latest in European fashion and urban luxury (along the lines of Doctor Glow's life in The Stock Market*).*

BLACK STUFF

Vicente Rossi

*Black Stuff (1926) by Vicente Rossi (born in Uruguay, 1871) demon-
strated that the tango has roots in the dancing of nineteenth-century
social organizations formed by slaves and free blacks. The book was an
iconoclastic slap at prevailing Eurocentrism, and its argument has never
been popular in Argentina or Uruguay. In the following excerpt, Rossi
recounts the tango's famous diffusion to Paris, the launching pad for its
international dissemination and rise to global celebrity on the eve of World
War I. This is a famous example of a general pattern whereby elements of
Latin American popular culture receive acceptance among the middle
class of their home countries only after gaining recognition abroad.*

The tango finally showed up in Paris, the great marketplace of dances
from all over, the place from which dance fashions are exported
around the world.

And if Paris expected to laugh at our "black stuff," it was terri-
bly mistaken, because, as things turned out, our blacks got the last
laugh. The tango, good Río de la Plata *criollo* that it is, shrewd and
resourceful from its long experience on the streets of Buenos Aires,
took the measure of the situation and immediately applied the limitless animal energy of its warm, silky, redolent flesh. It made the
Parisians dizzy with its languid sensuality of a pampered woman
gently stretching her limbs. The tango's suggestiveness reenergized
the hearts and minds and feelings of people who believed that they
had already exhausted all the strong sensations capable of enliven-
ing human existence without endangering it.

Parisian annals record no greater choreographical triumph than
the advent of the tango in the City of Light, and the same can be said
about all the other European cities that, observing the excitement of

---

SOURCE: adapted from Vicente Rossi, *Cosa de negros: Los orígenes del
tango y otros aportes al folklore rioplatense, rectificaciones históricas*
(Buenos Aires: Imprenta Argentina, 1926), pp. 181, 190–94.

Paris, hastened to extend their own invitations for a visit from the provocative Argentine traveler.

According to an Argentine chronicler, the tango arrived in Paris initially "carried there by lily-white hands," meaning that the first to introduce it were female members of Buenos Aires high society. They kept it hidden away in luxurious surroundings, and the street-wise tango felt ill at ease amid their tapestries and fancy furnishings. It was incapable of really showing its stuff until much later, when true tango-dancing Argentines, delegates of the common people, travelled to Paris and offered more authentic demonstrations.

These more authentic demonstrations occurred in unpretentious settings like popular taverns where the dance felt much more at home and which, quickly infatuated by the newcomer, invited it back night after night. Glad tidings flashed through the city, and other, more prestigious venues made attractive offers to the jaunty newcomer, adding the tango to the programs of music halls, cabarets, and places of diversion frequented by the pleasure-seeking upper class.

By 1912, our humble black stuff was rising to fame, not only in Paris, but also in the other cities of France and neighboring countries. By 1913, all Europe had become intensely preoccupied with the tango. It occasioned a general commotion, a scandal, a public issue that, for a time, absorbed the social and intellectual energies of the Old World, occasioning opinion surveys, journalistic discussions, and the creation of new Europeanized versions of the dance. Aristocrats, princes, and emperors, the entire hereditary ruling caste of the decrepit Old World weighed in.

By 1914, the popular triumph of our inimitable black stuff had reached delirious heights in societies that had once, in a now-forgotten past, burdened the ancestors of the black creators of the tango with the heavy chains of slavery. One could hardly imagine a more refined and amusing form of vengeance. In Europe, everyone could intuit the black stuff hidden in the irresistible twists and turns of the suggestive dance. But European intellectuals insisted on proposing the most farfetched sorts of tango origins, firmly discarding the memory of black people, as always, after having thoroughly exploited them. The intellectuals discussed the influence of Thebans, Assyrians, Chaldeans, Babylonians, and Lacedemonians. They noted remarkable similarities with dances of the much-cited Egyptians, Greeks, and Romans. They offered tribute to their own ancestors, the barbarians of northern Europe, and evoked the mysteries of Asia. Finally, they waxed metaphysical, the last resort of an intellectual who cannot identify the truth or simply wishes to avoid it.

This European consternation echoed across the Atlantic to the surprise of the Río de la Plata press, which ignored the tango's merits, and, if it paid the dance any attention at all, did so unfavorably. Our journalists could never understand how the five letters of the African word *tango* had achieved such prominence in a region of the world usually reserved, in our newspapers, for editorials and in-depth reportage on momentous matters.

No one, absolutely no one in Europe knew the geographic location of Argentina until only a few years ago. The European press never published a single thing about us, as if we did not even exist. The telegraph only transmits news in one direction, after all: from there to here. No European intellectual ever registers anything positive about us. Our América figures not at all in the curriculum of European schools. All anyone in Europe knew or cared about us is that we pay well and in hard currency and offer a lucrative market.

And now our black stuff has promoted international fraternization and cultural exchange between Argentina and Europe more efficaciously than the labors of white diplomats ever did. Here's what an English correspondent wrote to me from London in 1914:

> It would be an injustice to deny that the tango, the craze that has currently seized all Europe, has had a markedly educational influence. Because of it, the great mass of the public has learned the name and whereabouts of the Argentine Republic during the last six months. We now know more about Argentina than we cared to learn from many years of reports on crops and railroad construction. The tango, then, must be accounted Argentina's peaceful weapon of Old World conquest.

And ten years after that, we sent them boxers and soccer players who expanded European awareness of us further. In other words, we are educating Europe by means similar to those that Europe applied when supposedly *civilizing* us centuries ago, with punches, kicks, and black stuff.

> *Analyzing the Sources: Despite Rossi's precocious embrace of black cultural influences as a sign of Argentine identity, Europe retains an important role in this thinking. What is that role?*

DOÑA BÁRBARA

Rómulo Gallegos

Doña Bárbara (1929) by the Venezuelan Rómulo Gallegos (1884–1969) is one of the most famous twentieth-century novels of Latin America. Gallegos, who became president of Venezuela, was frequently used as an example of the great public respect accorded to men of letters. In regionalist fiction like Doña Bárbara, *Europeans or North Americans usually symbolize exploitation. That is certainly true of a man called Danger, who appears in the following passage from the novel. The man called Danger is, like doña Bárbara herself, a caricature: the efficacious and in some way impressive, but ultimately repulsive and untrustworthy "gringo," whose belief in his own superiority is among his most notable traits. Movies and telenovelas kept the character of Mr. Danger familiar enough to Venezuelans that the populist president Hugo Chávez could use the name at century's end to make fun of his favorite rhetorical target: US president George W. Bush.*

He was a great mass of muscles under sunburned skin, with a pair of very blue eyes and flaxen hair. He had arrived a few years earlier, with a rifle on his shoulder, hunting jaguars and alligators. He liked the region, as barbarous as his own soul, ready for the taking, because inhabited by people whom he considered inferior, lacking

---

SOURCE: Rómulo Gallegos, *Doña Bárbara* (Caracas: Biblioteca Ayacucho, 1929), 84–90.

his blond hair and blue eyes. The local people expected him to buy a ranch and implement new techniques of livestock management. They had high hopes and offered him a warm welcome, but the imagined new techniques never materialized. Instead, the new-comer built the simplest of huts on someone else's property, without asking the landowner's permission, slung his rifle and his hammock in the hut, climbed into the hammock, lit his pipe, and relaxed with his hands behind his head.

"*All right*," he said in English, adding in fractured Spanish, "I'm in home!"

He said his name was William Danger, an American from the north, a native of Alaska, in fact, son of an Irishman and a Danish woman who had gone to Alaska looking for gold during the Klon-dike gold rush. Whenever Danger said his name, he added the translation "Míster Peligro," and then laughed so much at his own joke that some doubted Danger was his real name. Perhaps he chose it only because of its unsettling translation.

There was also a mystery of some kind surrounding him. Sev-eral times in the early days he had shown people copies of New York newspapers with articles that protested injustices done to a certain unnamed "Man without a Country." Danger claimed to be that man, and although he never really explained the injustice, nor why the article called him "Man without a Country," everyone opened their doors to him expecting rivers of dollars.

In the meantime, Mr. Danger did nothing but shoot alligators (to export enormous quantities of their hides in annual shipments) and jaguars and any other sort of wild animal that came within range of his rifle, which he did just for fun. Once, when he hap-pened to kill a cunaguara that had just had cubs, he managed to raise one of them to full size. He used to tussle with it, displaying the perennial good humor of a rough, oversized boy. The cuna-guara's claws left scars that he loved to show, all over his forearms, scars that leant him almost as much prestige as the mysterious articles about him in New York newspapers. The hunter's hut soon turned into a comfortable ranch house surrounded by extensive corrals full of cattle. This reason for the transformation connects Danger's story to that of doña Bárbara.

Danger had gone to see doña Bárbara because he had heard she was a practitioner of all the famous superstitions of the llanos region, such as burying a horse alive to strengthen a newly built corral, which he wanted to witness personally. Besides, he needed to talk to her about the hut that he had already built on her property, for she (or more precisely, her ancient husband, Colonel Apolinar) was the landowner whose permission he had failed to get beforehand.

Within a few seconds of laying eyes on the foreigner and hearing the reason for his visit, doña Bárbara had fallen in love with him and made a plan to get him. She had Colonel Apolinar invite him for dinner, and that night she poured both men drinks with calculated generosity. Both had a fondness for drink, and the older man, weak and dissipated, soon became idiotically oblivious to the winks and nods exchanged at dinner between his wife and his guest as the two discovered their mutual inclinations across the table. In the meantime, at a different location, several ranch hands were digging a large pit for the horse that was to be sacrificed.

"We'll bury it at the stroke of midnight," doña Bárbara had said, "just the three of us. This sort of thing is not for the hired help.

"Bonito," exclaimed the foreigner. "There we'll be, under a starry sky, shoveling dirt onto a horse! Picturesque, to say the least."

As for the old colonel, he was in no condition to save himself even had he suspected anything, which he did not. Mr. Danger had to help him climb on his horse, as midnight approached, for the short ride to the place of sacrifice.

There, the pit stood open when they arrived, with an old nag, the proposed victim of the barbarous rite, tied to a post of the corrals under construction nearby. By the pit were three shovels, and overhead, stars that failed to dissipate the darkness of the deserted place.

Mr. Danger untied the horse and led it to the edge of the pit, alternating comforting words to the animal with loud bursts of laughter that the drunk husband celebrated idiotically. With a formidable shove, Danger tumbled the old nag into the pit.

"Now then, doña Bárbara, cast your spells to keep the spirit of the horse in this place. And you and I, colonel, can get to work keeping its body here."

Apolinar picked up a shovel but could not maintain his balance if he leaned over to fill it with the earth that had been left piled at the edge of the pit. So he staggered, muttered obscenities, and chuckled until he finally managed to fill his shovel and stood proudly, swaying slowly from side to side. Danger, meanwhile, had seized another shovel and set to work with great rapidity.

"You're a little drunk, colonel," he had just observed when the Apolinar dropped his shovel, trembled, raised his hands to his kidneys, exhaled a mortal groan, and plummeted into the pit face down with his own lance protruding from his back.

"Oh, poor colonel," exclaimed Mr. Danger, pausing in his task. "A slight change of plans."

"Don't feel sorry for him, William. He had it out for me, too. I beat him to it, is all. Now, give me a hand," said the new widow, taking up the fallen shovel. "You're not the sort to get all weepy over something like this. You've done worse, I reckon."

"I came for the ceremony, not for this. Don't change plans on Mr. Danger."

That said, he let go of the shovel, mounted his horse, and rode home to play with his pet cunaguara.

But he kept the secret, first, because the "man without a country" wanted to avoid drawing the attention of the authorities, and second, because in the eyes of this scornful foreigner, old Colonel Apolinar did not merit much more concern than the horse whose grave he shared. Consequently, Mr. Danger did not dispute the story that Apolinar had drowned and been swept away while trying to cross a swollen stream. When some ranch hands killed an alligator and cut it open to find a wedding ring in its stomach, doña Bárbara identified it as her husband's, and Mr. Danger smiled and said nothing.

In payment for his silence, doña Bárbara allowed him to transform his hut on her property into the ranch house with corrals that he soon began to fill with livestock branded as his own, every bit of it stolen.

Analyzing the Sources: What makes this strong, capable character negative?

Chapter 7

CULTIVATING
NON-EUROPEAN ROOTS

Latin America's cultural turn away from Europe intensified in the middle years of the twentieth century. First, the awesome destruction of World War I had called the long-assumed superiority of European civilization into question. Then came the world economic crisis that began with the crash of the New York stock market in 1929. The capitalist order instituted globally by European colonialism seemed to be unraveling along with colonialism itself. Nationalist self-awareness was the order of the day, and writers around the world sought inspiration in what was local and native. In Latin America, non-European roots provided the cultural touchstone.

One strong current of this intensified search for national identity was *indigenismo*. The word (from *indígena*, a common Spanish synonym for Indian) referred simultaneously to political attitudes, anthropological interests, and (our major focus here) literary developments. The unifying theme in all this was the idea that the indigenous people of Latin America, rather than being *defined out* of emerging national identities, as had been common in the 1800s, were now regarded as the *chief defining element* of national identity in many countries, particularly in Mexico and the Andes. In the 1800s, there had been an artistic motif—sometimes called "Indianism"—in which Latin American writers and painters portrayed Indian princes and princesses of centuries past, something safely remote, Romantic, idealized, and long-disappeared. Indigenista writers of the 1930s, on the other hand, focused instead on living indigenous villagers, and they did so in ways that were anything but idealized and tended, instead, to linger on the villagers' poverty and misery, denouncing their marginalization and advocating their assimilation into the modern life of the nation.

In retrospect, the indigenista emphasis on "modernizing" and assimilating indigenous people amounted to an assault on their culture. Indigensimo involved a large dose of paternalism, and indigenista writers were not free of stereotypes or airs of superiority. Yet, by their own lights, they meant to serve the interests of indigenous people, and many had a truly radical Marxist vision of revolutionary social transformation. In addition, indigenistas typically learned indigenous languages and had considerable experience with the people whom they portrayed in their fiction. Many had anthropological training. As a literary school, indigenismo was especially Andean. The two indigenista stories included in this chapter, "Runa Yupay" and "Three Silver Sucres," from Ecuador and Peru, respectively, illustrate both the penchant to denounce the exploitation of indigenous people and the tendency to espouse a vision of social amelioration based not on the indigenous people's own direction and agency but on the wisdom and leadership of paternalistic whites and mestizos. There is also an excerpt from the greatest indigenista novel of them all, *Wide and Alien Is the World,* which exemplifies the left-wing indigenista interest in the communal traditions of indigenous villages. The Peruvian political theorist José Carlos Mariátegui imagined the Inca Empire as the socialist forerunner of a modern revolutionary Peru.

In countries without large populations of indigenous peasants, writers located non-European roots in populations of African or mixed descent. In many parts of Latin America, African descent was defined as characteristic of particular regions within each country, most often coastal regions—the pattern in Venezuela, Colombia, Ecuador, and Peru, also in Central America and, to a lesser degree, in Mexico. There, non-European roots became a focus of literary regionalism that explored the traditional life ways of particular areas of the Latin American countryside. The protagonists of "The New Saint," a regionalist example included in this chapter, are people of African descent whose racial identity is never mentioned except to specify that they are people of the Ecuadorian coast. In this common pattern, African descent was subsumed into regional identities, building blocks of larger national identities because diverse regions add up to the nation. Brazilian literary regionalism, which flourished in the 1930s and 1940s, found its most vigorous expression among writers of the northeast, some focusing on coastal areas characterized by populations of African descent and some (as in the novel *Arid Lives*, excerpted here) on the mixed-race populations of the arid backlands, the same sertanejos whom the reader will recall from the da Cunha selection in the last chapter.

In sum, both indigenista and regionalist writers tended to present the non-European roots of the nation as distinctive marks of authenticity, providing Latin American countries with unique identities. Their point was parallel to what Gilberto Freryre and Fernando Ortiz, anthropologists both, were saying in these same years about Brazil and Cuba, respectively. Yet indigenistas and regionalists assumed that the protagonists of their stories would need to be modernized and assimilated into the national mainstream. Non-European roots, in other words, constituted defining ingredients which, when combined with other ingredients and properly cooked, added a signature element to national cuisines. But they were not to be served raw or by themselves.

TWO SHORT STORIES

José de la Cuadra

José de la Cuadra was born in 1903 in Guayaquil, Ecuador's chief port city. The coastal region of Ecuador was the focus of his fiction, and he figured importantly in the "Guayaquil Group" of writers who turned their attention to social issues in the 1930s. De la Cuadra wrote especially about Ecuador's coastal people of African descent. In addition, he wrote about the indigenous people of the Ecuadorian Andes, as in the first story that follows. Note the powerful compression of de la Cuadra's writing, which makes a few words go a long way. Also of interest is a clear contrast in his attitudes toward the indigenous people of highland Ecuador, on the one hand, and the people of the coast, on the other.

THREE SILVER SUCRES (1932)

Presentación Balbuca adjusted the drawstring at the waist of his white, pajama-like Indian's trousers. He threw his red poncho with its broad lead-colored stripes over one shoulder and remained standing, motionless, in the door of the small-town lawyer's shabby little office.

"You'll see, you'll see, Balbuca," the lawyer was saying. "The judge has ruled against us so far, but it doesn't matter. We'll appeal."

He added:

"Don't forget the three *sucres*."*

But the Indian was no longer listening.

He spat on the ground in front of him, the way llamas do, and trotted up the steep, narrow street to the town square. He seemed oblivious to his surroundings, and his face wore a dark frown. But the expression was merely external. In reality, he thought about nothing, nothing at all.

Every now and then, he stopped to rest for a moment.

He scratched the ground with his stubby toes, drew the air thickly into his lungs, and expelled it with a hoarse whistle, a sort of prolonged "hunhhh . . ." of exhaustion. Then he resumed his rhythmic trot up the hill.

When he reached the square, he sat on a stone bench attached to the wall of one of the buildings that faced it. He took a handful of toasted barley from a small cloth bag that hung around his neck under his poncho and tossed it into his mouth.

The starchy sweetness of the barley made him thirsty. He went to the fountain that enlivened the middle of the square with its cheerful sound and shooed away the mules that were drinking there.

"Away! Away," he cried, with a mule-driver's voice. "Away!"

SOURCE: José de la Cuadra, "Ayoras falsos" and "El santo nuevo," in *Obras completas* (Quito: Editorial Casa de la Cultura Ecuatoriana, 1958), pp. 410–14, 592–99.

*Ecuador (along with Panama and El Salvador) has now adopted the US dollar as its official currency, but formerly it used *sucres*, named after the patriot general who defeated Spanish forces near Quito in 1822.

The animals moved away, and Balbuca dipped his cupped hand into the dark, murky water and slurped. His thirst slaked, he returned to the stone bench.

There he sat for over three hours without the slightest movement indicative of boredom, his eyes fixed on his bare feet, over which green-and-black, shiny-winged flies buzzed and occasionally alighted.

Finally, the man for whom he was waiting passed by: master Orejuela.

"Master Orejuela, can you give me three sucres? My boy Pachito will work for you. Can you?"

Orejuela, who was the administrator of a nearby hacienda, prided himself on knowing how to deal with Indians.

He discussed the matter at length with Balbuca and finally agreed to advance him three sucres in return for three week's work on the part of Pachito.

"I know your son Pachito. He is still a little boy, eight years old, nine at most. What can he do all by himself? The sheep would get away from him! He can only be a helper."

Finally it was settled. Pachito would start early in the morning on the following day. But there was still a final difficulty to be resolved.

"Will you give him food to eat, master?"

Orejuela did not like that a bit. Food? Was he going to have to feed the child, too? That was too much! That would just be too expensive! The child would have to bring his own toasted corn and barley rations. The hacienda would provide water. . . .

Balbuca implored him. His hut was very far from the hacienda. If Pachito had to bring his own food he would eat so much on the way that it would last only two days.

Orejuela finally consented to give the boy food every day . . . except for Sundays.

He shouted with laughter.

"Sunday is a day of rest. That's a holy obligation, right? The owner of the hacienda is a big Conservative, you know, very Catholic. So let the boy fast on Sunday. The hacienda only feeds workers. If you don't work, you don't eat—just the way they say it is under Communism.

Balbuca accepted, and they closed the deal.

"Bring the sucres, then."

Orejuela indicated that they would have to draw up a contract first.

"The hacienda has to protect itself. The kid is a minor and you'll have to give your permission in writing as his father. The laws are very strict."

So they went to look for a government official, whose office was in the dim and foul-smelling little back room of an old house, to formalize the contract.

Presentación Balbuca did not know how to read or write, so he signed the document with a shaky, crooked X.

The document incorporated a number of innovations that the official implemented in response to certain silent signals given him by Orejuela. According to what was written and signed, Balbuca declared that he had received not three, but ten sucres, and that he committed his son to provide two full months of personal service.

Orejuela then paid the Indian with three coins that he carefully put into the cloth bag that hung around his neck.

"Don't forget to send the kid tomorrow bright and early."

Presentación promised to do so and went out the door. In the street, he hurried down the hill.

When he got to the lawyer's shabby little office, he stopped.

"Doctor," he called from outside, "I have brought the three sucres that you said."

The lawyer appeared at the door and extended his trembling hand, as avid as a beggar's.

He explained:

"These three sucres are the rest of the five that I needed to buy the stamps that have to go on your petition to appeal the judgment against you."

The lawyer squeezed the three coins between thumb and forefinger, and found that he could bend them.

He shook with fury:

"These are made of lead, not silver! They are as false as your mother!"

Indignant, he threw the worthless slugs of metal in the Indian's face.

"You wanted to fool me, Indian son of mule! *Me* . . . a lawyer!"

Balbuca silently gathered the slugs out of the dirt.

Once again he climbed the hill and looked around the square for Orejuela. He found him sitting at a table drinking chicha with the government official who had drawn up the contract.

"Master Orejuela, they are no good," he said, putting the worthless coins on the table. "Master doctor said so."

Orejuela reared up violently.

What! What was this piece of rubbish saying? That *he*, Felipe Neri Orejuela, had given out counterfeit money? Is *that* what he was saying? Accusing him of a *crime*, was he? In the presence of a government official?

He addressed his companion in dismay. Would the authorities allow this? Would they not impose a modicum of respect for a free Ecuadorian citizen publically insulted by a miserable Indian?

An outrage! What on earth had this corrupt country come to?

Balbuca listened without expression to Orejuela's histrionics. Then he said simply:

"Change the coins, or I won't send the boy."

At that point, the authority had heard enough. He turned to a couple of Indian day laborers who were passing by and commanded them:

"Grab hold of this lowlife."

Hesitant but cowed, they obeyed.

Turning to Balbuca, the official added:

"I'm taking you prisoner, and you'll stay in jail until your boy reports for work. Contracts are sacred and must be obeyed."

Balbuca struggled weakly in the arms of the men who held him. His eyes were very wide. His pupils were dilated. He bit his lips and said something unintelligible in Quechua under his breath. Then he fell silent and stopped resisting.

Orejuela now intervened sympathetically with the official. He offered to send a man to Balbuca's hut as soon as possible to collect the boy so that the Indian would not be in jail long. He, Orejuela, was not the sort of man who liked to see others suffer, not even uppity Indians who violated the rules of civilized behavior.

And, in fact, eight-year-old Pachito was brought at dawn the next day, with his sweaty little face and his ruddy cheeks that, chapped by the cold air of the high Andes, gave a misleading impression of robust health. . . .

Presentación emerged from jail and did not ask to see his son. He left town immediately and headed for his hut on a distant mountainside.

When he passed by the large gate of the hacienda administered by Orejuela, he picked up a small stone, made sure that nobody was looking, and threw it against the heavy wall in anger. The stone knocked a bit of white-washed plaster off the wall with a dull thud.

The Indian smiled expressionlessly, vaguely, stupidly. . . .

Then he looked in all directions, wiped his wild, glistening eyes on his sleeve, and quickly concealed his hand beneath his red poncho with its broad, lead-colored stripes. . . .

THE NEW SAINT: A STORY OF POLITICAL PROPAGANDA ON THE ECUADORIAN COAST (1938)

I

In the bottomland along the river, the rice crop was almost ready, its sprigs gradually turning golden in the equatorial sun, its roots refreshed by the dark waters that rose around the base of the plants twice daily at high tide and then subsided at low tide, as if the marsh were breathing. The wind came down the river flirting with its ripples, just as crystalline as the water, seemingly emanating from the same distant Andean source, and it gently shook the long, rough leaves of the rice plants. Small splashes made by the sudden swish of tails—a catfish, a small crustacean—occasionally shook the lower parts of the plants from below. The springs would soon swell to the bursting point, matured by the labor of the mud and the sun.

"You're going to make a pile of money this year, don Camilo."

"You never know. It depends on the price. And as far as I know, the price of rice in Guayaquil is rock bottom. Of course, who cares what we make, right? A poor man's sweat doesn't make anything but a stink."

"Relax, don Camilo, you'll see. The sucres are going to rain on you thicker than mosquitoes in the marsh."

"Maybe."

But Old Camilo Franco—whose unflattering nickname was "Bottles" because of his formerly limitless predilection to drain liter bottles of aguardiente—was not really thinking at all about the erect, parrot-green stalks of grain. Nor was he thinking about the potential produce of the stand of fruit trees that extended behind his riverbank dwelling with walls of woven cane. Nor about the egg-laying hens that clucked and pecked at caterpillars and dried corn in their little enclosure. Nor about his enormous white ducks, "big as a one-and-a-half-year-old goat," that floated in the surrounding ponds and drainage channels, dipping their bills in vain pursuit of fish. Nor about the hogs that awaited their judgment day in his pigsty, meanwhile getting fatter and fatter. Nor even about the young calves that frolicked around his cows, rubbing themselves against their mothers' thighs and tugging ineffectually at the wild grasses in the pasture.

You could have said to the man:

"Don Camilo, your house is falling down. . . ."

"Let it fall."

At most he might add:

"The termites have eaten through the supports, and I don't have any arsenic."

And, vaguely and slowly, he would make an ugly face signifying sadness.

And yet, Camilo Franco was, or had been, a tough, energetic man, strong as a thorny *guadua* cane as big around as your arm, and just as prickly, too, a man who had held firm against the ravages of age—never weakening even for a day—since he turned fifty a couple of decades back.

He had an adventurous past, one that he never bragged about, and, to the contrary, used to curse with regret.

Old Camilo had been born the son of agricultural workers who lived by arrangement with the landowner on a large estate, the descendant of slaves, still in the same place where both the slaves and their descendants had lived out their miserable lives for generations, always working for the same rich families. He did not conceal his family's long history of servitude:

"Until I was thirty-three years old, the age of Christ, as they say, I worked my whole life for the white Moreira family."

But then he had left, running away from everything, in order not to marry Magdalena.

"I had been in love with Magdalena. That was one pretty heifer! Everybody gawked at her. We were about to get married, on my saint's day . . . but the patrón got ahead of me. . . ."

The old man sighed when he told the story, even now, so many years later.

"He took advantage of her and wanted me to accept it and cover his tracks. But I couldn't accept it . . . how could I? Magdalena cried . . . and I loved her more all the time . . . but the patrón got ahead of me. . . ."

His voice became opaque and hoarse when he told the story, even now. And if his listeners were able to look deep into his eyes while he told it, they would no doubt see, against the background of his ashen grey pupils, the dark figure of that distant country girl, still wandering today, perhaps, on who-knows-what twisting pathway through this life. . . . Meanwhile, told from the angle of the patrón Moreira, the story would include a pastoral landscape, the blue sky, and lustful Love descending on fluttering wings. The rustic damsel would surrender herself to the conqueror's powerful arms as Pan, or some other similarly lecherous deity, watched with amusement from a nearby copse of trees.

The time that old Camilo spent in the inhospitable, virgin wilderness, deprived of the deliciously human virginity of Magdalena, had been full of countless, extraordinary adventures. The forest gave up all its secrets to him. He learned the magic of the plant kingdom: the herbs that cure and the herbs that kill, the trees that signal the presence of water or buried treasure, that ward off thieves or malicious spirits. He familiarized himself with the obscure lives of animals, from the most horrible creeping things to the fiercest of beasts.

"I've made plenty of money off that stuff, too. But I never did anything un-Christian, either. Not me! I'm a good child of the Lord."

People used to make fun of his religiosity:

"You, don Bottles, will believe in anything."

In fact, his fanatical religiosity led him to expect divine intervention in almost all matters, appealing to each saint according to his or her spiritual jurisdiction: "San Andrés, please look after my rice crop. Santa Ana, please watch over my cow. Santa Bárbara, I need rain! But, San Jonás, don't let it flood!" On the other hand, shrewd man that he was, he always took practical measures to facilitate the miracles that he so devoutly awaited, and he systematically applied the philosophy of old sayings. "God helps those who help themselves," he would say solemnly, or "He who find himself in the water should swim for shore," and he would then let out a shrill little laugh.

They say that when he supposed the danger to have passed, that the patrón had forgotten about his act of defiance in not marrying Magdalena, he finally came out of the hills.

"But I came here, to the bottomlands."

"And why didn't you go back to the Moreira estate, don Bottles?"

"Some say I refused to go back so as not to face the patrón, and some say it was so as not to face Magdalena."

"And how about you? What do you say yourself?"

"Nothing. I don't say anything. I don't say yes, and I don't say no . . . to anything."

Instead, he found a place as a sharecropper on lands belonging to the Echarri family, occupying a little piece of bottomland along the river, where he lived ever after.

"This is where fate brought me, where I found me a little piece of ground. This is where I married my wife, may she rest in peace. Here is where my daughter Carmen was born, the one they called Blackberry because she was so dark. And here is where Carmen died, too, in childbirth, leaving me my little filly, Marta. And here is where Marta has grown up, my only companion. . . ."

He adored his little filly. This big macho, as he liked to think of himself, seemed more like a woman when he was taking care of the girl. Every night before going to bed, he quietly approached the mosquito netting beneath which his granddaughter slept and contemplated her for a while. He carefully adjusted the netting to protect her from the mosquitos. And then, raising his calloused right hand, he made the sign of the cross and blessed her in the name of the Father, the Son, and the Holy Ghost. . . .

II

The cause of don Camilo's distraction was, precisely, his grand-daughter.

He knew that she was eye-popping pretty, an object of desire. He knew that her firm flesh was a morsel for any palate. He knew that her tender seventeen years were tempting, indeed. And, tireless watchdog, he suffered because he knew. He meant to get her married as quickly as possible, and he had already chosen a husband for her. The marriage would happen when the waters rose at the end of the season.

But he was still worried. . . .

The fiancé, Juan Puente, was an agricultural worker on a nearby estate, but he was not of peasant origin like Camilo. He was from the city and had held a good job on the railroad until he lost it, accused of being a labor agitator.

The old man liked to chat with Juan Puente. Or rather, he liked to listen to the young man's impassioned ideas about social reform, ideas that opened unexpected vistas before his tired eyes. When Juan Puente talked about the legitimate demands of workers and peasants, old Camilo got it. He got it, and he became pensive and, not understanding everything that Puente said, he squirmed, determined to master the ideas. Gradually, he incorporated the new ideas by mixing them with the old ones already in his head, and, without intending to, he modified the new ideas to make them fit.

Certain phrases danced in his mind: "Social Revolution," "the dictatorship of the proletariat," "Lenin is the great saint of the new religion."

Don Camilo thought of Vladimir Illych Lenin in a manner that harmonized with his ingenuous peasant religiosity. One time Juan Puente gave Camilo a magazine that contained a picture of the Russian leader, and the old man cut the picture out and put it up on the wall beside a number of saint's images in the corner that he devoted to them. The little kerosene lamp that flickered there on a tiny altar thus illuminated one more holy image for the old man to remember in his daily prayers.

Without confessing it aloud, old Camilo supposed that, in case of necessity, Lenin would be able to protect him, by some sort of miraculous intervention, from the depredations of the patrón.

And necessity seemed imminent.

The patrón's son, Dionisio, was prowling around Camilo's house on an almost daily basis.

"I don't like to see that hawk flapping around here," repeated the old peasant. "That bird's looking for prey."

And he could easily guess that the prey was his granddaughter, his little filly, who was not so little anymore.

"Just like the other one. Just like him. Whites are all the same, all cut from the same cloth."

He was afraid that the story of Magdalena might be repeated with his granddaughter, and so one day he communicated his fears to Juan Puente.

"You know, Juan Puente. I like you very well, obviously, and because I like you I'm going to tell you . . ."

"Tell me what, don Camilo?"

"I've had it with that Echarri boy, up to here . . ."

"Why?"

"He's after Marta. He'd like to have her."

"Really."

"It's God's own truth. I've seen him."

"Ah . . ."

Juan Puente then said firmly:

"I'll take care of that little twit. You'll see. I know how to treat his kind."

Don Camilo smiled, still worried.

III

But lo and behold, within a short time it became evident that young Echarri had discontinued his campaign.

He vanished completely from the vicinity of the humble house where he had appeared so often in the past, riding his fine thoroughbred horse with its expensive saddle and bridle, taking no care to keep the enormous animal's hooves from trampling the crops that old Bottles had planted.

And then came the news that the patrón's son had left the estate to travel to Guayaquil, and eventually, to Europe.

One day at dusk, when don Camilo was conversing with Juan Puente outside on the porch in the cool of the evening, he brought up the matter.

"What did you do, Juan Puente, to get him off our backs so fast?"

"Easy. I bumped into him one time, where your coffee bushes are planted. And I said to him: 'Look here, young man. You're after Marta, aren't you? Well,' I said, 'Marta is going to be my wife, and if you don't clear out of the way . . . I will *kill* you . . . understand? With this blade that I keep sharpened up just for you. Try it out. Touch it!' And I showed it to him right there."

"And what did the white boy say?"

"He got all pale and stuttered all over the place, making excuses, saying I'd made a mistake, that he wasn't after anybody, and that to prove it he was going to move up the date of a long trip that he was planning. . . . So I told him: 'Good idea, young man. You take the trip that you have in mind, because if you don't, I'm going to send you on a longer one . . . much, much longer. . . .' These bourgeois that want to ride us are really cowards, don Camilo. You just have to know how to deal with them!"

"Ah . . ."

The old man asked no more questions. He walked into the house and softly caressed the hair of his granddaughter, who sat in the corner near Camilo's little shrine, sewing her wedding dress. He lit the tiny kerosene wick and put it right in front of the portrait of Lenin. Then he went back out onto the porch to rejoin Juan Puente.

He took the younger man's arm and whispered into his ear:

"Listen, Juan Puente. I'm going to tell you something. . . ."

"What?"

"That white Echarri boy going away . . ."

"Yeah?"

"Lenin did it!"

And looking up at the low, heavy clouds, the old man obeyed a powerful impulse, and raised his tired voice to shout at the sky: "Viva San Lenin!"

A gust of wind that was passing on its way to the river at just that moment caught the last syllable of the shouted name and returned it with a clapping of leaves. . . .

Analyzing the Sources: Presentación Balbuca undergoes a subtle but meaningful transformation in the reader's eyes over the course of "Three Silver Sucres." What is the transformation, and why does it matter? "The New Saint," on the other hand, is not very subtle, but it does raise a question of broad importance in the 1930s: How would Latin Americans respond to Marxism? What answer does de la Cuadra seem to be giving?

ARID LIVES

Graciliano Ramos

Graciliano Ramos (1892–1953) was from the small state of Alagoas in the Brazilian northeast. Ramos may be considered the founder of northeastern regionalism, one of Brazil's literary highlights in the 1930s. The following excerpt is from the stark 1938 novel Barren Lives, *his most important work, which describes the daily life of sertanejos who tend herds of cattle in the scrubby, arid sertão region, their lives constantly menaced by recurrent droughts. Typical of writers in search of the non-European roots of national identities, Ramos espoused left-wing politics, and he spent time in jail as a result.*

Squatting beside the three stones that supported the pan over the cooking fire, her flowered skirt tucked between her thighs, Vitória*

SOURCE: Graciliano Ramos, *Vidas sêcas, romance* (Rio de Janeiro: J. Olympio, 1947), pp. 53–57, 60–63.

*In the Portuguese original, Vitória is always called *Sinha* Vitória, indicating her aspiration to status as a respectable married woman.

blew on the embers. A cloud of ashes billowed up and covered her face. Smoke flooded her eyes, and her rosary of blue and white beads swung forward, clinking against the pan. Vitória wiped the tears from her eyes with the back of her hand, pushed the rosary back into her blouse, squinted, and blew again with puffed-out cheeks.

The flames licked at the sticks of acacia, died away, arose again, and gradually filled the spaces between the stones. Vitória straightened her back and fanned the fire. A luminous shower of sparks descended around the dog, Baleia, who lay curled up nearby, dozing in the warmth, lulled by the aroma of food.

Sensing the movement of the air and the crackling of the fire, Baleia awoke, moved a prudent distance away for fear of singeing her fur, and gazed in wonder at the whirling red sparks that disappeared before touching the ground. She panted, wagged her tail approvingly, and tried to signal her admiration by standing erect on her hind legs and hopping toward her mistress. But Vitória was in no mood for the dog's admiration.

"Get away!"

She kicked at the dog, who withdrew, humiliated, contemplating rebellion.

Vitória had gotten up cranky that morning and, by way of nothing at all, had complained to her husband about their improvised bed. Taken aback by her unprovoked assault, Fabiano had simply grunted and, reflecting that women are impossible creatures to understand, had climbed into the hammock and gone back to sleep. Vitória had paced back and forth looking for a suitable target, and finding everything in order, she had vented at life in general, and now, at Baleia, by giving her a kick.

She approached the low kitchen window, saw the children under a tree playing in the mud, happily covered with it, shaping it into little clay cattle that they then put in the sun to dry, and she failed to find a reason to scold them. She thought again about the improvised bed of tree boughs that she and Fabiano slept on, and she silently cursed him. They had gotten used to the thing, but it would be much nicer to sleep on a real bed, the way other people did.

She had been telling him that for over a year. Fabiano had accepted the idea at first and had mumbled a few confused calculations. It would cost so much for the wooden frame, so much for the leather bottom. All right. They could save the money for it by economizing on clothes and kerosene. Vitória had said that was impossible because their clothes were rags, the kids ran around practically naked already, and they all went to bed with the chickens. The truth was that nobody practically ever lit a lamp in that house. So they had discussed other possible economies. Failing to agree on any, Vitória resorted to bitter comments on the money that her husband spent at the market, playing cards and drinking. Fabiano had retaliated with observations on Vitória's expensive and useless dress shoes. She looked ridiculous stumbling around in those shoes like a wobbly parrot. The comparison gravely offended her, and had she not been somewhat fearful of Fabiano's reaction, she would have told him a thing or two. In fact, though, the shoes really did not fit her very well. They pinched her toes and gave her calluses. She tripped and limped, and had trouble walking on the high heels. She probably did look ridiculous, but still, Fabiano's remark had wounded her deeply.

When the cloud of sadness lifted and she dispeled that bitter recollection from her mind, the bed reappeared on her narrow horizon, now in the guise of a totally unachievable goal. She mused about it unhappily as she went about the household chores.

She went into the main room, ducked under the end of the hammock where Fabiano lay snoring, took her pipe and a bit of tobacco from the shelf, and went out to the porch. A cowbell could be heard down by the river. It was the red cow. Fabiano might have forgotten about its medicine. She considered waking him up to ask him, but she became distracted looking at the prickly pears and mandurucu trees in the distance.

A haze rose from the scorched earth. She shuddered and grew pale, recalling the last drought, and her eyes widened. She did her best to banish the memory, fearing that it might become a reality. She said a Hail Mary under her breath and felt better, her attention caught now by a hole in the fence around the goat pen. She rubbed and crumbled the tobacco between the palms of her rough hands, filled the clay pipe, and went to repair the fence. She returned, walked around the house, and entered the kitchen.

"Fabiano might have forgotten about the red cow."

Squatting by the fire, she stirred it and, with a spoon, extracted an ember to light her pipe and puffed at the tar-clogged bamboo stem. The pot hissed and a warm, dusty breeze shook the cobwebs that hung like curtains from the underside of the roof. Baleia lay biting at fleas and snapping at flies. Fabiano's snores rang rhythmically in Vitória's ears, and their rhythm influenced her thoughts. Fabiano snored with assurance. Probably there was no danger of drought.

Once again Vitória began to daydream about the bed. But the thought reminded her of the "wobbly parrot" remark, too, and she had to make a great effort to focus her mind on the object of her desire.

Everything around her seemed so stable, so fixed. Fabiano's snoring, the crackling of the fire, the sound of cowbells outside, even the buzz of the flies—gave a sensation of fixity and repose. Would she have to sleep on a bed of tree boughs her entire life? And in the middle of that awful bed was a thick knot, a knot so thick that she had to sleep on one side of the bed and Fabiano on the other. Neither could stretch out in the middle. At first the bed had not bothered her. Limp and exhausted from work, she would have lain on a bed of nails. Lately, however, things had been looking up. They were eating better, getting a little flesh on their bones. They still owned practically nothing, of course. If they had to flee a drought, they could leave that house carrying only their clothes, the shotgun, and the small tin trunk full of odds and ends. But they were managing to live, thank God, one way or another. The owner of the place liked them, and things were almost all right. All they lacked was a bed. The idea dogged her thoughts. No longer so exhausted by hard work, she lay awake thinking part of every night. And going to bed as soon as night fell was just not right. People are not chickens.

From there Vitória's thoughts took a detour, but it led back to the original route soon enough. That fox had stolen the speckled hen. It had to be the speckled one, the fattest one, didn't it? She decided to set a snare for the fox by the hens' perch. She was mad now. That fox was going to pay dearly for the speckled hen!

"The thief."

Little by little, her anger shifted orientation. Fabiano's snoring became intolerable. Nobody snored more than that man. It would be good to get up and look for a bough to replace that damned one with a knot that didn't let you turn over in bed. Why hadn't they replaced the blasted thing already? She sighed. They didn't seem to be able to make up their minds. She'd have to be patient. Maybe it would be better to forget the knot altogether and think about a bed like the one that belonged to Tomás the miller. Tomás had a real bed, made by a carpenter, with a frame of sucupira wood, shaped and smoothed and neatly dovetailed at the corners. It had a bottom of rawhide tightly stretched across it and firmly tacked along the edges. Now, *that* was a bed where a body could rest her bones.

What if she sold both the hens and a pig? Too bad that the blasted fox had gotten the speckled hen. The fattest one. She needed to teach that fox a lesson. She was going to set a trap by the chickens' perch and break the back of that wretched fox.

She got up, went into the bedroom to look for something, and returned discouraged and empty handed, having forgotten what she went to get. Where was her head?

She sat down unhappily by the low kitchen window. She would sell the hens and a pig and stop buying kerosene. No use consulting Fabiano, who always got excited and made plans that came to nothing. She knitted her brow, a bit shocked at her bold idea, but confident that her husband would be pleased at the idea of owning a bed. Vitória wanted a real bed of leather and sucupira wood, like the one that belonged to Tomás the miller.

Analyzing the Sources: The sertanejos described by da Cunha in The Backlands *were admirable but exotic beings, viewed very much from the outside. Compare and contrast the portrait of Vitória in this selection from* Arid Lives.

RUNA YUPAY

José María Arguedas

José María Arguedas (1911–1969) was raised in the rural Peruvian highlands in intimate contact with the Quechua-speaking indigenous people of the Andes, whose language he grew up speaking. Later, Arguedas became an anthropologist and a leading voice of indigenista literature. During the 1930s, the Peruvian government commissioned Arguedas to write a story (finished in 1939) to prepare the country's schoolteachers for the 1940 census, which they were expected to help administer. In the story's Quechua title, Arguedas evoked the runa yupay, a census that had been carried out periodically in the Inca Empire.

In the Indian village of Huanipaca, honeysuckle flowers grow everywhere and perfume almost every street. Travelers look around for the plant and find it growing atop the stone walls of all the gardens. They go over to smell it close up and pause for a moment, as if listening to something, and when they return to their own villages, they say:

"In Huanipaca there is a plant so fragrant that, if God smells it, he will surely take it up to heaven."

The Indians have it in their patios, and so does Señora Amalia, whose house is the biggest in the village. Señora Amalia owns four sugarcane haciendas in the fertile valleys of the district and is served by five hundred Indians.

In front of Huanipaca rises the high cordillera of the Andes, blue in the distance, with snow-covered peaks. Beside Huanipaca runs the stream of that name, at the bottom of its narrow canyon, seeking the river that runs through a much larger canyon, at the foot of the snow-covered mountains, a canyon so deep that the river is almost always hidden. At intervals along the flank of the cordillera, other

---

SOURCE: José María Arguedas, "Runa Yupay," in *Agua y otros cuentos indígenas* (Lima: Editorial Milla Batres, 1974), pp. 115–16, 119–26, 134–35, 137.

streams run down to the river as well, each in a canyon of its own, wide and shallow toward the top, narrowing and deepening as it descends to the river until each stream has become a tumbling thread of white water at the rocky bottom of a vertical gash so narrow that it seems one could almost leap across it. The Indians use these streams to water the corn that they sow along the lower part of their course and to water the wheat, barley, potatoes, and quinua that they sow higher up. The great landowners of the region use the water, too, for their sprawling sugarcane haciendas in the valley.

Huanipaca is the administrative seat of its district. It has a church with a steeple of plaster-covered masonry and a large unpaved square where grass and broad-leaved *romaza* grow, where free-ranging little pigs root around during the day and toads and crickets sing at night. The little streets that lead away from the square are straight, sloping, and unpaved. Down the middle of each runs a shallow, stone-lined drainage ditch full of dirty water, pieces of glass, rags, corncobs, and corn husks. Pigs and ducks splash around in the pools that form along them in places, and in the stillness of the night one can hear the water burble musically in the tiny rapids between the pools. A peculiarity of this place is the frequency of goiter among its inhabitants, many of whom—men, women, and children—have the telltale lumps of that disease on their necks. Some say it is because of the water, some say the air. Huanipaca also has a school. The school teacher, who is not from the village, rooms in Señora Amalia's big house, and so does the village priest, who is not from there, either. The señora resides on one of her four haciendas.

The schoolhouse, one large room with an earthen floor, stands next to the church. It has a covered walkway on the front side, facing the village square, and a large patio overgrown with romazas on the back side. The students sit to do their lessons in the large room and in the covered walkway, and they play among the romazas at recess. The teacher has managed to get the students to carry woven bags for their notebooks and writing slates and to wear aprons of cheap fabric to protect their clothes against the chalk dust. They must pass a hygiene inspection every morning and afternoon, and so they always have clean faces and combed hair. The teacher, who studied in

Lima, is a mestizo of modest background, the son of a provincial storekeeper, and the villagers approve of him. With his low forehead, his thick black hair, and his indigenous-looking features, he could be a *cholo** from Huanipaca or any other town of the vicinity. Since the beginning of the year, he has been on a campaign to get all of the Indian boys into his schoolhouse, and to do so he has visited each and every family in the village and the surrounding countryside.

"*Jampuyki tayta!*" he says in Quechua to the father of each house he enters: "Send your boy to school! What he learns there will help him when he grows up. That way, they won't be able to take advantage of him. He'll know better. Look at how you and all your neighbors have goiters on your necks. Your son will learn to protect himself from goiters. Send him to school!"

"*Cumunú, Werak'ocha!*" they always say. "Of course, sir!"

But then they don't do it. So every month, the teacher repeats the visit.

"What's this, *tayta*? A man your age should speak the truth. Why do you lie to your friend? You must trust me. I will take good care of your boy. Send him to school!"

"But who then will care for our calf, *Werak'ocha*? Who?"

"Send him only in the afternoon, then. But send him! It's best for your boy. Do you want him to grow up ignorant?"

"All right, *Werak'ocha*, I will send him."

The teacher has been persistent, and gradually his school has filled with Indian boys.

After mass on Sundays, the people of the village usually gather in front of the church to receive the warming rays of the sun and hear the schoolteacher explain the news from Lima. The teacher subscribes to several newspapers mailed to him from the capital and also maintains correspondance with several friends in that large and distant city.

"What news, sir? What do they say about the so-called census? Will it really take place?"

---

*An Andean mestizo, more indigenous than European in appearance.

"Of course it will! It's nothing bad! The census is needed to take the pulse of Peru, to measure the health of our nation. The government needs to determine the number of our country's inhabitants and attend to the needs of each of its villages. It will be good for everyone. These are fortunate times, for it seems that all Peru now wants to progress rapidly into the future. The people are ready to work hard, so the government in Lima needs information to direct our labors, to choose the right path forward."

"They say that there are many construction projects underway in Lima."

"Many, indeed. Our palace of government is finished and should make us proud. It is even superior to similar buildings in other countries. And they are building many new parks and avenues in Lima, too. They have had to tear down entire blocks of old buildings to make the avenues properly wide and straight. . . ."

"That must really be something to see!"

"And the Pan-American Congress has just been held in Lima."

"What was that like, sir?"

"Something really big and important, a meeting of representatives from all the nations of North, South, and Central America. Around twenty nations, just imagine! And each nation has sent its very best and wisest men to represent it. They gathered in a great building to discuss what we all need, what is best for all the people of America, to educate them and improve their lives, to make them truly free and truly happy, to find ways for them to help each other, like brothers. Brotherhood and betterment is what the congress was all about."

More people arrive to hear the schoolteacher explain these matters. Even those who did not arrive in time for mass hurry from their distant houses to join the group in front of the church. When he is through with mass, the village priest comes to stand beside the schoolteacher and help explain the news of the day to the Indians, who usually do not speak, but rather, listen attentively. From time to time, however, when discussion is called for, the villagers voice their own ideas.

For various Sundays in a row, the teacher and the priest have mentioned the projected national census, the public works underway in Lima, and the many highways that are being constructed to bring the automobile to even the most isolated villages of Peru.

"So much progress!" exclaims a villager. "To think that in an airplane you can fly across the entire world in the blink of an eye! What are a hundred leagues now, or even a thousand leagues? Nothing is impossible."

"Forget airplanes," says the priest. "With automobiles alone you can hurtle through these cordilleras the way an ant scurries through the cobblestones. Think of it. In the old days, who would have considered going to Cuzco or Arequipa, much less Lima, except for reasons of extreme urgency? The Indians had no idea of such places. And now? Thanks be to God, now, even Indians can pay a *sol*** or two or three, climb into the back of a truck, and go to any of those places. And what's more, they pass through town after town where they find other Indians speaking Quechua like themselves, who tell them, 'This, too, is Peru, just like your own village.' And hearing Quechua, they feel deep down that it is true. They think, 'This is our country, a country called Peru.'"

"It's true! We have to travel through our country to see what it really is. A Peruvian should be ashamed if he goes to foreign lands and is asked about Cuzco or Arequipa or Trujillo and can't describe those important cities."

"Well, he should be even more ashamed if they ask him, 'How many inhabitants does Peru have?' and he can't answer with confidence and has to mumble something ignorant."

"That's exactly right," says the schoolteacher, taking advantage of this turn of the conversation. "The purpose of the census is precisely to avoid that sort of ignorance. And look at how this works," he goes on, addressing the entire group. "When we know how many inhabitants Peru has, we will also know how may tailors, how many engineers, how many doctors, lawyers, teachers, and priests there are. We'll know how many know how to read and how many suffer the misfortune of not knowing so much as how to write their own names. Town by town and village by village, the census will tell us how

**Peruvian currency.

many children there are, according to their ages. So the government will be able to calculate the number of teachers that will be needed at various levels, one teacher for every fifty children. . . ."

The Indians and mestizos listen and learn. It is true. They know more or less how many people live in their village, but they have no idea how many people live in Peru. And not just them, because sixty-three years have passed since the last national census!

As the hour of the midday meal approaches, the people drift away in the direction of their houses, and one can hear their appreciative remarks:

"Huanipaca is a lucky village. We have a good teacher, a good priest, a good mayor. All the authorities are good. That's why we get along. . . ."

"It's not that way in other villages where neighbors tussle like dogs and cats."

"That's the way it is if you don't have good local authorities."

When the schoolteacher goes to get his mail on the following Friday, he finds a large envelope addressed to him and bearing an official seal. It is from the national census bureau, and he opens it eagerly. Inside are a number of circulars and pamphlets.

"Now it's really happening! It's about time! I bet they are asking schoolteachers for their cooperation. It makes sense! We teachers ought to help because nobody is in a better position to do so. And our students can help as well. I've already spoken to mine about that."

He looks at the materials as he walks home and reads the title of the thickest pamphlet: *The School Teachers of Peru and the Census of Population and Occupation.*

"Wonderful! This is exactly what I had hoped and exactly what ought to be done! It is absurd not to know how many Peruvians there are. When the last census was done in 1876, I had not yet even been born. There were just a little more that two and a half million of us then. I wonder how many of us there are now? Now we are going to find out! I'm going to work like the devil!"

The schoolteacher of Huanipaca practically runs the rest of the way home, and that night there is a light burning in his room into the wee hours.

Before long his students are moving excitedly through the streets of the village to collect trial census data. They greet the residents of each house respectfully and explain that they have come in the name of their teacher before entering. Then they draw a small notebook from their pocket and request all the necessary information. They take the process very seriously, asking the questions and noting the responses as if they were quite grown up. And the people of Huanipaca answer all the questions. The teacher has impressed upon them their obligation to collaborate with the government, and they consider it a matter of village pride to do so. Some behave just as seriously as the students, answering the questions in the manner of one who discharges a civic duty. Others do it with humor and applause for the boys, offering them a little something to eat or drink. In Indian houses the census-takers are Indian students, and all the questions are asked and answered in Quechua.

The teacher watches the students run from house to house, filling their notebooks with details for the national census.

"Look at them, busy as ants. Incredible! Being a schoolteacher is the most rewarding thing there is."

The national census is a great event in Huanipaca, involving all the inhabitants of the village. The students feel great enthusiasm for the census because the teacher has communicated to them a sense of its enormous significance. And their enthusiasm is contagious. Their elders, too, have come to understand the benefits that the census would bring to them, the Indian inhabitants of Peru, who have for so long lived half-forgotten and abandoned to their fate. Now they will be counted!

Analyzing the Sources: How does the indigenista vision presented here relate to earlier selections dealing with the indigenous people of Peru? What common thread links it, for example, to Matto de Turner? What theme links it to Guaman Poma, Carrió de la Vandera, and de la Cuadra?

WIDE AND ALIEN IS THE WORLD
Ciro Alegría

Ciro Alegría (1909–1967) was a Peruvian journalist and political activist who lived many years in exile because of his participation in APRA, Peru's Popular American Revolutionary Alliance. Neocolonial ideology had dictated the dissolution of Indian communities to promote individual ownership of property, but nationalist ideology revered the powerful community ethos of indigenous people. The following passage from Alegría's 1941 novel Wide and Alien is the World, *written and published in exile, gives a lyrical picture of indigenous villagers harvesting their community crops, then depicts the exploitation of Indian labor outside their communities. Where neocolonial authors had portrayed the Indians as beaten and fatalistic, Ciro Alegría paints them as future revolutionaries. The novel centers on a Peruvian highland village called Rumi.*

The villagers of Rumi began the harvest. Men and women, old and young, even children, went out into the corn field. Their dark faces and brightly colored clothing leapt to the eye amid the pale gold of the ripening crop. The morning was soft, warm, and luminous, and the land itself seemed to glow with satisfaction at having made the grain swell so fat.

The harvesters broke through the husk encasing each ear of corn with a finger nail or with a wooden point that they carried, attached to their wrists with a string. Then they pulled the leafy casing apart to reveal the dry, shiny grains, yellow and white, but also red and purple, finally pulling the ear free and letting it tumble into the cloth bags that they carried over their shoulders. Other harvesters gathered the bean pods that hung from vines that climbed the stalks of corn. Still others gathered the large white

SOURCE: Ciro Alegría, *El mundo es ancho y ajeno* (Caracas: Biblioteca Ayacucho, 1978), pp. 108–09, 130–32.

melons that grew there, too. The ears of corn were carried to a structure where they were stacked on end and exposed to the sun to dry. The name of the structure (*cauro*) and the name of the operation (*mucura*) were words from Quechua. The Spanish spoken by whites and mestizos had tended to displace the Quechua in northern Peruvian villages like Rumi, but the agricultural vocabulary had remained Quechua, rooted in people's hearts the way their plants were rooted in the ground. The cauro full of stacked corn stood in front of the mayor's house on Rumi's modest plaza. Other fruits of harvest were heaped beside the cauro. The harvesters who watched the heaps rise as they returned repeatedly to empty their sacks praised the bounty of the earth.

Everyone harvested, from the very young to the very old. Old Rosendo, the mayor of Rumi, moved more slowly than most, but worked right alongside the rest. He did not seem like the mayor at all, only a happy, hard-working grandfather. Anselmo, the harp player, seated on a stool to one side of the cauro, his large instrument reclining on his shoulder, played for the harvesters. The notes of the harp, the sounds of laughing voices, the rustling of dry corn shucks, the crack of ears coming loose from the stalk—all mingled to form the happy sound of the harvest. Girls carrying gourds went back and forth between the harvesters in the field and the large earthenware jugs of chicha corn beer, distributing the red, celebratory brew. The chicha sang in the harvesters' veins of its fermented-corn origins. And the corn field, shorn of its pregnant fruits, was gradually transformed into a patch of forlorn stalks robbed of their former plumes.

And whom did we see chatting over there but Juan Medrano, son of a village official, and Simona, one of the young women we saw helping with the cows on a certain morning. The two were beginning to feel close in the last couple of days. And the afternoon, shimmering with heat, had just begun. A penetrating fragrance was rising from the earth to mingle with the smell of overall ripeness. Juan was strong as a tree limb, Simona, succulent as a fruit, and neither was over twenty years old. They began to tussle, slowly separating from the other harvesters. Simona ran away laughing and

Juan pretended he couldn't catch her. Finally, he did catch her, and they looked deeply into each other's eyes.

"Bet I can trip you."

"Bet you can't."

They struggled playfully for a moment—Simona was strong, too—finally rolling amid the stalks of corn. The corn patch covered the joyous alliance of their brown bodies with its interminable rustle, its obedient ears, its yellow beard. Above arched the deep blue heavens, bending harmoniously over the earth. Simona discovered the joy of her own body and of a man's, and Juan, who had tripped up many young women in his travels, discovered that powerful call that eventually leads men to settle on just one woman.

The setting sun struck the corn flowers and the brown faces now in profile. The long shadow of the neighboring Andean peak grew longer, creeping over the ground to cover the corn field. The day's work was finished, and the harvesters returned to the village. In the plaza stood the cauro, brim full, and the towering heaps of beans and melons.

The harp is still playing. Someone sings. All the villagers of Rumi feel happy and, without stopping to think about it, they are fulfilled at having used their days for peace, cultivating the earth for the common good.

Meanwhile, far away, Rumi's native son Benito Castro suffered greatly as a salaried hacienda laborer. Benito remembered Rumi and his heart ached. He remembered his horse, Lucero, and his heart ached even more. The agricultural labors of the hacienda were *so* different from those of the indigenous community. In Rumi, people worked quickly, laughing and singing, and their daily labors were a pleasure to them. On the haciendas, they moved slowly and sadly, like step-children of the land. They might have a little strength left, but they had no spirit left at all.

Time passed and, not suspecting what grave events were occurring in Rumi, Benito labored with a hundred other indigenous workers in the mud under heavy rains, cultivating the crops of the "patrón" who owned the hacienda. The hacienda was enormous, and the huts provided for the workers were so far away from the field that Benito and the others had to sleep together in a large shed while they worked there. In these quarters, he came to know Indians from all over, people who spoke Quechua (when they spoke, which was not often), and had mostly melancholy things to say. Benito had not been raised speaking Quechua, which sounds sometimes like a raging wind and sometimes like water seeping through the earth, but now he began to learn.

Their stories were rarely the old folktales, but rather, lamentations of their labors and sufferings. In low voices, a tight circle of listeners gathered around them, the oldest of the group told of the great rebellion led by Atusparia more than a generation earlier.

Here is the story: The year is 1885. The Indians are groaning under the weight of the oppression they suffer. Each of them has to pay a personal tax of two *soles* twice a year. They have to contribute their labor without pay to build roads, barracks, cemeteries, churches, and public buildings in the name of the Republic. The overseers devastate the indigenous communities to force them to work. The Indians have to work for nothing just to escape persecution. They have to endure in silence.

But one time they protested, presenting a petition in Huaraz. No one paid any attention. Instead, Pedro Pablo Atusparia, an indigenous mayor who led the petitioners, was insulted, jailed, and whipped. Fourteen mayors of indigenous communities went to protest this abuse. They, too, were insulted, jailed, and whipped.

They pretended to give in. And then on March first the Indians came down from the mountains toward Huaraz carrying bundles of straw to roof a building—public work for the Republic. But at a signal they pulled clubs and machetes from the bundles of straw, and the fight began. They told this story in the present tense.

The first wave of Indians is thrown back. A squadron of cavalry charges, scattering their forces. Encouraged by this success, the squadron attacks Pumacayán, a steep-walled Inca fortress where the Indians have taken shelter. Pumacayán has beautiful stone carvings of mating pumas on walls that the government prefect of Huaraz intended to dismantle, planning to use the materials for the city cemetery and several private mansions. Pumacayán is defended by Pedro Granados and a handful of brave men. Granados wields a huge leather sling with which he hurls rocks the size of a person's head with deadly accuracy. Alone he topples seventy of the attacking cavalry. The squadron falls back, and the Indians besiege Huaraz. It fall the next day. The Indians drink the blood of the most valiant of their enemies to feed their own valor. They want to destroy the families of the rich who cower in their houses. But Atusparia, the leader of the rebellion, is against that. "I do not want crimes," he says. "I want justice."

The revolution begins to spread. The Indians cover themselves with sheep fleece and crawl on all fours to take the city of Yungay by surprise. The countryside of Huaylas, too, rises up, and assaults all the towns there. In some of them, the rich form "urban guards" and fight bravely. Other indigenous leaders emerge.

Emissaries are sent to other parts of the highlands asking for help, asking for revolution. But the battalions of the government arrive with good rifles, with artillery. They massacre the Indians like so many ants. To save ammunition, the army stands indigenous prisoners in rows to execute six at a time with one bullet. The leaders of the rebellion are captured and executed, too. As the blows and bullets rip the body of José Orobio, the White Condor, he scorns his executioners: "A little more. Give me a little more." Uchcu Pedro, who brought dynamite from the mines to arm the revolution, turns his bare buttocks to the firing squad and bends over. Atusparia falls wounded, and his bodyguards fall dead on top of him, defending him even in death.

These are the things that were whispered among the workers, exhausted by their days of ceaseless toil, in the nights when they gathered together. They remembered the victories more than the defeats. And the night was filled with hope and tragedy, with images of legendary heroes, with the memory of those who struggled shrewdly and powerfully against their tormentors. They were not yet beaten. Any day now, the revolution would begin again.

Analyzing the Sources: The power of Alegría's story comes from its contrast between the idealized village life and the stark, "alien" world beyond. What are those contrasts, and where do you see the novelist exaggerating them?

THE AFRICAN ROOTS OF CUBAN MUSIC

Fernando Ortiz

Cuban anthropologist Fernando Ortiz (1881–1969) is a foundational figure in Latin American studies, who pioneered the historical exploration of Afro-Cuban culture. Like his contemporary Gilberto Freyre, in Brazil, Ortiz became a leading spokesman for the nationalist ideology of mestizaje, which rooted Latin American national identities in race mixing. Cuban mestizaje was black–white. Popular music offered examples and metaphors to represent the process. In the following passage from the opening of his 1950 book, The African Roots of Cuban Music *(1950), Ortiz announces his theme. The genius of Cuban music, and the qualities that make it Cuban, lie in a creative encounter between Europe and Africa. The passage thus updates Vicente Rossi's celebration of the tango and exemplifies highly influential, and eventually official, attitudes of mid-twentieth-century "mestizo" nationalism.*

No one can accuse a Cuban writer of hyper-patriotism for writing that Cuban music has had a wide international resonance for centuries, both in the New World and the Old, because it is an undeniable fact. Cuba possesses a genuine, national musical culture, all its own, yet imbued with cosmopolitan values.

Both Cuban cigars and Cuban dance music have been acclaimed universally. But neither is attributable solely to European colonizers; both of them, instead, are the product of an intercultural embrace. Cuba was where Europeans first "discovered" tobacco in November 1492, already in the exquisite, tightly rolled form of the cigar that remains to this day an unsurpassed gift to world connoisseurship. A legacy of vanished indigenous life, adapted by white masters and black slaves, a "mestizo" product of racial and cultural mixing. Cuba's other great gift to the world has been, and remains,

SOURCE: Fernando Ortiz, *La africanía de la música folklórica de Cuba* (Havana: Ministerio de Educación, 1950), pp. 1–2, 4–5.

its popular dance music, the creation of blacks and whites, "mulatto" so to speak, if the cigar is "mestizo." Of these two great Cuban contributions to world culture, moreover, music is the more unique. Tobacco was known and used throughout indigenous America, but Cuban music sprang forth on Cuban soil exclusively, like our royal palms.

Once again, as has happened repeatedly over two centuries, Cuban music (which means *Afro*-Cuban music, by definition) is in style internationally. Our music is fire, sugar, and smoke, rum to drink through your ears. It brings people together on the same level and enlivens their senses. What accounts for the intense musicality of the Cuban people?

It seems beyond question that the answer must lie in the confluence of diverse cultures that have mingled in the Cuban people. Europe and Africa provided the materials, but they were assembled on this side of the Atlantic by people of Europe, and of Africa, and most especially, people of mixed European and African descent. In other words, this mixture is not superficial or eclectic, but rather, integral to the creation of the music. The result is something new and original, a unique product of transculturation.

My purpose in this book is to uncover the African wellsprings of Cuban popular music through historical and ethnographic study. This project must start with the Spanish conquest and colonization of Cuba, because it is from that time, centuries ago, that blacks and whites have been interweaving their cultures, along with a few surviving pre-Columbian influences, to create Cuban national culture. Elements of Old World background must be teased from sources on West Africa and early modern Spain. Indeed, the African influence in our music reaches back to Iberia, where slaves were imported and race mixing occurred before that happened in the New World. Columbus himself heard African music in Lisbon and Seville, and even in Guinea, before he made his first transatlantic voyage into the unknown. Euclides da Cunha and others have already made this point concerning African influences in early modern Portugal. If Cuban music descends from a love affair between the Spanish lute and the African drum, it was in Europe that the two met, and from there they eloped to the New World.

The European and African preludes must be our starting place. The colonizers' first musical renditions in the New World, whether black or white, simply repeated what the musicians had learned in the Old World, the same genres, styles, and instruments, simply accommodated, as well as could be, to new circumstances. Medieval Spanish music has been well studied and does not require an extended discussion here. We will get to it. Let us begin, however, with an equally important topic that has been comparatively much less studied, the music of Africa. To reconstruct that history, I will draw from African ethnographies and travel accounts, as well as from my own earlier work on African cultural survivals in Cuba.

Analyzing the sources: How do ideas of transculturation and mestizaje compare with the melting-pot metaphor in the United States?

Chapter 8

COLD WAR VISIONS

During the Cold War, the vision of the revolutionary left was thoroughly dominant among Latin American writers. Marxism had exercised a growing influence among the region's intellectuals and artists since the 1920s and 1930s, and their efforts were increasingly influential. After World War II, Latin American letters gained even more international recognition with a string of Nobel Prizes for Literature—Gabriela Mistral (1945), Miguel Angel Asturias (1967), Pablo Neruda (1971), Gabriel García Márquez (1982), Octavio Paz (1990)—representing political attitudes that ranged from Mistral's feminism and antiracism to Neruda's militant communism. Over all, the vision of the revolutionary left set the tone for poets, artists, folksingers, and culturally engaged university students throughout the region from the 1950s to the 1980s. The framework of the Cold War, viewed by both sides as a titanic struggle for the fate of the planet, intensified the anti-imperialist critique of US involvement in Latin America that had been developing since the early 1900s.

During the 1950s, the US government skimped on economic aid to Latin America and directed it preferentially to European countries where communist parties were gaining electoral popularity or where it was feared that they might do so. Encouraging Europe's economic recovery would dim the communist appeal there, hoped US policy makers. They were less concerned about Latin America, whose military establishments had become firmly allied with the United States and received substantial support in equipment and training. At the same time, both government and business leaders in the United States were determined, after World War II, to win back Latin American markets for the products of US industry, an initiative that conflicted with the region's efforts at import-substitution industrialization. Meanwhile, US-based multinational corporations rapidly expanded their operations in Latin America. The activities of such multinationals as United Fruit, Standard Oil, and the International Telephone and Telegraph Company were not generally perceived in Latin America as providing useful investment or developmental impetus but, to the contrary, as bleeding the region economically and controlling its destiny in the interest of foreign investors. Latin American writers thus echoed popular denunciations of US neglect or US meddling, both deemed inimical to the welfare of the region's poor majority. Meanwhile, wealthy Latin Americans became more closely connected with, and more strongly oriented toward, the United States than ever before.

This chapter explores Cold War visions by focusing principally on a single event, the overthrow of Guatemala's revolutionary government of 1944–54. Following decades of reactionary dictatorship, Guatemala had enjoyed ten years of popularly elected progressive government that advanced a series of not-very-radical projects, such as land reform to benefit the long-oppressed indigenous Mayans who made up roughly half the national population. To garner resources for these reforms, the government expropriated vast and underutilized landholdings of the United Fruit Company in Guatemala. Mexico's revolutionary leadership had carried out land reform and expropriated foreign companies in the 1930s without provoking dire social consequences or US intervention, of course, but in the context of the Cold War, and under the influence of "Red Scare" McCarthyism, the United States reacted differently to the Guatemalan "threat." While there were, in fact, no important connections between the Soviet Union and the Guatemalan government, US policy makers feared that revolutionary attitudes alone would produce a dangerous anti-US alignment and that, were the Guatemalan revolution to succeed, its example would be followed throughout the hemisphere. The 1954 intervention toppled the government of Guatemalan president Jacobo Arbenz with the collaboration of his own military. The intervention got widespread approval (to the degree that people paid any attention at all) in the United States. Within a few years, however, the revolutionary challenge was renewed, this time more durably and very influentially, in the Cuban Revolution of 1959.

The initial selections in this chapter set the stage, the eve of the Cold War, when the nationalism of Brazil's Getúlio Vargas and Argentina's Juan Perón dominated two of Latin America's largest nations. Not Marxist revolutionaries by any means, Vargas and Perón were populists who rallied the masses, established a special rapport with workers, and proclaimed their allegiance to the common people, the *povo* or *pueblo*. Evita Perón waved the populist banner even more vigorously than did her husband. Then come the sources on Guatemala, which exemplify the extreme polarization of Cold War visions, when Latin America was seen as a battleground in a geopolitical contest that would decide the fate of the world. The first is an example of US-style anticommunist discourse, dictated in Washington for broadcast in Guatemala during the 1954 intervention. The Guatemalan army officers who turned against the revolutionary government (and other strongly anticommunist Latin Americans, of whom there were many) surely identified with that discourse. Following that are two examples of the contrasting revolutionary leftist vision: one selection that portrays the Guatemalan land reform and the forces arrayed for and against it, and another that recounts the machinations of the intervention itself.

MESSAGE TO THE WORKERS

Getúlio Vargas

Getúlio Vargas of Brazil ranks among the great populist leaders of the twentieth century. He read this "Message to the Workers" on the first of May, the international labor day of the twentieth-century left, in 1947. At that moment, he had recently left office, having ruled Brazil as provisional president, elected president, and then dictator from 1930 to 1945. Vargas had developed a warm relationship with organized labor and, when forced to resign, he founded a political party for workers as he went out the door.

(This PTB became a forerunner of the PT, or Workers' Party, that ruled Brazil in 2015.) Labor unions were a rising influence in major Latin American countries in the post–World War II world, and rapport with workers characterized populism. Vargas gave speeches that were carefully crafted but rarely dramatic. Here he affirms his relationship with the workers, whom he treats as synonymous with the Brazilian people, o Povo, in Portuguese, as a whole. Vargas was able to reactivate this relationship a few years later by being reelected president.

Workers of Brazil!

Every year, on this day dedicated to the People, it has been my custom to address you in a perfect harmony of ideas and sentiments. My government and the workers fraternized effortlessly, bound together by constructive energies flowing from our common purpose. The workers saw themselves differently, no longer as opponents, but rather, as part of the power structure.

The first of May was an occasion, then, to commemorate the legal gains of organized labor and to build the social conscience of our People, affirming their rightful aspirations for continued advancement. My administration strove constantly to build the social consciousness of workers, encouraging them to study public issues. The workers became aware of how we were promoting social equilibrium. We encouraged suggestions about how to eliminate inequities of social class.

How unlike the behavior of our political adversaries, who promised that they would benefit the People without saying how, as they could wave some sort of magic wand to make things better! Now that they're in office, they see that I didn't invent the problems with which I had to deal. And still, they devote their energies, not to governing, not to resolving those difficulties, but to destroying what I built. The predictable result is that progress has been reversed on

SOURCE: Getúlio Vargas, "Mensagem aos Trabalhadores lida a 1.o de maio de 1947 ao microfone da Rádio Mayrink Veiga, do Rio de Janeiro," in *A política trabalhista no Brasil* (São Paulo: José Olympio Editora, 1950), pp. 187–89.

many fronts. Now we are facing a rise in the cost of living that effects society as a whole, and they threaten to control it in ways that will increase unemployment. Now the workers feel menaced, disheartened, neutralized. Everyone can see the emptiness and sterility of our adversaries' political posturing. Everyone suffers from the flip-flopping policies that have only one overall goal: to conceal their true purpose, which is to bilk the workers.

Brazilian workers never had political allies in power before my administration. No wonder they were happy with a government that listened to them, put social issues at the center of its program, and acted as referee for fair industrial relations, in which labor had both rights and responsibilities.

Today, the world agrees in placing the first of May among the most significant annual holidays. It is the day that commemorates the workers' struggle for social equality. We commemorate what has been accomplished so far, and we resolve to advance further toward the goal. To do so, the working class must stick together. Workers need a powerful party for the overall good, the progress and unity, of the Brazilian national family. The Brazilian Workers' Party is the political arm of the working class. Never doubt it.

Nor can we lose, in the long run. The desire for social equality has become firmly established in the spirit of our People. This struggle can never be in vain. In the future, society will not be divided between rich and poor, powerful and humble. We will understand one another and work together to achieve our common happiness. Then the first of May will become a different sort of holiday, no longer about class struggle and worker aspirations, but about brotherhood across classes, an exaltation of social equality and unity.

Workers of Brazil! I close by reaffirming my confidence in your ultimate triumph. Fear not, for your destiny is the destiny of Brazil.

Analyzing the Sources: What are the major goals of this speech, and how are they achieved without ever being explicitly stated?

HISTORY OF PERONISM

Eva Duarte de Perón

Evita, the world-famous second wife and political partner of Argentine president Juan Perón, taught a short course on the History of Peronism at the regime's Peronist School for Advanced Studies in 1951. Her course was a rambling collection of ideas gleaned mostly from her own experience at her husband's side, addressed to an audience of true believers and Peronist militants. They illustrate the powerful populist emphasis on the idea of a somehow unanimous and unified common people, el Pueblo. As with the radio message of Getúlio Vargas, Evita Perón's lessons also point to the populist idea of a mystic unity between the Pueblo and an idolized, charismatic Leader. Here, though, she is not addressing the common people, but rather, a party cadre. Her "lessons" to them suggest that the reality of Peronist politics fell considerably short of the ideal of selflessness.

EXTRACTS FROM CLASS FIVE
"THE PEOPLE VS. THE SPIRIT OF OLIGARCHY"

In earlier classes I spoke of world history and of its two key elements: on the one hand, masses of people waiting for great leaders to meld them together into one People, united and self-aware; on the other hand, those great leaders, men like our General Perón. In today's class, we focus on Argentina, specifically on Peronism and its connection to the common People.

The connection is essential. In an earlier class I pointed out that the Argentine people, the workers, are extraordinarily content precisely because Perón has brought them security. Now they don't worry about the future. When I was recently in Europe I sensed fear among the common people of France and Italy. They are great centers of civilization but the people there face an insecure future.

SOURCE: Eva Duarte de Perón, *Discursos completos* (Buenos Aires: Editorial Megafón, 1985), pp. 3:52, 71–91 (extracts).

That's why, when I walked through the streets of both countries, everyone shouted, "We'd rather be in Argentina with Perón!" Perón is all about the People.

In fact, the best way to know who's a true Peronist, and who isn't one, the best way to identify traitors in our ranks, is to look at their relationship to the People. Do they consider themselves part of the People? Do they loyally serve the People's best interest, or are they attending mostly to their own personal ambitions? To free themselves totally from lingering traces of the oligarchic spirit, good Peronists must learn to love the People just as they love Perón, and they must base their actions on spiritual values, on the disposition to self-sacrifice for the good of the collective, not just in appearance but in deep conviction, not just in words, but in deeds.

I have closely studied the biographies of the world's great men, as some of you may have done as well. We learn from history that every great man has some flaw, perhaps a fatal one, but we normally pardon their flaws because of their transcendent genius. Perón is the exception, however, a genius without any flaw at all, or if he had to have a flaw, it would be this one: that his heart is just too big, the most sublime of defects, in other words, the flaw of Christ who pardoned even those who crucified him. We should all meditate on the greatness and virtues of General Perón, and above all, on his humility, which makes him greater still.

Perón says it and I say it: Argentina doesn't want and doesn't need more than one class of men. The authentic working people of this country are *the* People in Perón's eyes, and mine. And what an enormous contrast between this new ruling class and the old oligarchy!

The oligarchy was a closed caste, a club that accepted no new members. They more or less owned the government, as if nobody but an oligarch were capable of ruling. They displayed in all ways the oligarchic spirit, prideful, vain, and selfish. Eventually, the oligarchs were ready to sell Argentina to the highest bidder, just to keep a semblance of their precious wealth and power.

Now we want only one class of Argentines. Of course we want people to get rich, and become intellectuals. It's good to strive to be superior. That's the great thing about Peronism. It allows all

Argentines to achieve their dreams, even if it's to become president of the Republic. The proof? Today we've got workers all over the government—workers in the legislature, workers in the ministries, a worker attaché in our embassies—everywhere.

In terms of culture, we've got worker theaters and even art galleries, though we've got a lot more to do, in that regard, before General Perón will be satisfied. Thanks to Perón, our universities, once reserved for a privileged few, are now open to the People. The children of workers can now become doctors and lawyers if they possess the inclination and the talent.

I can boil down everything that I'm trying to say to this. Peronism is above all a victory over the selfish spirit of oligarchy. The greatest danger to Peronism occurs when the oligarchic spirit infects Peronist hearts. Forgive me for emphasizing that point so much. It is really fundamental for our movement. Remember: A Peronist never says "I." A Peronist always says "we."

The doctrine of Perón is pure brilliance. The faults in our movement lie in ourselves. Unlike the general, we are made of common clay. But we can and must strive each day to become better and more worthy of the name Argentines. And we can do that by becoming better preachers of Peronist doctrine, and not merely preachers. We must practice what we preach, realizing that each of us, individually, is nothing. The People, and Perón, are everything.

Analyzing the Sources: A subtle reading of this document strongly suggests an ongoing problem in the Peronist movement. What is it?

DECLASSIFIED MESSAGE

Central Intelligence Agency

This secret communication was sent to CIA operatives in Guatemala by their superiors in the United States on June 18, 1954, as part of the planning for the US-sponsored overthrow of President Arbenz. It begins with instructions on how to translate the text and broadcast it on the radio, claiming without any basis in fact to be a message from an antigovernment "National Liberation Committee," supposedly in consultation with a (nonexistent) antigovernment Assembly of the Guatemalan People. The text to be translated begins with point two. It is written in a "telegraphic" style that omits many words such as prepositions and articles, some of which have been supplied in brackets at the beginning to facilitate comprehension by readers unfamiliar with that style.

1. D DAY TODAY, 18 JUN. H HOUR 20:20. BROADCAST AT 20:20 FOLLOWING OPENING APPEAL WITH MAXIMUM IMPASSIONED INSISTENCE, INTRODUCE [with] FANFARES, CLOSE [with] NATIONAL ANTHEM. USE LIVE VOICE, MAKE ANY LAST MINUTE FACTUAL CHANGES IN [the] TEXT WHICH SUBSEQUENT INFO MAY NECESSITATE, BUT DO NOT DEVIATE FROM POLICY LINE BELOW. ELABORATE AS NEEDED, BUT DON'T MAKE TOO LONG, REPEAT [at] HOURLY INTERVALS.

2. (BEGIN TEXT) NATIONAL LIBERATION COMMITTEE COMPOSED [of] REPRESENTATIVES [of] ALL GROUPS OPPOSING COMMUNISM, ARBENZISM, DEFENDING CONSTITUTION AND PEOPLE'S LIBERTIES, HAS CONSULTED LAST NIGHT WITH THE ASSEMBLY OF THE PEOPLE, SECRETLY CONVENED NOT FAR FROM [the] CAPITAL TO REPLACE CONGRESS WHICH HAS OUTLAWED ITSELF. AFTER MATURE DELIBERATION, [the] FOLLOWING APPEAL TO [the] PEOPLE [was] ADOPTED.

3. AT THIS MOMENT, ARMED GROUPS OF OUR LIBERATION MOVEMENT ARE ADVANCING EVERYWHERE THROUGHOUT THE COUNTRY. WE ARE STILL HOPING

SOURCE: Central Intelligence Agency, "Cable to Director from Lincoln re Guatemalan Coup, 6/18/54" (Declassified document), www.foia.cia.gov/browse_docs.asp?doc_no=0000921724.

THAT FAST, DECISIVE ACTION BY OUR LOYAL ARMY, DEPOSING OUTLAW ARBENZ AND HIS MOSCOW-CONTOLLED REGIME, WILL PREVENT MORE BLOOD-SHED. BUT THERE CAN BE NO MORE DELAY, NO MORE FENCE SITTING, NO MORE WISHFUL WAITING. THE HOUR OF DECISION HAS STRUCK.

4. WE, REPRESENTING ALL GROUPS OF THE NON-COMMUNIST POPULATION, DO SOLEMNLY DECLARE: THIS IS NOT A FOREIGN INTERVENTION, BUT AN UPRISING OF THE HONEST, CHRISTIAN, FREEDOM-LOVING PEOPLE OF GUAT TO LIBERATE OUR HOME-LAND FROM THE FOREIGN INTERVENTION WHICH HAS ALREADY TAKEN PLACE, FROM CONTROL BY THE SOVIET UNION WHICH HAS MADE GUAT AN ADVANCED OUTPOST OF INTERNATIONAL COMMIE* AGGRES-SION, FROM RULE BY SOVIET PUPPETS ARBENZ, TORI-ELLO, FANJUL, FROM TERROR, MASS ARRESTS, TORTURES, EXERCISED BY COMMIE AGENTS JAIME ROSENBERG, CRUZWER, AND OTHERS.

5. YOU ALL HAD DURING LAST FEW WEEKS AMPLE FORE-TASTE [of] COMMIE DICTATORSHIP, ABOLITION [of] CONSTITUTIONAL LIBERTIES, ARRESTS [of] THOU-SANDS [of] NON-COMMUNISTS, ARRIVAL [of] SOVIET ARMS SHIPMENTS, COMMIE MILITARY INSTRUCTORS, RUSSIAN SECRET POLICE OFFICERS. WE MUST PUT END TO ALL THIS TODAY, MUST SETTLE ACCOUNTS WITH THOSE RESPONSIBLE FOR THIS SITUATION TODAY OR OUR COUNTRY WILL BECOME BATTLE-FIELD FOR WARS AND CIVIL WARS PRESCRIBED BY MOSCOW, WHICH SEEKS ANOTHER KOREA IN CEN-TRAL AMERICA. OUR EXPORT CROPS WILL HELP RUS-SIAN PEOPLE WHO ARE UNDERFED BECAUSE OF

---

*Cold-war slang for *communist*.

DISASTROUS FAILURE [of] COMMIE AGRARIAN REFORM IN RUSSIA AND EVERYWHERE. OUR PROUD, BEAUTIFUL COUNTRY WILL BE SUBMERGED IN DISASTER.

6. HEED OUR INSTRUCTIONS COMING FROM THE NATIONAL LIBERATION COMMITTEE AND FROM THE ASSEMBLY OF THE PEOPLE:

A. ARMY TO TAKE ARBENZ, MEMBERS OF CABINET, OTHER LEADING OFFICIALS INTO CUSTODY, OCCUPY KEY GOVERNMENT BUILDINGS, SEIZE PGT, CGTG, CNCG** HEADQUARTERS, ARREST ALL COMMIE LEADERS, CONFISCATE WEAPONS IN HANDS OF COMMIE GROUPS.

B. POLICE TO RID ITSELF OF COMMIE CHIEFS ROSENBERG, CRUZWER, OTHERS, RELEASE ALL POLITICAL PRISONERS, PLACE ITSELF TEMPORARILY UNDER ARMY ORDERS OR SUFFER FATE OF COMMIE AGENTS.

C. WORKERS, PEASANTS: JOIN LIBERATION MOVEMENT WITH THE WEAPONS COMMIE LEADERS GAVE YOU. DO NOT PARTICIPATE IN ANY COMMIE-ORDERED STRIKES, PARADES, OTHER MOVES. DISPOSE OF COMMIE UNION LEADERS AND THEIR DUPES, NOT THE LOYAL REGULAR ARMY.

D. CIVILIAN GOVT EMPLOYEES: DISREGARD ANY UNLAWFUL ORDERS FROM ARBENZ REGIME, REPORT ANY SUSPICIONS TO NEAREST ARMY COMMANDER, LOCAL LIBERATION COMMITTEE. STAY ON YOUR JOBS, BUT WAIT FOR RE-ESTABLISHMENT [of] LAWFUL GOVT.

E. NEWSPAPERS, RADIO STATIONS: REFUSE IMMEDIATELY PUBLISHING ARBENZ REGIME PROPAGANDA. DISCONTINUE PUBLICATION, BROADCASTS, UNTIL

**Labor organizations.

ILLEGAL COMMIE CENSORSHIP WIPED OUT BY LIBERATION.

F. POPULATION AT LARGE: JOIN IMMEDIATELY ARMED FORCES OF LIBERATION MOVEMENT. HELP YOURSELF TO COMMIE-ISSUED ARMS OR ARMS CACHES. WOMEN, OLD AND SICK MEN, CHILDREN TO STAY CLOSE TO HOME. OBSERVE, REPORT ALL SUSPICIOUS MOVES, EXPOSE COMMIE LEADERS TRYING TO SNEAK OUTSIDE COUNTRY, PREVENT POLICE FROM MURDERING POLITICAL PRISONERS BY KEEPING JAILS, POLICE STATIONS UNDER MASS SURVEILLANCE.

G. EVERYBODY CONTINUE [to] LISTEN [to] VOICE [of] LIBERATION.

7. IF WE ALL, SOLDIERS AND CIVILIANS, ACT IMMEDIATELY, WITH DETERMINATION, COURAGE AND DISCIPLINE, WE SHALL SOON SUCCEED IN WIPING MOSCOW'S SHADOW OFF THE BLUE SKY OVER OUR BELOVED HOMELAND, RESTORE OUR CONSTITUTIONAL LIBERTIES, REESTABLISH GOOD, SINCERE RELATIONS WITH ALL NEIGHBORING COUNTRIES, BUILD A TRULY DEMOCRATIC ORDER WHICH WILL PREVENT FUTURE COMMUNIST CONSPIRACIES, BUT ALSO ANY RETURN TO REACTIONARY DICTATORSHIPS. BUILD AN ORDER BASED ON THE PRECEPTS OF CHRISTIANITY, POPULAR SELF-GOVERNMENT, EQUAL POLITICAL AND ECONOMIC OPPORTUNITY FOR ALL, REGARDLESS OF COLOR, RACE, OR SOCIAL STATUS, AND ON PEACEFUL COOPERATION BETWEEN ALL NATIONS, BIG OR SMALL, ON BASIS OF EQUALITY.

8. NONE OF YOU IS ALLOWED TO ABSENT HIMSELF FROM THE STRUGGLE FOR THESE IDEALS, FROM THE FINAL BATTLE AGAINST THE FORCES OF DARKNESS, COMMUNIST CONSPIRACY, AND SOVIET RUSSIAN IMPERIALIST EXPANSION UPON OUR SOIL. DEATH TO ARBENZ AND

HIS COMMIE ADVISORS! FORWARD FOR GOD, FATHER-
LAND, AND LIBERTY!

Analyzing the Sources: Why does the CIA-*authored broadcast so
emphatically deny its true origin?*

WEEKEND IN GUATEMALA
Miguel Angel Asturias

*In the immediate aftermath of the 1954 US intervention, Guatemalan
Nobel laureate Miguel Angel Asturias (1899–1974) wrote a collection of
short stories,* Weekend in Guatemala, *that was rushed into publication
outside Guatemala in 1956. A good example of the revolutionary vision
that diametrically opposed the anticommunist vision of the US government, the book is dedicated as follows:*

TO GUATEMALA, *my Country,*
Alive in the blood of its student heroes,
Its peasant martyrs,
Its slaughtered workers,
Its struggling People.

*The collection begins with a title story narrated by a caricatured US
sergeant who brags of his exploits during a "weekend (intervention) in
Guatemala." A second story features an English-speaking tour guide who
has taken US citizenship. He is almost killed by US bombing during the
intervention and, disillusioned by the indiscriminate violence of US-hired
mercenaries brought from other Central American countries, goes mad
with self-hatred. A third story translated here in its entirety, displays the
indigenismo for which Asturias is best known. The story is set in the
Guatemalan highlands on the eve of intervention, when the revolutionary
government is carrying out its policy of land reform.*

La Galla

High on the mountain, a matasano tree swayed in the wind and spread its branches over a green hollow. The color of the matasano leaves, matasano green, a sort of ashen yellow-green, contrasted with the unchanging, emerald green of the hollow below. Beginning with those two colors, the eyes of Diego Hun Ig began to count the the eleven other greens of that place, the Grandmother of Waters, until he had observed all thirteen shades necessary to complete his happiness that morning. Diego Hun Ig, leader of the Great Brotherhood, was on his way down to meet with the council of the brotherhood, where the Councilor of the village would explain about the land reform. And that is how and why the Councilor and Diego Hun Ig met that day under the covered walkway of the village hall.

They saw one another, approached one another, greeted one another. Simultaneously, they took off their white hats and exposed their jet black hair. They extended their hands and touched them together in what seemed more a priestly gesture than a handshake. Following the greeting, the Councilor turned and moved along the walkway, bathed at that hour by the slanting rays of the morning sun, toward the meeting room, and Diego Hun Ig followed him. There was little furniture in the meeting room, only wooden benches along the walls and, at the center of the far end, a single table and heavy chair. Nothing more. The sandals of the Councilor and his visitor echoed on the stone floor.

In a corner of the room, in the semidarkness fragrant with the smell of mahogany from the big exposed beams supporting the roof of the structure, each man ceremoniously took his seat on the end of a long bench. Then they spoke of the matter at hand.

"Land reform . . . ," said the Councilor. From inside his shirt, he drew a bound notebook no larger than those which one uses to intone the devotions due to Catholic saints, and extended it to Diego Hun Ig, who accepted it respectfully and raised it to his forehead

Source: Miguel Angel Asturias, "La galla," from *Week-end en Guatemala* (Buenos Aires: Editorial Goyanarte, 1956), pp. 95–107.

as a sign that it would enter his mind, then to his chest, as a sign that it would enter his heart.

The enormous drums echoed all that afternoon and all that night in the doorway of the assembly house of the Great Brotherhood. The incessant thunder of the enormous drums called all the members of the brotherhood—all the men, young and old, all the women, all the children—to assemble on the morning of the following day, a Saturday. It had been a very long time since the last such call. An atmosphere of gathering storm accumulated, moment by moment, with the thunder of the drums. The afternoon came, icy chill. But the crowds—who swept the patio of the assembly house of the Great Brotherhood with wide bunches of tree roots, then sprinkled it with water to control the dust, and covered it with leaves and flowers—were hardly aware of the cold or the setting of the sun. Meanwhile, Diego Hun Ig and the other elders, Procopio Cay, Circuncisión Tulul, Julián Aceituno, Santos Chavar, and Pedro Roca, placed the insignias of the brotherhood on an altar composed of green branches.

There were nine principle insignias. Atop a wooden staff, a large silver disk with the image of Santiago Matamoros on one side, and on the other, the letters J-H-S, signifying Jesus Christ. Diego Hun Ig would hold this staff during the ceremony. The other shining insignias comprised a series of lesser silver disks. Some had borders of tiny bells that tinkled when they were moved. Some were surrounded with projecting solar rays. Some had crosses emerging from the top. Once the insignias had been placed on the altar and candles lit before them, Diego bent his knee and crossed himself, followed by the others, who did the same.

Now it was night. The village, poorly lit by a moon that could not quite get out from behind the clouds, lay deserted, empty, throbbing with drums.

The drums echoed loudly in the tiny general store that people called "the store of doña Bernardina Coatepeque" because the owner was a native of Coatepeque, although everyone referred to her as "La Galla" because her feistiness resembled that of a fighting cock. The owner paced back and forth without attending the customers who had entered to make small purchases of this and that. The drums were driving her crazy.

"Those damned Indians of the brotherhood . . . bunch of savage beasts . . . are going to keep us up all night again! Who can sleep a wink with that noise . . . and no government to put the quietus on them. . . . What do you want girl?" She turned to one of the customers.

"Five-cents' worth of incense."

"Incense . . . what for?"

"To burn . . ."

"I know it's to burn . . . what I'm asking is . . . God in heaven, those drums are going to make me puke. Damned Indians! What I'm asking is why are you going to burn incense?"

"Because today is the last day of the novena of the Dulce Nombre. . . ."

"And you, missus, what do you want?"

"Twenty-five pounds of flour . . ."

"And you?"

"One of those machetes . . ."

"Why do you want a machete?"

"To have one . . ."

"Good Lord, Good Lord, those drums!"

A hoarse voice issued from the mysterious spice-scented darkness in the shadowy recesses behind the counter of the store: "You might as well close up, Bernardina. That way it won't be so loud, and for what you're selling it's not worth staying open anyway. . . ."

"You might as well close," answered La Galla in irritation. "Get off your tail and do it yourself. . . ."

A bony man with a hat, a big moustache, and a half-smoked cigarette in his mouth raised himself from a bench, half-closed the double door, and stood waiting for the last customers to leave before closing the other half of the door and barring both halves with a plank.

The resounding drums were immediately muffled. In the dim light, the cat awoke, arose, walked over to its dish—which, though smelling of milk, lay empty, washed, and ready for the morning ration of milk. In disgust, it leapt away between the stacks of straw hats that stood in a row on a table beside the door.

"I'm going to see what we did today," said La Galla, "and then we'll have supper."

From underneath the counter she extracted the drawer that contained all the profits, in coins and bills, from that day's sales, along with a pencil and a notebook, in which she proceeded to do the accounts.

"I know why you can't stand the sound of those drums."

"You know everything, don't you? . . . Let me do the accounts."

"It gets on your nerves. . . ."

"Leave me alone or get out of here. I don't need hassles in my own house."

"It gets on your nerves."

La Galla clutched the braided leather whip that she always wore at her waist and struck the counter with it, where it lay like a dead snake.

"Shut up, I said!"

The bony man looked sideways at the menacing whip, then shrugged in protest without saying anything further, went to one of the shelves, and helped himself to a bottle of beer.

"That's better, right. Go ahead and drink all the beer in town, and don't bother me with bad memories."

The bony man did not respond. He had gone through the door that led into the house behind the store and into the dining room, where he was drinking his beer with his head hunched sullenly between his shoulders.

La Galla's voice could be heard from the store.

"Hey, Freckles . . . I was rude because these damned Indians and their drums are driving me crazy, okay?"

"Rude! You threatened me with that whip that I don't know why you have to wear at your waist all the time . . . and I do know why . . . because it was what your father liked to beat the daylights out of the Indians with."

La Galla burst through the door, whip in hand.

"Shut up or you'll be sorry."

"I'll shut up, but the drums won't. . . ."

"What did you say?"

"That I'll shut up. . . ."

"Let's see what the cook left me," said La Galla. "They take work as cooks and can't scramble an egg . . . and you read the newspaper. Do something useful. I pay for that subscription, and I've never seen you read it."

"Freckles" extracted a newspaper from a sleeve bearing his real name, Luis Marcos, and moved closer to a lamp.

"Bernardina," he said loudly, the moment that he laid eyes on the paper. "No wonder they are drumming. Listen to this." And he read: "Land Reform Law. Property to be distributed tomorrow to the Indians of the Great Brotherhood . . ."

"Steamed potatoes are what she left, with parsley. Do you like parsley, by any chance? And fruit salad, but without bitter orange, so it's as bland as can be. What did you say about the newspaper?"

"It says property to be distributed tomorrow to the Indians of the Great Brotherhood."

"How awful to take land away from the rightful owners to give it to those Indians! I was hungry, and now . . . pass me the bread . . . no, no, I can't swallow it," she said nibbling a bit of fruit salad. "The sound of those drums will make it stick in my throat. You eat, and excuse me for not keeping you company. . . ."

Of moderate height and weight, La Galla normally walked with feminine grace, but now she dragged herself toward her bedroom like a prisoner condemned to death and not fully in control of her body. Cold tears on her cheeks, her lips not quite closed, sobbing, she threw herself headfirst on the bed. The drums would not let her sleep. They rumbled just as loudly in the distance, it seemed, as in the doorway of the Great Brotherhood.

Just the way they had sounded all night on the eve of the Indian uprising in which her father was killed. Her father, a personal friend of the president of the Republic, had been all-powerful in the locality, much feared and hated among the Indians. "Shepherd boys" was his term for the Indians, because the young ones watched over his flocks. He more or less owned them, and when they grew up, he "sold" them to the other owners of nearby coffee haciendas or banana plantations on the coast.

Luis Marcos folded the newspaper, or rather, half-folded it, and left it on the table. He lacked, not exactly the strength, but the willpower, for certain things. He flattened the paper with a thump of his fist. That's the way the drums had rumbled on and on, he thought, as he stretched, got up, and went into the store to get another beer. The store was dimly lit by a single candle that flickered in front of a saint's image.

That's the way the drums had rumbled on and on when they killed the old man, or rather, when his secretary Rafael Procol put him out of his misery with a bullet so that the Indians wouldn't kill *him*, as well. A treacherous favor. But if Procol had not shot the old man down point-blank at that moment, the Indians would have cut both of their throats. As it was, when the Indians finally got to them, they found the old man stretched out on the ground and let Procol live.

Poor Galla, thought Marcos, running his tongue over the beer foam on his lips. That's the way she grew up, and she just can't get used to treating the Indians like people. The idea revolts her, makes her blood boil. Her father, who has a terrible hold over her even now, had a kind of dungeon at his plantation on the coast, with stocks to put the Indians in if they got uppity. And his accounts were crooked as a corkscrew! He never paid the workers what he really owed them. Indians who started to work on the old man's plantations could never leave because the more they worked, the more indebted they got. And when they died, their children inherited the debt and had to stay on the plantation. . . .

Diego Hun Ig paused in the door of his hut to tell his wife that he would be back after midnight, and then he went like a nocturnal bird along fences and across fields to the Quebrada de Melgarejo, home of Tucuche, the eldest elder of the locality. Hun Ig took the old man coffee, bread, and a piece of hard cheese bundled in a handkerchief. Tucuche was pleased. He motioned his visitor to sit on the ground, and then sat there himself like a stone idol.

"Consider, father, that the whites are going to give us land," said Diego, after bowing his head deeply. "How can we know if their offer is for good or ill? One must always take care in dealing with *them*."

Tucuche's eyelids lowered over his milky, ancient eyes, and he sat for a long time, breathing deeply, a dancing whirl of wasps inside his head, his hands—dark spiders of bone and hide—resting on the ground, to either side.

"Do you consider it for good or evil, father?"

"It is not an evil thing, Diego Hun Ig. But evil will come with it. The time is not ripe for the land to return to our hands. We must wait more years before the return of Big Feathers. Nine times I have been within the wheel of the moon, and nothing indicated this offer of lands to be the will of Big Feathers. I already knew, yes. I knew about it all."

"What will be the evil, father?" implored Diego with an anguished voice.

"More whites will come. There will be new struggles and new tributes. And great suffering."

Very far away, like waves pounding on a distant beach, the echo of drumming could be heard.

"Whites?"

"Yes, with demands and more demands. There will be a . . . very strange war. Unseen enemies, enemies we will never know, will rain death upon us. Those who understand will say nothing. To take away the lands, war will come against us from the sky, and we will never understand the reason, Diego. It will be a secret and a mystery."

"Father, father . . ."

"Many of our leaders will bow their heads and allow the whites to take our people and our money in tribute once again."

The midnight wind blew in his ears like the cold and leathery wings of a bat as Diego Hun Ig made his way home, stumbling at every instant in the dark, unable to find where to put his feet. The drums swelled the heart of the sky, the immensity of the night, within the circle of the mountains that surrounded his town with their emerald walls.

It was unthinkable for a *principal* of the Great Brotherhood to tell anyone of the secrets confided to him by the eldest elder of the town, and dawn was a long time coming for Diego. His wife had left him food: six tortillas above the dying embers of the fire, a jar of coffee nestled in the ashes, and a piece of dried meat on a plate nearby. He did not eat when he got home after midnight, but he got hungry before dawn. The food was cold by then, and his teeth colder. Around him everything was cold, cold and damp. He thrust his hand into the ashes, so much did he want a glove, and his eyes observed that the remaining, tiny embers spilled between his fingers like rubies without burning him. He thought it odd.

The sound of drums continued. The steady, sleepy rhythm made him think for a moment that the sun might never rise, and that everything—stars, waters, hearts—might simply stop, suspended in time. The sleeping birds might never awaken to greet the rising sun, and everything, for a time, a time of innumerable years, might simply stop. Only old Tucuche would continue to breathe and await the Plumed One, the Bejeweled Lord of Green Feathers, who would finally descend to return the lands to them—finally, and this time, truly.

The ceremony was a simple one. The principal leaders of the Great Brotherhood, with their insignias and crosses, went out to receive the government commission that had come to distribute lands. At the head of the group walked Diego Hun Ig with his round silver sun on its silver staff, flanked by other principals. They practically had to push their way out through the crowd around the door of the assembly house of the brotherhood. Everybody wanted to see— young men and old men, women and children. Everybody wanted to see what the famous "distribution" would be like.

The members of the brotherhood formed a line to receive a piece of paper giving them title to a parcel of land. Some tried to kiss the hands that extended the title, but the commissioners withdrew their hands and would not allow it. They explained that they were doing no more than carrying out the program of the Revolution. Luis Marcos had run his sleepy sick-man's eyes over the ceremony without getting very close to it because he did not like the smell of Indians, and being in a crowd of them made him feel that he was drowning. He climbed on a pile of earth and stones at a construction site in front of the assembly house of the brotherhood to watch the ceremony.

Diego Hun Ig and the chief commissioner stood front-and-center with the other principals arrayed on either side. In front of them was a table covered with the national flag. Each Indian filed past to receive his title, and the commissioner gave a speech with so many and such dramatic gestures that the speech seemed to issue more from his sleeves than his mouth. Diego answered him briefly. Then the drums started again, the Indians played marimbas and fired rockets that exploded high in the air, and a military band played.

"Shall we play the national anthem?" the bandleader came to ask.

"No," replied the commissioner. "Play the anthem when we go to the lands being distributed at the moment when each of the new property owners occupies his parcel."

And that was what they did. The parcels had already been marked, and each Indian family went to stand on its new property, each family in sight of the next. The groups of property-owning parents, surrounded by their children and grandchildren, all dressed in their bright clothing, their faces shining with happiness, formed multicolored splotches on the green mountainside, some of them large and nearby, some tiny and far away. From a distance one could count hundreds and, eventually, thousands of them, and when all were in place, they sang the Guatemalan national anthem with one voice, not like poor and disinherited Indians, but like people with their feet on their own ground.

Months later, La Galla got a visit from one of her old schoolmates, whom she was astonished to see. They understood each other immediately, however. A simple comment about the "difficult situation" was all it took for them to know each other's mind and agree. La Galla's task would be merely to write down the names of all the local communists on a piece of paper.

"Are there a lot of them, Bérnar?" asked Bernardina's visitor, with her best long-toothed smile, remembering the high-school nickname.

"Everybody in the Great Brotherhood, how's that for trivia?"

"But brotherhoods like that are a church affair, dedicated to devotion of a patron saint or the Virgin. . . ."

"Right, it's the Brotherhood of Santo Domingo. They're the ones who got the land that was distributed around here. They call it the Great Brotherhood."

"They have infiltrated everything. But they're not going to enjoy things for long because our plans are already in place, and that's why, remembering how your daddy died, I came to talk to you. Our people are making lists of communists for every locality, so that not a single one escapes."

When her visitor left, La Galla's eyes got hard. Amid her soft features, those two dark coins fixed their gaze on a single point, never wandering.

Luis Marcos entered with a young man who carried a large camera and said he was a journalist.

"He's the son of a friend of mine," explained Marcos, and turning to the journalist, he added: "I worked with your father on the boundary-survey commission. That's where I got this cold that never goes away. . . ." He coughed. "And how's your father?"

"Father died three years ago."

"I didn't know. You can't imagine how sorry I am. We were such good friends."

"Is he going to interview somebody?" said La Galla, prompt and curious. "Who's he going to interview, unless it's the Indians?"

"It's the Indians that I'm coming to interview," said the journalist, looking at the tip of his shoe, as he frequently did when speaking.

And, accompanied by Marcos, he marched off in search of the head of the Great Brotherhood, Diego Hun Ig.

They called from the gate in front of the house, through the ample fenced-in yard shaded with fruit trees, asking if the owner were at home. A small woman's form appeared, Hun Ig's daughter. She quickly covered her face behind her hands. They asked for Diego's whereabouts.

"He is home," answered the girl uncertainly.

"Then run tell him a man's here to see him. . . ."

"I'll tell him," she said and vanished.

Then the figure of the principal appeared, his hair combed with pomade, his shirt very clean, his calf-length pants embroidered, his sandals new.

He approached and said hello to Marcos. They told him that the journalist was going to interview him. They had to explain what that meant: "ask a few questions."

"He's not with the police?" objected Diego.

"What a brute!" said Marcos. "A newspaper reporter, you know, the kind that writes for the newspapers? Understand?"

"I understand," he said, and addressed the younger man: "And what do you want to ask?"

"Let us inside first," said Marcos.

"Doesn't matter," said the journalist, who had not spoken until then. "The interview has more character this way." He could just imagine: communist leader interviewed, an exclusive for *Visiones* magazine, international edition.

"If you would like, of course you can come in," said Diego stepping out of the doorway.

"No, no, I don't want to bother you. Just two or three questions. Are you a communist?"

Diego did not know the word. His daughter, bringing with her the fragrance of verbena, came to stand at his side, and six other children of a variety of sizes also appeared to surround their father.

"What's that mean?" It was Diego's turn to ask.

"It's uh . . . free love, having a lot of women," Marcos explained, "and turning over your children to the state."

"I've got just one woman and these children," said Diego, confusing a Spanish gender distinction in even so simple an utterance. "The big ones go to school, and I'm going to send all of them so that all will learn."

"That's it, communism," clarified Marcos. "You want to turn your children over to the state."

"Well, I don't know, but I want to send them to school to learn to read."

"Tell me, please," said the journalist, "if, now that your brotherhood has received land, you plan to buy a tractor and other equipment and build a silo."

"Yes, sir, that's just what we want to do."

"Fine," chortled the freckle-faced Marcos, "that's just fine."

"Write this down," said the Indian, with a different attitude. "Now that we're all property owners with land of our own, we're going to get rich and have money."

"Just one more question. Is what you have just yours or does it belong to everybody?"

Diego answered instantly:

"Mine, just mine. Everybody's got their own. Now, what's going to be everybody's is the image of our patron saint, Santo Domingo, which the brotherhood commissioned three months ago."

"And the tractor and the silo?"

"All that will belong to everybody, too, sure, like the image of Santo Domingo. Everybody will contribute, sure."

"There you go," said Marcos. "Communism comes from the idea of community ownership."

"Whatever it is, the land belongs to individual families. The land that they gave me is mine and only mine and nobody is going to take it away from me. That's why they gave it to me."

And it was in that very spot that the guns later cut down Diego Hun Ig. A time of great suffering for the Indians. La Galla, with the support of Luis Marcos, not only supplied a list of all the supposed communists in the locality, but also gave the mercenary invaders a guided tour, pointing out houses. In the meeting house of the Great Brotherhood the invaders set up a sort of tribunal chaired by La Galla, and the henchmen that arrived from far away blindly obeyed her orders to cleanse the village and the surrounding countryside.

After the first day of killing members of the brotherhood, La Galla collapsed on her bed without taking off her scarf or removing the combs that adorned her hair, without turning on the light, and in the dark she said to Luis Marcos, who stood at the door, locking it:

"Let them try to play their drums . . . now . . . the drums . . . can shut up. I order it."

Marcos did not reply. He stood there in the dark not knowing whether to turn on the light, unsettled by the tone of her voice, which was unusual, anguished, and violent.

Each of them turned toward the other in the dark, two fluttering shadows.

"The drum," shouted La Galla. "The drum! Are you hearing it?"

He heard nothing but did not say so.

"Go tell those damned Indians to make less noise! Orders of La Galla, Bernardina Coatepeque. Kill the owners of those drums. Are you listening to me?"

"I'll go . . ."

"Me, too . . ."

He went out, with La Galla right behind him, her face transformed by visions, raising her skirt to her knees as if she were wading through a shallow river, screaming for the drums to stop. The village smelled of gunpowder and blood. Only the two of them were in the street. The bodies of a number of Indians still lay unburied. They tripped over them.

Then a sound of drums made "Freckles" think that he, too, was losing his mind. They were in the town square, not far from the door of the meeting house of the Great Brotherhood, when he heard drums, huge, enormous drums in the sky, rumbling through the clouds.

Quickly he realized that they were airplanes. He tried to hold on to La Galla and squeeze her against his ribs, but she was stronger than him, bag of bones that he was, and she barely brushed the two-day growth on his cheek as she got away.

"Galla, don't worry, they're the airplanes . . . the airplanes of our allies . . . bombing. Those aren't the Indians' drums. They're the gringos' airplanes! Galla!"

Tucuche, the eldest elder, climbed to the edge of the Quebrada de Melgarejo to look around at the sky. His hands of hide-covered bone grasped at the air, at something invisible in the air, like a fluid, and when he had taken it to himself, his entire body turned green.

"Diego Hun Ig," he said, speaking to the absent dead man who remained just as alive for Tucuche as the water, the sun, and the air. "Now they don't hang us, they shoot us. Now the disaster is complete. Many have been killed secretly in villages, on roads. It is not yet time for the land to return to our hands, but the time will come. . . ."

"Ha, ha, ha, ha!" laughed La Galla in the village square, snapping her whip. "I thought they were drums, but they're airplanes. I like gringos and how they shut up the drums with their airplanes! Ha, ha, ha! Indian idiots, trying to use rawhide-covered drums against modern warplanes!"

The next day, the sons of Diego Hun Ig all went to work on the highway, without pay, without food. Diego's daughters carried them lunch in baskets. That is when the road boss, Cirilo Pilches, went after one of the daughters and took her by force. "Indian communist," he said as he raped her. "This is the free love that your father wanted to proclaim around here. Now you can have children for the state, because that's what your daddy wanted, he wanted you all to belong to the state. So here's for your tractor and your silo. . . ."

The Indian girl hardly resisted. She just let him do it, like an animal. The road boss, on the other hand, was a person. He had a military rank, two pistols, and a sword. He was valiant, a distinguished hero. After they triumphed over a bunch of defenseless peasant drummers, the gringo bombardiers had decorated him. Satisfied, he walked away from his victim, who left without picking up the remains of the broken dishes, and returned to his job of watching over the forced laborers doing road work. In his back pocket, he carried the most recent issue of *Visiones*, which he continued reading. . . .

"The Communist ringleader Diego Hun Ig, fearing, no doubt, that we would discover Marxist literature and pictures of Lenin, Stalin, and Mao-Tse Tung in his house, met us in the doorway. And there, clutching a machine gun and surrounded by fierce dogs, he confronted the author of these lines, who had appeared in the company of a respectable man of the neighborhood, merely to ask a few questions . . ."

The sun came out again. High on the mountain, the matasano tree still swayed in the wind and spread its branches over its always-green hollow. The golden, ashen green of the matasano leaves contrasted with the emerald green of the hollow below. Beginning with those shades of green, now that the eyes of Diego Hun Ig were forever closed, other eyes, other generations of eyes would continue to count the eleven further shades visible at that place, the Grandmother of Waters. Together, thirteen shades of green would be necessary to adorn the image of Our Lord of the Quetzal Feathers when, on a certain one of nine mornings, he returned to make his definitive distribution of lands to his Indian drummers.

> *Analyzing the Sources:* How does the author help readers understand
> the mentality of people such as "La Galla" as well as villagers such as
> Diego Hun Ig? Why was it so necessary to brand the people who wanted
> land reform as communists?

MEMORY OF FIRE

Eduardo Galeano

Uruguayan writer Eduardo Galeano (1940–2015) was another of the many Latin American writers presenting a sharp anti-imperialist vision of US intervention in Latin America during the Cold War. Like many other artists and intellectuals, Galeano spent years in exile because of his leftist allegiances. Galeano's most influential works, The Open Veins of Latin America *(1971) and* Memory of Fire *(1986), are "works of remembering," history written with fiery conviction and a literary freedom of style. The excerpt that follows, from the second of those works, gives an overview of the 1954 Guatemalan intervention from a top-down perspective.*

1953: BOSTON
UNITED FRUIT

Throne of bananas, crown of bananas, a banana held like a scepter: Sam Zemurray, master of the lands and seas of the banana kingdom, did not believe it possible that his Guatemalan vassals could give him a headache. *"The Indians are too ignorant for Marxism,"* he used

---

SOURCE: Eduardo Galeano, *Memory of Fire, Volume III: Century of the Wind,* trans. Cedric Belfrage (New York: Pantheon Books, 1988), pp. 149–54, 157.

to say, and was applauded by his court at his royal palace in Boston, Massachusetts.

Thanks to the successive decrees of Manuel Estrada Cabrera, who governed surrounded by sycophants and spies, seas of slobber, forests of familiars; and of Jorge Ubico, who thought he was Napoleon but wasn't, Guatemala has remained part of United Fruit's vast dominion for half a century. In Guatemala, United Fruit can seize whatever land it wants—enormous unused tracts—and owns the railroad, the telephone, the telegraph, the ports, and the ships, not to speak of soldiers, politicians, and journalists.

Sam Zemurray's troubles began when President Juan José Arévalo forced the company to respect the union and its right to strike. From bad to worse: A new president, Jacobo Arbenz, introduces agrarian reform, seizes United Fruit's uncultivated lands, begins dividing them among a hundred thousand families, and acts as if Guatemala were ruled by the landless, the letterless, the breadless, the *less*.

1953: GUATEMALA CITY
ARBENZ

President Truman howled when workers on Guatemala's banana plantations started to behave like people. Now President Eisenhower spits lightning over the expropriation of United Fruit.

The government of the United States considers it an outrage that the government of Guatemala should take United Fruit's account books seriously. Arbenz proposes to pay as indemnity only the value that the company itself had placed on its lands to defraud the tax laws. John Foster Dulles, the secretary of state, demands twenty-five times that.

Jacobo Arbenz, accused of conspiring with communists, draws his inspiration not from Lenin but from Abraham Lincoln. His agrarian reform, an attempt to modernize Guatemalan capitalism, is less radical than the North American rural laws of almost a century ago.

1953: San Salvador

Dictator Wanted

Guatemalan General Miguel Ydígoras Fuentes, distinguished killer of Indians, has lived in exile since the fall of the dictator Ubico. Now, Walter Turnbull comes to San Salvador to offer him a deal. Turnbull, representative of both United Fruit and the CIA, proposes that Ydígoras take charge of Guatemala. There is money available for such a project, if he promises to destroy the unions, restore United Fruit's lands and privileges, and repay this loan to the last cent within a reasonable period. Ydígoras asks time to think it over, while making clear he considers the conditions abusive.

In no time word gets around that a position is vacant. Guatemalan exiles, military and civilian, fly to Washington to offer their services; others knock at the doors of US embassies. José Luis Arenas, "friend" of Vice President Nixon, offers to overthrow President Arbenz for two hundred thousand dollars. General Federico Ponce says he has a ten-thousand-man army ready to attack the National Palace. His price would be quite modest, although he prefers not to talk figures yet. Just a small advance . . .

Throat cancer rules out United Fruit's first preference, Juan Córdova Cerna. On his deathbed, however, Doctor Córdova rasps out the name of his own candidate: Colonel Carlos Castillo Armas, trained at Fort Leavenworth, Kansas—a cheap, obedient burro.

1954: Washington

The Deciding Machine, Piece by Piece

Dwight Eisenhower President of the United States. Overthrew the government of Mohammed Mossadegh in Iran because it nationalized oil. Has now given orders to overthrow the government of Jacobo Arbenz in Guatemala.

Sam Zemurray Principal stockholder in United Fruit. All his concerns turn automatically into US government declarations, and ultimately into rifles, mortars, machine guns, and CIA airplanes.

John Foster Dulles US Secretary of State. Former lawyer for United Fruit.

Allen Dulles Director of the CIA. Brother of John Foster Dulles. Like him, has done legal work for United Fruit. Together they organize "Operation Guatemala."

John Moors Cabot Secretary of State for Inter-American Affairs. Brother of Thomas Cabot, the president of United Fruit.

Walter Bedell Smith Under-Secretary of State. Serves as liaison in "Operation Guatemala." Future member of the board of United Fruit.

Henry Cabot Lodge Senator, US representative to the United Nations. United Fruit shareholder. Has on various occasions received money from this company for speeches in the Senate.

Ann Whitman Personal secretary to President Eisenhower. Married to United Fruit public relations chief.

Spruille Braden Former US ambassador to several Latin American countries. Has received a salary from United Fruit since 1948. Is widely reported in the press to have exhorted Eisenhower *to suppress Communism by force in Guatemala.*

Robert Hill US ambassador to Costa Rica. Collaborates on "Operation Guatemala." Future board member of United Fruit.

John Peurifoy US ambassador to Guatemala. Known as *The butcher of Greece* for his past diplomatic service in Athens. Speaks no Spanish. Political background: the US Senate, Washington, DC, where he once worked as an elevator operator.

1954: BOSTON
THE LIE MACHINE, PIECE BY PIECE

The Motor The executioner becomes the victim; the victim, the executioner. Those who prepare the invasion of Guatemala from Honduras attribute to Guatemala the intention to invade Honduras and all Central America. *The tentacles of the Kremlin are plain to see,* says John Moors Cabot from the White House. Ambassador Peurifoy warns in Guatemala: *We cannot permit a Soviet republic to be established from Texas to the Panama Canal.* Behind this [fuss] lies a cargo of arms shipped from Czechoslovakia. The United States has forbidden the sale of arms to Guatemala.

Gear I News and articles, declarations, pamphlets, photographs, films, and comic strips about communist atrocities in Guatemala bombard the public. This educational material, whose origin is undisclosed, comes from the offices of United Fruit in Boston and from government files in Washington.

Gear II The Archbishop of Guatemala, Mariano Rossell Arellano, exhorts the populace to rise *against communism, enemy of God and the Fatherland*. Thirty CIA planes rain down his pastoral message over the whole country. The archbishop has the image of the popular Christ of Esquipulas, which will be named Captain General of the Liberating Brigade, brought to the capital.

Gear III At the Pan-American Conference, John Foster Dulles pounds the table with his fist and gets the blessing of the Organization of American States for the projected invasion. At the United Nations, Henry Cabot Lodge blocks Jacobo Arbenz's demands for help. US diplomacy is mobilized throughout the world. The complicity of England and France is obtained in exchange for a US commitment to silence over the delicate matters of the Suez Canal, Cyprus, and Indochina.

Gear IV The dictators of Nicaragua, Honduras, Venezuela, and the Dominican Republic not only lend training camps, radio transmitters, and airports to "Operation Guatemala," they also make a contribution to the propaganda campaign. Somoza calls together the international press in Managua and displays some pistols with hammers and sickles stamped on them. They are, he says, from a Russian submarine intercepted en route to Guatemala.

1954: GUATEMALA CITY
THE RECONQUEST OF GUATEMALA

Guatemala has neither planes nor anti-aircraft installations, so US pilots in US planes bomb the country with the greatest of ease.

A powerful CIA transmitter, installed on the roof of the US embassy, spreads confusion and panic: the Lie Machine informs the world that this is the rebel radio, the Voice of Liberation, transmitting the triumphal march of Colonel Castillo Armas from the jungles of Guatemala. Meanwhile, Castillo Armas, encamped on a United Fruit plantation in Honduras, awaits orders from the Deciding Machine.

Arbenz's government, paralyzed, attends the ceremony of its own collapse. The aerial bombings reach the capital and blow up the fuel deposits. The government confines itself to burying the dead. The mercenary army, *God, Fatherland, Liberty*, crosses the border. It meets no resistance. Is it money or fear that explains how Guatemala's military chiefs could surrender their troops without firing a shot? An Argentine doctor in his early twenties, Ernesto "Che" Guevara, tries in vain to organize popular defense of the capital: he doesn't know how or with what. Improvised militias wander the streets unarmed. When Arbenz finally orders the arsenals opened, army officers refuse to obey. On one side of these dark, ignoble days, Guevara has an attack of asthma and indignation; on another, on midnight after two weeks of bombings, President Arbenz slowly descends the steps of the National Palace, crosses the street, and seeks asylum in the Mexican embassy. The army of Castillo Armas takes over Guatemala.

1954: GUATEMALA CITY
NEWSREEL

The archbishop of Guatemala declares: *"I admire the sincere and ardent patriotism of President Castillo Armas."* Amid a formidable display of gibberish, Castillo Armas receives the blessing of the papal nuncio, Monsignor Genaro Verrolino.

President Eisenhower congratulates the CIA chiefs at the White House: *"Thanks to all of you. You've averted a Soviet beachhead in our hemisphere."*

The head of the CIA, Allen Dulles, assigns to a *Time* journalist the job of framing Guatemala's new constitution.

Time publishes a poem by the wife of the US ambassador to Guatemala. The poem says that Mr. and Mrs. Peurifoy are *optimistic* because Guatemala is no longer *Communistic*.

At his first meeting with the ambassador after the victory, President Castillo Armas expresses his concern at the insufficiency of local jails and the lack of necessary cells for all the communists. According to lists sent from Washington by the State Department, Guatemala's communists total seventy-two thousand.

The embassy throws a party. Four hundred Guatemalan guests sing in unison "The Star-Spangled Banner."

1955: GUATEMALA CITY
ONE YEAR AFTER THE RECONQUEST OF GUATEMALA

Richard Nixon visits this occupied land. The union of United Fruit workers and five hundred thirty-two other unions have been banned by the new government. The new penal code punishes with death anyone who calls a strike. Political parties are outlawed. The books of Dostoyevsky and other "Soviet" writers have been thrown into the bonfire.

The banana kingdom has been saved from agrarian reform. The vice president of the United States congratulates President Castillo Armas. For the first time in history, says Nixon, a communist government has been replaced by a free one.

> *Analyzing the Sources: The importance of anticommunism is clear in all the readings for this chapter. What other factors, revealed here, clearly influenced the US decision to engineer the overthrow of the Guatemalan government in 1954?*

Chapter 9

GUERRILLA WARFARE

The triumph of the 1959 Cuban Revolution suggested to revolutionaries and counterrevolutionaries alike that guerrilla warfare would shape the political future of Latin America. Insurgent groups, both rural and urban, soon appeared in virtually every country of the region. Meanwhile, the armed forces of Latin American countries had entered into firm alliances with the US military, which encouraged, aided, and advised their counterinsurgency operations.

While inspired by a Marxist analysis of social conflict and by a sense of participating in a global process, Latin American insurgents believed themselves to be, above all, reenacting a centuries-old struggle against imperialism. That is why many of them took the names of past rebels whose fight they envisioned themselves to be continuing. Uruguay's Tupamaros were remembering Tupac Amaru (the eighteenth-century rebel, as well as other historical rebels who called themselves Tupamaros), Nicaragua's Sandinistas were remembering a rebel leader of the 1920s who fought against US marines, and so on. Guerrilla warfare—an "asymmetrical" battle waged by "irregular" forces (without uniforms or a state organization behind them) against a "regular" army (with both)—has a long history in Latin America. The word *guerrilla* itself (meaning "little war") was coined in Spanish around 1810. Many of the patriot fighters who won independence from Spain were guerrillas, and Argentine insurgents of the 1970s were invoking independence-era guerrillas when they called themselves Montoneros. This sense of history was largely absent in the US State Department as it organized a hemispheric counterinsurgency war against Latin American guerrilla movements.

As guerrilla insurgents proliferated in the 1960s, Latin America's regular armies began to specialize in counterinsurgency. In this they had the aid and encouragement of their allies in the US military, which established a training center, called the School of the Americas, where Latin American army officers were invited to study counterinsurgency techniques. Because guerrillas were always fewer and less well-armed than their adversaries, they relied on surprise and concealment. Once their precise location was known, however, regular troops could quickly annihilate them. This vulnerability was especially true of urban guerrillas. Therefore, counterinsurgent organizations made systematic use of torture to break the secrecy of insurgent organizations. Counterinsurgent wars often became "dirty wars" that involved large-scale violations of human rights. To cover their tracks, counterinsurgent torturers often simply "disappeared" the people whom they interrogated, arresting them without warrant, taking them to secret detention centers, and finally executing them and disposing of their bodies without a trace. Such practices, as well as the creation of "death squads" (composed of out-of-uniform soldiers and police) unceremoniously murdered anyone believed to be supporting guerrillas, became widespread in Latin America from the 1960s to the 1980s.

This chapter provides views of insurgency and counterinsurgency in various countries of the region. The narrative of a Colombian army officer illustrates the way in which counterinsurgents tended to define guerrillas as "common criminals," rather than people fighting for a political cause. If the guerrillas were merely common criminals, after all, then there were no political issues to discuss. Unsurprisingly, the published writings of the guerrillas themselves tend to make a precisely contrary point, placing great emphasis on the idea that insurgents were involved, above all, in "revolutionary education" and "armed propaganda." The energy that guerrilla armies actually devoted to this "battle for hearts and minds" varied, of course. Uruguay's Tupamaros were famous for it. The FARC (Armed Forces of the Colombian Revolution), which has outlasted all but a handful of guerrilla organizations thanks to its ruthlessness and its incessant mobility in the labyrinthine terrain of the northern Andes, does not seem very ideologically driven today. But revolutionary education is highlighted in the 1960s *Diary of a Guerrilla* that chronicles the FARC's creation in the 1960s. The important role of women in Latin American guerrilla movements is brought out in several selections, principally the one on El Salvador. Women's experiences, especially the tension between their commitments to their children and their political cause, throw a different sort of light on the matter. A Chilean interrogator, interviewed years after his activities as a torturer, admits the political motivation of the people whom he tortured, without expressing any remorse about his actions. Like those who calmly defend the "enhanced interrogation techniques" applied by the United States in the early twenty-first century, "Fat Romo" justified his actions simply by claiming that they achieved the desired results.

A final source (though first in chronological order) represents Mexico, where no major guerrilla movement developed during the Cold War. Mexico's government already claimed to be revolutionary, but student unrest led to major confrontations with the authorities in the months before the country was to host the Olympic Games. The demonstrators' slogans and banners offer succinct statements of what was on their minds.

MASSACRE IN MEXICO

Elena Poniatowska

Elena Poniatowska (born in France, 1932) became a leading voice of twentieth-century Mexican literature. Her book Massacre in México (La noche de Tlatelolco *in the original Spanish) is a loose assembly of documents, testimony, and oral history regarding the 1968 massacre of protesters in Mexico City's Plaza de Tlatelolco. Student unrest led to major confrontations with the authorities in the months before Mexico was to host the Olympic Games. Among the words that Poniatowska recorded were the slogans chanted in the streets and carried by the protestors on hand-lettered banners. Note the tensions around the idea of participation by the common people,* el Pueblo.

SLOGANS CHANTED IN THE STREETS BY PROTESTORS

Mex-i-co, Lib-er-ty! Mex-i-co, Lib-er-ty! Mex-i-co, Lib-er-ty! Mex-i-co, Lib-er-ty!

Join us, Pueblo! Join us, Pueblo! Join us, Pueblo! Join us, Pueblo! Join us, Pueblo!

Che Che Che Guevara! Che Che Che Guevara! Che Che Che Guevara!

Dialogue! Dialogue! Dialogue! Dialogue! Dialogue! Dialogue! Dialogue!

Fidel, Fidel, give the Yankees hell! Fidel, Fidel, give the Yankees hell!

WRITTEN MESSAGES CARRIED, POSTED, OR WORN BY PROTESTERS

Who are the agitators here? Ignorance, Hunger, and Misery!

We don't want Olympics! We want Revolution!

Soldiers, don't shoot! You are Pueblo, too!

Literacy training for riot police!

Pueblo, open your eyes now!

Juárez, what should we do?

Analyzing the Sources: How would you characterize the apparent relationship between the demonstrating students and el Pueblo?

SOURCE: Elena Poniatowska, *La noche de Tlatelolco: Testimonios de historia oral* (Mexico City: Biblioteca Era, 1971), pp. 15, 17, 20, 21, 41, 54, 86, 97.

ZARPAZO: MEMOIR OF A COLOMBIAN ARMY OFFICER

Evelio Buitrago Salazar

The memoir of Evelio Buitrago Salazar, a Colombian army officer, was published by the country's Ministry of Defense in 1968. The following extracts are the book's prologue (by another army officer), the author's account of his family background, and some remarks about the guerrilla leader, Zarpazo, whose group Buitrago had successfully infiltrated. Both the prologue and the opening passages exemplify the anti-Communist vision whereby guerilla enemies of the government represent a malevolent, foreign, criminal force lacking any sort of political legitimacy. Buitrago also exemplifies the conservative discourse associated with Colombia's central coffee-growing region.

PROLOGUE

Evelio Buitrago Salazar, Sergeant 2nd Class in the Colombian Army here presents his memoirs of the difficult struggle against banditry, or *bandolerismo*, as we call it in Colombia.

Buitrago Salazar is 100 percent soldier, and the account of the role he played in the region of Quindío, Tolima, and Valle del Cauca is free of vanity or exaggeration. The modesty of this meritorious author, who has been decorated with the Cross of Boyacá, certainly speaks well of him. Without diminishing the well-deserved fame of Sergeant Buitrago, one can affirm that in this memoir many Colombian army veterans will find echoes of their own heroic deeds, their own blows struck for social peace and order.

In Colombia, it has been said, politicians start internal wars and leave military men to make peace. The quotation indicates the singular vocation of the Colombian army to defend our national Constitution. To restore peace to our violence-stricken cities and

SOURCE: adapted from Evelio Buitrago Salazar, *Zarpazo: Otra cara de la violencia (Memorias de un suboficial del ejército de Colombia)* (Bogotá: Ministry of Defense, 1968), pp. 5–16.

countryside the police and armed forces have given their best: their youth, their enthusiasm, and their blood. What more can we ask of these selfless heroes?

Thanks to their efforts over a period of years, the peace of God, preached with peerless love in Christ's Sermon on the Mount, reigns once again in the Republic of Colombia. The *bandolero* spawn of barbarism has been pursued, driven to its lair, cornered, and destroyed. All that remains of the bandoleros is the sad memory of an epoch that will never come again.

Buitrago merely tells his story and does not discuss the causes of violence in Colombia, which would clarify nothing, serve no useful purpose, merely arouse passions, provoke a polemic, and perhaps raise devastating flames from the smoldering ashes. Buitrago shows us uniformed soldiers using their weapons honorably for the betterment of society, just as the dying Simón Bolívar commanded. He also reveals the moral bankruptcy of our bandolero foes, stripped here of the romantic aura that sometimes surrounds them and which they have, in fact, never deserved. Bandoleros like Zarpazo do not really fight for a political ideal. Cruelty, crudity, greed, treachery, cowardice, wantonness, ignorance, and insanity—these are the true attributes of bandoleros like Zarpazo. Bandolerismo constitutes a dangerous running sore that, if unattended, threatens the life of our whole society. This book indicates the proper treatment, strong, painful, but indispensable if the patient is to be saved.

These bandoleros appeared at an unfortunate moment in the history of Colombia, taking advantage of our prolonged and bloody political controversies to rob and murder and establish their gangs in certain key economic regions of the country. Had it not been for the energetic intervention of the armed forces, Colombia would soon have bled to death, and Communist forces from the other side of the world, taking advantage of our confusion and weakness during the period of *la Violencia*,* would have invaded, grinding the privileged land of our founding fathers Santander and Nariño under foreign boot heels. Instead of our yellow, red, and blue tricolor, the Colombian flag would today bear the hammer and sickle of

---

*A period of protracted political strife from the late 1940s to the late 1950s.

Communism. We all owe a debt of eternal gratitude to the officers and soldiers who sacrificed their lives in order that such a travesty should not come to pass.

May our children and grandchildren never witness the return of bandolerismo, and may this book, with its salutary lessons, contribute to the preservation of the peace of God.

Retired Col. Guillermo Plazas Olarte

I Was Born in Sevilla

I was born and raised in the town of Sevilla in the Cauca Valley, at 1,500 meters above sea level, nicknamed the Coffee-Growing Capital of Colombia. My father, a true son of Sevilla, owned pastures and groves of plantains just ten minutes outside of town. My mother was from a good family, a woman selflessly devoted to the care of her numerous children, in the conservative tradition of the coffee-growing region. But mine was not a family of those rich and powerful "oligarchs" that the subversives talk about. Rather, I grew up in what was, for that part of Colombia, an average family—religious, ambitious, and hard-working.

My town was a privileged place, carved out of the tropical forest by resolute men who felled and burned its trees to bless Colombia with the gift of fertile soils. Sevilla had about 70,000 inhabitants back in the 1930s, when I was christened. The houses were of plastered brick or mud-daub construction, and the climate was perfect for the cultivation of our leading national crop. Coffee bushes grew on the surrounding hillsides in the protective shade of plantain and guamo trees. Red coffee beans tumbled from the calloused hands of hired pickers into harvest baskets and from there into burlap sacks. One saw coffee beans spread out to dry in the sun everywhere in the outskirts of town. The smell of the beans impregnated the roads outside of town, as mule trains and shouting muleteers passed at irregular intervals carrying sacks of coffee to market. The aroma of roasted coffee saturated people's houses, floated through the long streets of stores, schools, banks, hospitals, and churches, and rose to the heavens. Coffee from Sevilla provided good money for everyone in town—the pickers, the processors, the wholesalers—and then off it went across the oceans of the world to distant ports, where it was converted into dollars!

That was Sevilla at the time of my birth in the Year of Our Lord 1936, a land where people lived intensely, working hard and making money, wheeling, dealing, and of course, eating plenty of good Colombian food—*arepas* and *sancocho*. It was a land for both rich and poor, for elegant women and self-made men, horse traders and horse breakers, where the mules were even better than the horses, a place where a man could drink aguardiente and shoot a game of billiards any time of day, dancing to the blaring music of a jukebox with one of those painted girls that made plenty of us lose our heads. Fluffy clouds filled the skies, unfurled above the green Andean mountainsides of Sevilla like banners of peace.

Only later did I learn of the horrors of violence, the violence that carried away my father, devoured my uncles, and diminished my inheritance. In 1953, my mother, my seven brothers and sisters, and I moved to the big city, to Cali, where we went to school and started to spend a fortune on tuition, uniforms, and books. My father stayed behind to administer our property. He was a real man. Our property was steep and hilly, but it produced plenty, and soon we had electric lights at our big house in the county, and we owned four other houses, as well. We had sugarcane, and a mill, and in the evening the smell of molasses was in the air and one of the young day laborers would pull out an instrument and play a *bambuco*.** The roosters of the early morning crowed with jubilation, as if announcing the success of the sugar milling. We accepted day laborers belonging to any political party, without hateful discrimination. On Sundays, my father would lead them to church to give thanks to heaven and, after mass, buy supplies for the coming week.

The Peace of God reigned until 1954, when violence reared its ugly head in Sevilla. The undeclared civil war of the late 1940s had left a number of guerrilla gangs out in the mountains, pardoned by the government but accustomed, by then, to the easy profits of rob-

---

**The same dance as that of the "happy slaves" in the nineteenth-century novel *María*.

bery and pillage. Let the "new wave" of academic sociologists make their exhaustive studies of the causes of violence in Colombia. Who cares about their interesting theories! The fact is that the gangs who remained from the civil war turned into simple bandoleros, without political ideals, lacking human feelings, devoted to kidnapping and murder. Their leaders were the famous Sangre Negra, Chispas, Zarpazo (whom I came to know so well), and others who had traveled every inch of the terrain they dominated and could therefore easily outmaneuver and ambush the army contingents sent to control them. They terrorized the rural people, who collaborated with them and paid them protection money for fear of losing their lives and property.

As all this is well known, I might have omitted a description of these fiends. But outside of Colombia there are some perfectly decent people, and even influential authors, who remain entirely misinformed about the true character of our bandolerismo, as I have described it here. Eventually, my hand would punish these bloodthirsty monsters who had managed to escape the control and just retribution of society, sadly famous delinquents whom foreigners and sociologists have tried to justify and defend. I am one of so many military men whose duty it was to face the criminal bandoleros. I write these truthful memoirs two thousand kilometers from Colombia, in Lima, the beautiful capital of Peru, where nothing can disturb my impartiality. This is my story.

> *Analyzing the Sources: What were the basic characteristics of Colombian society, according to this author, before "common criminals" known as* bandoleros *began to "masquerade" as revolutionaries? How does he account for the violence plaguing Colombia?*

DIARY OF A GUERRILLA

Jacobo Arenas

During the years in which Evelio Buitrago was fighting "bandolero" groups, some of those groups were coalescing into Colombia's largest and most durable rural guerrilla army, the FARC, or Armed Forces of the Colombian

Revolution. The following selections from the diary of FARC commander Jacobo Arenas, published in 1969, can be read as a direct counterpoint to Buitrago's narrative. Arenas quotes at length the teachings of a man that Buitrago regarded as a bandolero, Manuel Marulanda (commonly called Tirofijo, meaning Sureshot), who led the FARC for more than three decades after the death of Arenas.

PROLOGUE

Here is a book written by a guerrilla fighter, comrade Jacobo Arenas, a member of the Executive Committee of the Communist Party of Colombia and ranking leader of the FARC. It is a war diary that recounts the assault launched by the Colombian army, under the guidance of Yanqui military advisors, against the rural, guerrilla-controlled zone known as Marquetalia. The book gives the profile of true popular heroes, such as Manuel Marulanda, whom the government presents as "the bandit, Tirofijo," and who has escaped a dozen times from efforts, carried out by thousands of soldiers, to surround and capture him.

The armed struggle of the Colombian revolution has not been dreamed up by a few leaders, however. To the contrary, it responds to urgent, concrete social needs. It is a prolonged popular war that has gone through three stages: in 1949–1953, the masses responded to the assassination of the popular leader Jorge Eliécer Gaitán; in 1954–1957, the masses responded to the attack on them by the military dictatorship, creating rural strongholds in the heights of the central Andean range, the most important being Marquetalia; from 1964 to today, guerrilla activity has spread through much of the Colombian countryside. In 1967, the commander of Colombia's armed forces claimed that this is merely a local manifestation of a global struggle "between Communism and democracy," but that is clearly the influence of his North American strategic advisors.

SOURCE: adapted from Jacobo Arenas, *Diario de la resistencia de Marquetalia* (Bogotá: Ediciones Abejón Mono, 1972), pp. 7–15, 21–23, 33–36, 47–56.

Colombia's rural guerrilla war is, in fact, an act of self-defense on the part of peasant combatants who seek merely their own liberation.

The Fall of Marquetalia

Marquetalia is an area centering on a small plateau high in one of the three Andean cordilleras that run through Colombia, the middle one, not far from the snowcapped heights of the Nevado del Huila. Altogether, Marquetalia has an area of about three hundred square kilometers. Since colonial times, the basis of the population has been the Páez people, Indians who fought hard against the Spanish invaders and since then have coexisted with the Spanish-speaking peasants who also live in the mountains. In April 1964, when we learned of the Colombian government's decision to liquidate it, Marquetalia was also the redoubt of guerrillas who had migrated in from more northerly, coffee-growing areas of the cordillera in search of a safe haven.

Against Marquetalia, where we had taken refuge, the government was planning to send sixteen thousand troops, combining infantry and artillery, the first ones to be brought in by air transport, following an aerial bombardment. Marquetalia would be surrounded and besieged, and we expected any sign of resistance on the part of the peasants to provoke the army's deployment of biological weapons. Furthermore, the assault was to commence almost immediately.

The leadership called a general assembly to discuss our tactics. As it happened, the assembly began on 17 May 1964, the day before the radio announced that the army was launching its Operation Marquetalia. The assembly debated a number of matters, beginning with the problem of evacuating the numerous families of noncombatants. Other discussions turned on the option of constant mobility—without a permanent home base, living off the land—a new form of rural guerrilla warfare that we decided to adopt.

The government forces advanced against us, and we eluded them, striking back at moments of our choosing. We pitched our tents here one night, there the next, moving ever deeper into the jungle, fighting often, but also discussing issues and reading and writing like a bunch of revolutionary philosophers. At one peasant hut, I established a sort of rustic office and study. My desk was a three-legged table which we also used for eating and the chair was a section of tree trunk. That tilted "seat" killed my back. I wrote on an old typewriter that my guerrillas had taken turns carrying day after day. When I typed, it made an infernal racket. Yet, nothing is more important than communications, propaganda, and the effort to awaken a revolutionary consciousness among peasants and workers.

THE TEACHINGS OF TIROFIJO

In my notebook I have collected the teachings of our Comandante Manuel Marulanda, which I transcribe here:

Every guerrilla, every member of our movement must study political as well as military problems so as to be able to explain our revolutionary aims, such as freeing the country from North American oppression and, for the peasants, a true land reform that would destroy the monopoly hold of the great estates. And education is vital, too, to counteract the enemy's systematic attempts to confuse and misinform the People. The revolution cannot triumph without massive popular support.

Our own self-discipline is also a form of political education. If we hold ourselves to a high standard and adhere closely to the regulations that we have made for the good of the revolution, the People will learn from our example. If they see true, principled revolutionaries in us, we will win their support for our struggle. And their support is the greatest good for the revolution.

Guerrillas must be morally strong, maintain a positive spirit, and reject fear. Don't worry about the airplanes. Let them strafe us, bombard us, photograph us, drop their leaflets, try to infect us with bacteria, and spend and spend money, because the faster they spend it all the sooner this oligarchic government will come crashing down. A fearful guerrilla cannot do political work among the masses, nor can a guerrilla do so successfully without high moral standards. When a guerrilla moves among the People, among his class brothers and his potential comrades in the struggle, he should not lay a finger on anything that does not belong to him. Now, we do take things from the enemy, but that is entirely another matter, and the difference must be clear to all.

Let no one mistake us for bandoleros. We are revolutionaries, not thieves, and if it were not an imperative of the struggle, we would not take things from the enemy, either. We are not fighting for personal interest or gain. Profit is the principle of capitalists, but it should not be ours. We are against that philosophy. Our motto must be the good of the People, and our behavior must be selfless and blameless. A true communist revolutionary believes in collectivism. As guerrillas, everything that we have, we have in common. Our life of constant movement reinforces this goal. When the revolution triumphs, some of us may want to own individual property again, but the majority, having absorbed the new revolutionary spirit, will surely be beyond that.

Our greatest enemy is imperialism. These uniformed soldiers who shoot at us here in the mountains are just puppets, after all, the puppets of generals, politicians, bankers, industrialists, great landowners— the Colombian oligarchy, in a word. But the oligarchs are puppets, too, in the end, and do the bidding of Yanqui Imperialism, which is not only our greatest enemy, but the enemy of all the Peoples of the earth. In any poor country where downtrodden people rise up and reach for a better life, a Yanqui invasion happens immediately. But if the countries of Latin America rise up together, the United States won't be able to occupy them all at once. The people of Cuba have set the great example, in that regard, for our entire continent.

Those are the words of Manuel Marulanda, thirty-five years old, married, and the father of five children. He is a peasant and the son of peasants. Circumstances made him a guerrilla, and now he is among the movement's most important leaders. Reactionaries and imperialists call him "the bandolero Tirofijo," trying to undercut the political prestige of this ranking member of the Colombian Communist Party, precisely because he has caused the army so many nightmares during his fifteen years of revolutionary struggle.

Analyzing the Sources: *The discourse of Marxist revolutionaries is an opposite mirror image of anticommunist discourse. Contrast this author's* *picture of the background, motives, character, and aims of the insurgency against the picture presented by Evelio Buitrago.*

THE TUPAMAROS IN ACTION

Movement for National Liberation

The Tupamaros of the 1960s and 1970s (formally the Movement for National Liberation, appearing here as a collective author) were urban guerrillas who carried out flamboyant actions, a sort of guerrilla theater calculated to win public sympathy for their revolutionary struggle. The following discussion of tactics and the role of women in urban guerrilla warfare is taken from materials that the Tupamaros published in Mexico in 1972, shortly before the Uruguayan government succeeded in destroying the movement.

THE TACTICS OF URBAN GUERRILLA WARFARE

It is a characteristic of urban guerrilla warfare that practically *all* the enemy's assets are vulnerable to surprise attack. Ambushing and annihilating an enemy contingent—quite an arduous maneuver for rural guerrillas—is a simple, everyday operation for urban guerrillas. The urban guerrilla struggles in the very bosom of the enemy. Absolutely all the regime's personnel, beginning with the president himself, are close at hand and exposed in an urban environment. The regime's communications systems and strategic installations are always vulnerable to bombing by an urban guerrilla force willing to sacrifice human lives to achieve its goals. However, urban guerrilla warfare does not consist in the constant and indiscriminate application of such violent methods. Rather, its tactics conform to its larger strategic objectives, both military and political. Failure to apply dras-

SOURCE: adapted from Movimiento de Liberación Nacional, *Los tupamaros en acción* (Mexico City: Editorial Diogenes, 1972), pp. 56–61.

tic methods can be a critical mistake at a decisive moment. The application of revolutionary violence can be counterproductive, on the other hand, when the consciousness of the people has not yet become sufficiently indignant owing to the crimes of the regime. Guerrilla warfare must always be, in part, political warfare, and this is especially true for urban guerrillas, who live and fight in intimate contact with the urban multitude. Any violent action without clearly evident and understandable political objectives can result in a setback for the movement in the eyes of the people.

In pursuit of its strategic goals, the Movement for National Liberation has experimented with a variety of tactics.

Sabotage. Sabotage such as cutting telephone or power lines, which may cause disruptions affecting workers, should be sparingly used in the initial stages of a conflict because of its potentially adverse impact on public opinion. Sabotage of purely military and state targets is much more acceptable to the people.

Attacks against the repressive forces themselves. This is surely the most direct method of bringing down a regime: eliminating the human agents of repression, the army and the police. The simple destruction of the regime's armed forces may be sufficient to cause regime collapse in many cases.

Reprisals. Both the people and the repressive forces of the regime more clearly understand the political logic of revolutionary violence when it constitutes a reprisal for acts of regime injustice, such as a specific official murder or torture, an abusive judicial verdict, or the arbitrary mass firing of workers.

Use of explosives. A timed explosive device in a public place may cause unnecessary casualties among the population, which means that such operations rarely produce an overall positive outcome for the movement.

The people's prison. Abducting regime personnel and imprisoning them in a secret location (whether they are murderous agents of repression or key public figures) can be a highly effective tactic. It protects our own prisoners in the hands of the state, forces it to moderate its repression, and obliges it to spend considerable resources searching for the people's prison and protecting government officials around the clock. It can also be used against employers who abuse their workers and is particularly good as a reprisal for specific misdeeds.

Supply operations. Vehicles, houses, and other spaces constitute the physical refuge for urban guerrillas, comparable to the Sierra Maestra for the rural guerrillas of Cuba, and operations that help procure these elements are of vital importance to the struggle.

Houses of the enemy. The houses of revolutionary fighters are constantly occupied by the forces of repression to intimidate the families. Urban guerrillas can retaliate in kind by temporarily occupying the formerly untouchable mansions of ranking members of the armed forces, the government, and the oligarchy, as well as those of foreign imperialists.

Armed propanganda. All guerrilla warfare expresses itself primarily through armed actions, but urban guerrillas also employ other means of communication with the people. Radio and television studios may be occupied in order to transmit proclamations, for example. Movie theaters may be occupied for the same purpose, and the proclamations projected on screen, read over a loudspeaker, or distributed on printed handouts. Factories may be occupied to create a dialogue with workers.

WOMEN'S ROLE IN URBAN GUERRILLA WARFARE

Women witness and experience social injustice just as men do, and just as men, they experience the need to become revolutionaries. Women therefore contribute equally to the revolution, even providing service as combatants. Today, not without considerable effort, the Movement for National Liberation offers roles of political militancy to women, abandoning outmoded social prejudice for the good of the revolution. Women have to overcome many difficulties in order to become revolutionaries, because capitalist society assigns a particular, highly limited role to women and educates them for that role, depriving them of adequate physical education and limiting their initiative, creativity, and assertiveness. A traditional woman's education in Uruguay contributes almost nothing to the formation of an urban guerrilla fighter. Every new female recruit must therefore fight a double battle against the forces of repression, on the one hand, and against her own upbringing, on the other. But the double battle only tests and strengthens her revolutionary commitment.

Women have a privileged role in urban guerrilla warfare. Compañeras of all ages can serve to great advantage in communications, as carriers of messages and small objects. The ability of women to modify their dress and appearance allows them to blend into a variety of social contexts and escape the detection of agents of repression. The presence of women is absolutely essential in safe houses located in whatever neighborhood of the city. The compañera posing as the housewife can establish friendly relations with the neighbors, deflect suspicions, and scout the surroundings for possible threats. Her daily round of shopping allows her to learn the neighborhood routines and detect anything abnormal. Women contribute to our political work among the masses, as well as helping train new recruits to the MLN in the basics of the urban guerrilla's clandestine life.

In addition, almost every strike team will include at least one woman. Considerable experience has indicated the advisability of this approach. Once, the MLN used women on strike teams only exceptionally, to accomplish some particular task. Today, however, women participate routinely at all levels of military operations, from initial planning through final execution, drawing fully on their revolutionary potential.

Finally, and importantly, women contribute constantly, by their mere presence, to maintaining the revolutionary unity and camaraderie, thanks to the feminine touch mentioned by Che in his writings on guerrilla warfare. The contribution may be a delicious meal cooked at a rare opportunity for relaxation, possibly a sisterly gesture that helps alleviate the stress of a combatant's life, or perhaps a woman's habitual cultivation of social relationships that help her compañeros deepen their collective commitment to the revolution.

Consider a Tupamara's actions in the following scene. The agents of repression are carrying out a dragnet operation, surrounding a number of city blocks and systematically searching them, house by house. They have arrived at a corner near an MLN safe house, which is also the residence of a compañera. Aware of the immediacy of danger, the Tupamara quickly and decisively puts crucial organizational materials into a gym bag and covers them with a towel, leaving it partly visible in the opening of the bag. When she steps onto the sidewalk, the uniformed agents of the regime are only twenty meters away from the door. With relaxed grace, the young compañera steps into the assembled crowd of curious onlookers. Almost immediately, she notices an agent of the regime following her. Although nothing disturbs her apparent calm, her thoughts are racing. Upon arriving at the bus stop, she turns and smiles at him.

"Where are you headed, babe?" he inquires.

"To the swimming pool." The towel visible in her bag corroborates her statement.

"What a shame that I'm on duty."

The Tupamara gets on the bus. Her training and quick thinking have preserved her own liberty and saved important organizational materials from falling into enemy hands.

Analyzing the Sources: What is the difference between the sort of tactics employed by the MLN on the one hand and terrorist tactics on the other? Were the Tupamaros protofeminists?

THEY WON'T TAKE ME ALIVE

Claribel Alegría

The lives of several Salvadoran guerrilla fighters were narrated in 1983 by the writer Claribel Alegría on the basis of personal interviews. The main subjects are female guerrilla leaders, as indicated by the book's subtitle: Salvadoran Women in the Struggle. *The book particularly follows the life of a couple, Eugenia and Javier, Eugenia being the more important guerrilla leader, but Javier, the chief witness, because the interviews were done after Eugenia's death at an army roadblock. The book's title,* They Won't Take Me Alive, *records Eugenia's last words.*

Javier: One of the great drawbacks of life in the clandestine underground is the way that it limits personal relationships. That was especially true for Eugenia, who had thousands of friends. She accepted the limitations of that kind of life as an inevitable aspect of the revolutionary path that she had chosen in joining the Popular Liberation Forces. Her clandestine life began in 1977 and lasted until her death.

Interviewer/narrator: Tell us a bit about the life of a couple in the clandestine underground.

Javier: Our love sprang not only from personal attraction, but also from very many shared values, from the way that we both regarded the plight of the common people, from stuff that had been on our minds since the events of 1974, from the whole process whereby we both became involved in the revolutionary struggle for national liberation. We went through all of that together. And what we felt about each other grew during our work with rural laborers in the early years. So it was a relationship that started with an initial attraction but really developed and deepened over time. We were very much in love by the time that we decided to get married, and our marriage was born and existed totally within the framework of the revolutionary struggle. Both of us were clear that the struggle of our people and our participation in the Popular Liberation Forces were the most fundamental things in our lives.

Going underground obliged us to accept that we couldn't necessarily be together all the time. We knew that there were risks of losing one another that we couldn't foresee. We were very aware of that aspect right from the start, and we talked about it a lot. We

---

SOURCE: adapted from Claribel Alegría and D. J. Flakoll, *No me agarran viva: La mujer salvadoreña en lucha* (Mexico City: Ediciones Era, 1983), pp. 64–65, 68–69, 97–99.

also talked about the matter of children, whether to have them or not, and even though both of us wanted very much for our love to bear fruit, we decided that during our first year we wouldn't have any children because we did not yet know what life in the underground would be like. Until then we had worked openly as political organizers. We were able to stay together during the first two years of our clandestine life, but only relatively together, because our revolutionary assignments were different ones. . . .

After many months underground, we went back to talking about having a child and still found it a very tough proposition. We began to consider the probable risks and consequences in detail, beyond pregnancy and childbirth, the challenges of raising and educating a kid under such difficult circumstances—living in a "safe house," as parents always under threat, and so on. But after a couple of years, when we had thought the whole matter through, we decided to go ahead. Both of us really wanted to have a child. Eugenia had her own very personal vision of what motherhood would mean to her. One of the things that she always said was that she wanted the child to belong to the movement, to belong not just to us, but also to the comrades who were fighting beside us. She was sure that, if something happened to her and to me, our comrades would become the parents.

Eugenia was already taking responsibilities that entailed a very heavy work load, and before deciding the thing about a child, she had a medical checkup and found out that she was extremely anemic. The doctor recommended that she should not become pregnant for at least three months. That was around July, and before those three months were up the enemy captured me. (*Eugenia and Javier were eventually able to have a daughter.*)

Interviewer/narrator: The Salvadoran National Guard captured Javier along with Eugenia's sister, Marta, and other comrades at a safe house on the outskirts of San Salvador on 16 October 1978. Marta was nine months pregnant at the time. I questioned Marta and several other women commanders on the subject of children.

Marta: It's a big problem. You get tremendously attached to kids, and yet you have to be ready to leave your child at a moment's notice.

Having children is the most beautiful experience that there is, and the most revolutionary experience, too, I believe. Our strategy of a prolonged people's war doesn't mean you can't have a child. Our organization always encouraged us to go ahead with our family lives despite the war and all its limitations. The problem was that each stage of the fighting got harsher and harsher.

When I had my first child, for example, the situation was a bit better, though still very dangerous. So you raise children with all the limitations of the work you do, but in a more proletarian and collectivist setting than otherwise, and that allows you to do the work and be a mother, too. Out in the countryside it is more difficult to have a child with you, right now, on one of the guerrilla fronts, but until 1980 kids could still live with us there and carry on family life. It is a beautiful experience that requires great sacrifices. Mothers who are revolutionaries have to make more sacrifices than mothers who aren't. We have to sleep less, for example, to keep up with our work.

As far as it is able, the organization takes responsibility for our children in our absence. The policy is to keep them and raise them in the spirit of the organization and not turn them over to relatives unless we really have nobody to take care of them. You turn them over to relatives, and they could be raised according to different political principles.

Nadia: I got married pretty young. Sometimes I think that I grew up prematurely because I started this work so young. A seventeen-year-old girl who becomes involved in underground military operations acquires a different mindset. The comrade I married belongs to the same organization. I recruited him. We joined only a few months apart. We've been separated now for about three years, on very good terms, and we're still good friends. There were just some things that he never could understand. I'd get home late or not get home at all some nights, and even though he knew that I was out doing revolutionary work, he couldn't avoid his machismo in spite of all his political education. He comes from a peasant background. And I, on my side of it, wasn't able to make him understand the demands of the work that I was doing.

Anyway, we have a son who is seven years old now. He was with us until he was one year old, and then it just became impossible to keep him, carrying him around in the woods, to meetings, and so on. And we didn't want to leave him with anybody. It didn't make sense. So after that he went to live with my parents, but I went to see him often until 1975, when my older brother and his wife were killed in combat. That created a very difficult situation for my family. The police were constantly after me. They knew where my son was and thought I was bound to turn up there sooner or later. So for safety reasons I didn't see him for fourteen months. It was the most difficult time in my whole life. He's still with my parents. When the surveillance finally relaxed, I was able to get back in touch with him, but not daily or even weekly. I've tried to concern myself with his emotional and political development as much as possible and have talked about it a lot with my parents. Despite the fact that my husband and I are separated, we have an excellent relationship with our son.

He is in contact with both of us and knows that we are separated but that we both love him. Now that he is seven years old he is beginning to understand that his mom and dad are off doing important work to help the poor. That's the way that he thinks of it. He knows that he should not talk about the things we tell him, and that doesn't bother him. It isn't easy for him, naturally, because it's not easy for any of us. We've managed to stay in touch and to guide him in basic ways so that he identifies with us, but we know that ordinarily a child ought to be with his parents.

The way things are in this country, though, under wartime conditions, I don't think that my concern as a mother can be restricted to a single child, because there are millions of children in El Salvador. I even think that if I didn't participate actively in the struggle to liberate my people I would not be morally qualified to raise my own child. Concentrating just on him would make me a hypocrite who allows things in this country to continue as they are. It's a contradiction that we have to face. The interests of our people as a whole must come first, even in the way that we organize our personal lives. That was a hard lesson for me to learn, because it is a painful thing sometimes, but I believe wholeheartedly that maternity is not merely a personal matter, that it has a historical dimension as well.

Analyzing the Sources: Even the most committed anticommunist could hardly view these Salvadoran revolutionary women as "common criminals." And yet some might consider them excessively wedded to their ideological vision. What do you think?

CONFESSIONS OF A TORTURER

Nancy Guzmán

In the following selection, Chilean journalist Nancy Guzmán interviews Osvaldo Romo, alias "Fat Romo," an infamous interrogator and torturer who worked for Chile's military government following the 1973 overthrow of the popularly elected Marxist president Salvador Allende's Popular Unity government in the US-backed coup led by General Augusto Pinochet. By 1994–95, when Romo was interviewed by Guzmán, he had been extradited from Brazil by the restored democratic government of Chile, where he had been tried and imprisoned for his crimes. However, he was quite unrepentant.

Nancy Guzmán: Why don't you tell me how you got involved in intelligence work?

Romo: The armed forces realized that they couldn't get all those Marxist-Leninist MIR* guys without my help. And that's why Lieutenant Miguel Kraanoff Martchenko showed up at my house one day. He showed up in a military vehicle and my wife got upset when she saw it, but I calmed her down and told her that I had to converse with him in private. She got upset because she had no idea about my work. Us intelligence people couldn't even tell our mothers what we were doing, see, and my wife thought that I was a community organizer.

SOURCE: adapted from Nancy Guzmán, *Romo: Confesiones de un torturador* (Santiago: Editorial Planeta Chilena, 2000), pp. 69–70, 117, 140, 159–160, 172.
*Movement of the Revolutionary Left.

The lieutenant told me that they'd been having a tough time catching those MIR guys and that I could help them out, because they'd arrest people sometimes and get fooled by them and let them go. I listened to his proposal and accepted it because the working conditions that he offered were very good. Anyway, it was patriotic duty, because the Popular Unity government was really corrupt and the army was basically saving the country, see? Saving the country . . .

Nancy Guzmán: Why do you repeat that? Are you maybe not so convinced that it's true?

Romo: No, look, I know that you don't understand what went on here in Chile, because you're too young to remember. But it was anarchy, okay? Hey, maybe those MIR guys had some good ideas, right? But nothing practical. The army isn't going to let a revolution happen here. They've got that Prussian discipline, you know. And anyway, Pinochet made his own revolution, is what I say. He really changed the country. In Chile only the army can make revolutions. And anyway, a civil war would have been worse and a lot more people would have died.

"El Chicho" (that was Allende's nickname) got half the country to go along with him. He was full of lies, but they believed him. I'm going to put all that in the book I'm writing. Oh yeah, Allende liked living high, all right. He always wanted the best, and meanwhile he had everybody else eating crap and standing in long lines to get it, too.

I saw all that before the military takeover, and the army didn't just barge in, either, because everybody was clamoring for them to do it. That's why I decided to collaborate with their project of national reconstruction.

Nancy Guzmán: You weren't working for national reconstruction but for the secret police, which stand accused of killing many people.

Romo: Look. It was an intelligence organization.

Nancy Guzmán: Explain to me what you mean by that.

Romo: An intelligence organization infiltrates the population to find out who might be extremists and what they are planning to do. . . .

Nancy Guzmán: Explain to me what you understand by "extremist."

Romo: Look, I learned to identify extremists at the US School of the Americas in Panama. Because I was there, you know. And I was around extremists, too, after all, in those poor neighborhoods. Extremists are smart. They aren't dummies, a little crazy, maybe, but very intelligent. They are Marxists or Marxist-Leninists. Have you read Marx or Lenin? That's what the extremists read and what they base their actions on. They try to create the necessary conditions for a popular uprising, so that they can install the dictatorship of the proletariat and cut off a lot of heads. Heck yeah, I studied Marxism. Those MIR guys used to go to my house to ask me about it, and we would talk.

Nancy Guzmán: Do you think that the MIR prisoners of the secret police could have avoided what happened?

Romo: Well, they were the tough guys who said that they planned to seize power by force, in defiance of the armed forces, right? But they were all talk, pure blah blah blah, because at the moment of truth some of them wet their pants.

Nancy Guzmán: You call them cowards. But what would you have done, Romo, if somebody kidnapped you, tied you up, tortured you, and said they were going to kill you?

Romo: I already told you. I have military training and would be able to resist any form of torture because that's what they teach you at the School of the Americas. Look. (Romo rolled up a pants leg to show some barely visible scars.) These are the marks that I got in Panama when they taught me to torture and to resist torture. Yep, that's what they train you to do. They tortured me there, so don't come telling me that the Chilean secret police torture so much, because that's nothing. And, anyway, those MIR guys were no bunch of harmless doves, because they had weapons, and they were criminals who didn't really care about Chile. They were "internationalists," see? Their country was supposedly the whole world.

Nancy Guzmán: Don't tell me that these seventeen- or eighteen-year-old kids were dangerous criminals. Why didn't you turn them over to the regular police so that they could be punished in the manner indicated by law?

Romo: There wasn't anybody there as young as that.

Nancy Guzmán: Martín Elgueta was only twenty-one years old.

Romo: Look. I am the one who arrested Martín Elgueta, and I tell you that he was no saint, okay? He had Cuban training and went around armed to the teeth. He carried a magnum pistol here (lifting his pants leg again to show his ankle), and do you have any idea what kind of hole a magnum bullet makes? But, of course, you catch these folks and afterward their mothers cry and say that their little doves would not hurt a fly. But it wasn't so.

Nancy Guzmán: What were the tortures like?

Romo: That depends. There was the electric grill, as we called it, like a set of bed springs made of metal strips on which the prisoners would lie tied spread-eagled, and we'd put electrodes on their genitals, in their mouths, in their ears, any place there was a bit of moisture. Sometimes we'd toss a bucket of water on them, too. Then (laughing and rubbing his hands together) we'd crank them up a little.

Nancy Guzmán: What do you mean by "crank them up"?

Romo: We had a little generator that you crank to produce electric current.

Nancy Guzmán: How did the tortured people react?

Romo: Oh, they'd jump and scream and twist around, and yep, it's true, sometimes they'd piss and shit on themselves. But nothing would happen to them. They don't die. They feel like they are going to die, but they don't. Sometimes it actually does them good.

Nancy Guzmán: Were you present during the tortures?

Romo: Yes, but not torturing. I was interrogating them to determine what organization they belonged to, this one or that one, where they fit. I figured that out.

Nancy Guzmán: And you did the same with the women?

Romo: Well, sure. They were doing the same stuff as the men. Hey, let me tell you, the women are even tougher than the men. They're tougher and they're meaner. They get into political stuff without thinking about their families and what they're getting into, and then they whine about daddy and the kids.

Nancy Guzmán: And did the women who disappeared die under torture?

Romo: I don't know because they were fine when I last saw them. Look, I'd go home in the afternoon, and the next day I'd ask where what's-her-name was, and they'd say she was transferred, and that's all I know.

Nancy Guzmán: And how about the rapes?

Romo: You're really stuck on that. It's a big lie, a story that the Marxists tell. Who was going to rape a bunch of dirty, filthy, disgusting women with urine and blood running down their legs? You've got no idea what you are talking about. Those women were in a room without a toilet, and they did everything in there, everything, in a bunch of cans, yep, cans like house paint comes in, and they never washed. There were places where they just did it on the floor and then slept there. So just imagine how they smelled. And there wasn't any toilet paper there, uh uh. You think somebody was going to touch them and risk getting some kind of infection?

Analyzing the Sources: How did Romo view the people whose torture he supervised? How did he view the act of torture itself?

Chapter 10

Speaking for Themselves

Beginning with the Caminha Letter and the narratives of Cabeza de Vaca, this book has endeavored to illuminate the social and cultural history of Latin America and, above all, the history of its indigenous, African-descended, and mixed-race majorities. Ironically, beginning with Caminha and Cabeza de Vaca themselves, the sources that speak of the non-European majority are, inevitably, more European than not. The ideas and attitudes of the majority, their own stories, were basically not written down and preserved because of European cultural hegemony, so one reads what did survive, the story told by outsiders. Even twentieth-century indigenistas and exponents of Afro-Brazilian culture were likely to be well-off white anthropologists rather than people like those that they portrayed. A different, intersecting vein of silence affected women, redoubling the silencing effect of race and class for women of color. Even Sor Juana Inés de la Cruz, born into the upper crust of colonial New Spain, was silenced for speaking up, and the writings by women in this collection of Latin American voices are few, indeed.

Fortunately, though, Latin America's formerly silenced people are now speaking for themselves. Their most important venue is no doubt the Internet, despite the inequality of access—which varies greatly from country to country and from urban to rural—but it is rapidly expanding and already notably widespread in Brazil. A book like this is no place to try to explore the explosion of Latin American popular culture occuring in social media and music videos. Fortunately, again, old-fashioned literary traditions still command respect. A short story or novel written from within indigenous traditions, poetry or essays about being black by someone who has actually had the experience—these things are no longer impossible to find in Latin America. After so much ventriloquism of indigenous and African-descended Latin American voices, we deserve a bit of the real thing.

"It's No Use" is a short story by a Mayan author of Yucatán, Ana Patricia Martínez Huchím. Yucatec Mayan is one of the important living indigenous languages in Mexico, along with several other living Mayan languages in Guatemala. As well as being a Mayan's story about Mayan life, this is a woman's story about women and about men's treatment of women. It is a powerful denunciation that nonetheless maintains a humane and ironic attitude toward its flawed characters. It is also formally intricate, almost a micronovel with its several chapters and various points of view. Its compression and simplicity also make it poetic, but it is a stark poetry, without the exoticism one finds in the indigenous characters of Ciro Alegría or Miguel Ángel Asturias. Finally, it incorporates a number of elements of indigenous storytelling that clearly relate it to oral traditions.

Cherrufe: The Ball of Fire, by Mariela Fuentealba Millaguir, is the first novel to be written in Spanish from a Mapuche perspective. The novel directly addresses matters such as identity, memory, and conflict with the nonindigenous. A *cherrufe* is a flying ball of fire of Mapuche belief. The novel begins when the narrator, a young girl, dreams of a cherrufe that announces the death of her ancestor, Chief Millaguir, who had been murdered decades earlier for refusing to sell the land than belongs to his people. In the dream, she sees the chief's funeral. Thousands of native riders have traveled great distances from up and down and across the southern Andes to see him laid to rest in a great hollowed tree trunk. The little girl has had no previous knowledge of these events, and she surprises her grandmother by describing her dream. Thus the girl's dream expresses a mystical connection with her people's experience across time. Her ancestors are evidently trying to communicate with her.

Shirley Campbell Barr represents the African diaspora, one could say, although that is my idea, not hers. True, her ancestors came to Costa Rica from Jamaica with many other black workers of the English-speaking Caribbean, most of whom labored on Costa Rican banana plantations. But she does not write about being black generally or in the abstract. She writes out her own experience and does not try to formulate anybody's identity but her own. Nor does she believe that racial identities are one-size-fits-all. To the contrary, Campbell Barr writes about the individual experience of race from the perspective of one who understands it to be a social construction, but no less real because of that. She is also an international traveler who attends literary gatherings around the hemisphere and has lived in several countries outside of Costa Rica. She invites you to visit her blog at rotundamentenegra.blogspot.com.

IT'S NO USE

Ana Patricia Martínez Huchím

The original Mayan version of Ana Patricia Martínez Huchím's story about mothers' struggles to save their daughters from repeating their mothers' mistakes won first place in the Fourth Literary Games of the Autonomous University of Yucatán in 2005. She dedicated it to the people who work to strengthen Mayan culture in the contemporary world, as she does in this story, with its sharp critique of indigenous machismo. There is blame to go around here—feckless men, heedless girls, ineffectual mothers—but there are no villains. Instead, there is painful clarity and no simple answer. The story begins and ends with what seem to represent traditional elements of indigenous storytelling. "There's a story told . . . ," opens the first section, invoking traditional storytelling and wisdom. "The other day, I was passing by . . ." begins the final section, confirming the validity of the story by invoking a collective judgment in the street. The body of the story is divided into chapters, each of which has an epigraph.

THERE'S A STORY TOLD . . .

There's a story told about young girls. All day long their mothers warn them, "See what happens to girls who run away with their boyfriends?" But it's no use. Many ignore the advice of their elders. Not until the girls run away do they remember what their mothers said, when it's too late. So, no, it doesn't work out for many girls. They don't find what they're looking for.

THE DESPERATION OF FLOREANO BATUM

Although you sow the choicest seed,
The harvest may not fill the need.

Thud!

It was a slight sound muffled by the tenacious barking of the dogs. Yet even in a placid sleep, Floreano Batum heard the sound of a stone coming to earth. He was used to the noise of the dogs, at this hour of the early morning, but not the sound of something heavy dislodged from the dry stone wall that surrounded the house. The sound woke him up to reality. His daughter's hammock hung empty.

Next to him in his own hammock, his wife started to sob. Sadly, Floreano dropped one foot to the floor and pushed gently. The hammock swayed in the darkness as a succession of memories flooded his mind:

"Yano, Yano! Come see your newborn daughter. She was born while you were out hunting. She's got the same birthmark as you on her shoulder. She looks a lot like you!"

"How the devil can she look like me if I'm a man?"

SOURCE: The author thanks José Manuel Tec Tun and Svetlana Larrocha for their stylistic advice. Ana Patricia Martínez Huchím, "It's No Use," *K'aaylay: El canto de la memoria, Revista de cultura maya* 2:31 (2008): 268–74.

He spat and kicked the dirt floor, then hung up his machete and his shotgun and went outside to sit in the shade of the ramón tree.

"Bad day," he grumbled. "I came home from hunting empty handed, the animals are eating up the corn in the milpa, and now they tell me that I got a daughter instead of a son. I wanted a son to help me with the work in the milpa." Angrily he crushed a round ramón fruit under his foot and vented his anger that way.

Floreano's foot pushed the floor to keep the hammock swaying.

"Yano, Yano! The baby's got diarrhea and she won't stop crying. X'ma Soco says that she's got the evil eye because you didn't hug her when you came home upset."

The man moved closer to the hammock where the little girl lay bundled like a cotton ball with a fuzzy little head. He gazed at hear and found himself enchanted by her eyes like little black beans.

"My little one," he burst out, "you're going to be my good luck charm, my *tuunich kéej*." And he lovingly kissed his daughter on the forehead.

Floreano's hand pushed the floor to keep the hammock swaying.

"My-f-fa-ther-plants-th-the-corn. My mo-ther-cooks-the-f-food. I-am-learn-ing-to-r-read."

The small voice sounding out words was music to Yano's ears. His daughter, a Batum, was going to school and, very quickly, learning to read. What did it matter than he had sold his shotgun for less than its worth to buy her school supplies? His daughter, a Batum, was going to *be* somebody—a school teacher, at least, or a graduate of some kind.

The hammock continued to sway.

"Yano, Yano! We've got a young lady in the house. Today our daughter got her period!"

Floreano was shocked, speechless. But how could that have happened? His little one . . . a young lady.

The hammock swayed.

When his daughter turned fifteen, Yano thanked God that she had grown up strong and healthy. His girl was as pretty as a flower. She was at the age in which all women are pretty.

Lying face up with his hand and foot dragging on the floor, Yano remembered:

"You've got to lift a gourd to know if it's hollow!"

That's what that good-for-nothing Heculano Och had shouted yesterday afternoon in the cantina. Now he understood the meaning, because that night, Och (which meant "fox") ran off with Floreano's little girl.

Thud! The sound of the falling stone echoed in Yano's ears and constricted his heart.

THE DESOLATION OF REFUGIO KU

Her own daughter had run away
To try the taste of suffering.

Refugio Ku lay in her hammock and sobbed. Why had her daughter run away like a thief in the night? Hadn't she told the girl so many times about what it was like for her when she ran away with Floreano Batum?

Floreano's mother had made her return home the next day and ask her sisters for her clothing. Her sisters threw her dresses to her over the high stone wall.

"Didn't you run away with a man? Then let him buy you clothes, and everything else you need!" said her sister x'Mos.

"You're going to get it now!" predicted her younger sister x'Ponsa.

And Floreano never bought her anything. She started selling fruit, plums, guayabas, anonas, and huayas, and that's how she made her living from then on. The first day in Yano's house he threw the tortillas on the floor because they weren't cooked well enough for him.

"Your tortillas are bad. Learn to make better ones," he demanded. But he didn't give her any money.

Refugio sobbed and remembered how sweetly Yano had spoken to her before she ran away with him.

"Your first name means 'refuge' and your last name means 'nest,'" he had said. "And that means you are the perfect woman to make a home for me."

His words had lifted her almost to heaven. Once she ran away with him, though, all she heard from his mouth was insults.

"Come with me and you won't eat just beans anymore. You'll always have meat to cook. And you'll have a beautiful shawl, lipstick like those fancy ladies, and perfume so you'll always smell nice. At my side, you'll lack for nothing at all," promised Yano.

Years earlier, Refugio's own mother had married a man who promised the same thing, saying come with me and you'll eat when the sun comes up, at midday, and when it goes down, without ever having to work.

What a lie!

But Refugio's mother believed it, and then, when she went to live with him, the man took her with him to cut firewood, and he made *her* carry two thirds of it home on her back.

The night when Refugio ran away with Floreano, she had danced with him. The young man even bought her mother a drink as a courtesy before asking Refugio to dance. The drink, along with exhaustion and the late hour, put Refugio's mother halfway asleep in her chair as her daughter danced and her husband played a "rascabuche" gourd-scraper with the band. Refugio's father was a musician who played percussion at dance halls and private parties. He saw his daughter leave the dance with Floreano as his wife nodded off.

"X'Rejuch (her Mayan name) has an itch between her legs," he thought. "She's needing a man." He scowled and kept time loudly with the gourd scraper, rritchi rritchi, rritchi rritchi.

When Refugio's mother finally opened her eyes, the girl had disappeared. The poor woman ran out into the night to find her daughter. She went to Yano's house and tried to spy the interior through the cracks in the dried mud-daub construction. A somber voice spoke to her.

"It's no use, *mamacita linda*," said Refugio tenderly from inside the house. "No use. What had to happen has already happened. It's no use . . . no use at all."

The Itch of Esperanza Batum Ku

A woman in love
Gives herself fully.

"Come eat, x'Lancha!" called Refugio to her daughter Esperanza, many years later. "Enough conversation for now!"

They'd been at it long enough, and there wasn't enough food in the house to invite the young man who was chatting with her daughter.

"Ay mamacita linda," answered the girl, "talking is the best thing ever, I like it better than beans with pork!"

The suitor, young Herculano, meanwhile, murmured in the girl's ear that he wanted to see her hair ribbon on his hammock. He had a way with words, thought Esperanza.

"What on earth does she see in that snot-nosed good-for-nothing?" wondered Refugio in the kitchen. "Maybe he's got a golden bird, as they say."

That night Esperanza put on lots of underwear, two bras, and several changes of clothes without being observed. Then she climbed into her hammock and rolled herself tightly in a blanket so that nobody would discover that she was wearing her entire wardrobe to bed. Herculano Och would buy her lots of clothes later on, but he couldn't yet, poor guy, because he had no money, not having found work yet. Soon. Meanwhile, Och himself had suggested that the girl wear all her clothes when he came for her.

Just before dawn, Esperanza heard a low whistle and the barking of the dogs. She slipped from her hammock in silence and went to the door, but when she unbolted it, the sound woke her mother.

"Where are you going?" asked Refugio.

"Outside, my stomach hurts. Those beans made me sick."

"Wait, I'll go with you."

Esperanza didn't wait. She ran across the bare yard and leapt over the high wall of dry stone surrounding the house. That's when a dislodged stone fell with a thud on the top of her foot. It hurt, but she bit her lip and did not cry out.

In spite of the darkness, she could see that Herculano Och was crouching among the weeds, waiting for her. She hesitated and turned back toward the house, but it was no use. Och pounced before she had time for another thought.

The fox took his first bite of the unfortunate little chicken right there by the dry stone wall, and then he dragged it back to his den, where his mother and sisters lived.

The dogs at the Batum Ku house stopped barking and started long howls that sounded like bad luck.

THE OTHER DAY, I WAS PASSING BY . . .

The other day, I was passing by the Batum Ku house, and nearby I heard a group of women talking about Esperanza.

"She was doing so well in her studies," said a woman whose husband has a reputation as the village drunk. "Who knows how high she would have risen? Now I see her pass every day carrying a bucket of corn on her head to mill for tortillas. She doesn't even have shoes!"

"Yesterday I saw her with a black eye!" said another whose husband is known to beat her.

"She wears the same dress every day," said another whose husband is even worse.

"It's her own fault," said a woman who lives "shacked up," as they say. "She had an itchy crotch, that girl!"

"In her family, they all run away, grandmother, mother, and finally, daughter," said a woman whose husband has abandoned her.

"She had to give it to him, otherwise he'd lose interest," confirmed another runaway. "That's how men are."

"So young, and such an itch!" said an old maid.

"Hush, all of you!" shouted an old beggar widow passing by. "Men make you whores, even if you're married to them. I'm happy to be a señorita again!"

Analyzing the Sources: A narrative like this one makes a critique without formulating it in so many words. How would you state the story's message in a sentence or two?

CHERRUFE

Ruth Mariela Fuentealba Millaguir

Ruth Mariela Fuentealba Millaguir's novel Cherrufe: The Ball of Fire *is based on the traditions of her own family. The novel is narrated from the point of view of a little girl, Charito, who is living at the house of her grandparents in the historical Mapuche homeland of southern Chile in the middle of the twentieth century. Charito seems to have inherited a special spiritual vocation, which is not uncommon among Mapuche women. The following excerpt is the final chapter of the novel, in which Charito is initiated into the family's spiritual connection with its ancestors at a ritual that may remind readers of the sweat lodges used by various native peoples of North America. The ritual includes elements, such as animism, out-of-body experience, the sensation of flight, and transformation into animal form, that are common to shamanic practice around the world.*

My brothers Tope and Paolo liked to play "Indian." What a pair of dummies! They ran after the chickens to grab tail feathers and stick them on their heads like the red skins at the movies. They shot arrows at each other and jumped and danced around a maqui bush, tapping their mouths with their open hands, singing, and shouting. They were trying to make it rain or something.

I don't know if it was a coincidence, or if they really managed to awaken some slumbering spirit, because I thought I felt a slight tremor, and soon the skies darkened as scattered clouds knotted themselves together. Then, wind and rain.

My grandfather ran to take care of his precious animals, and the kids piled into the house all wet and startled, drying faces on sleeves.

SOURCE: Ruth Mariela Fuentealba Millaguir, *Cherrufe: La Bola de Fuego* (Santiago: CONADI, 2008), pp. 53–56.

"What were those boys up to?" asked Mother.

"Nothing," they said, "just playing!"

When the young boys joined the other children already inside, the noise in the small house got shriller by the minute. Grandfather told a little of one of those stories that have been passed down for who knows how long. This one was about a "chained-up dog" that scares children who have to go out by themselves at night.

"And . . . boooo! Out jumps the chained-up dog!" shouted Aurelio, and we were appropriately thrilled and frightened.

But that night promised a totally different sort of excitement, something a lot bigger, that I could clearly sense without knowing at all what it was going to be. By the time that our elders, in single file, led us children to the smoke hut, I begin to feel the invisible presence of something or someone.

The old construction of rough walls and smoke-stained roof-tiles, which we called the "fogón," had been built by the sweat of my grandfather. It had only one window, high and small, to let in the light of the moon as it slid out from behind the clouds.

The world seemed not to sleep that night, as if each and every living thing were awake. I heard the toads, the crickets, and the birds talking to one another. Trees called back and forth across the fields. Flowers raised their voices in song, and the rustling breeze applauded them. Spirits were everywhere, invisible but drawing close to us, all with something to say.

The wisps of smoke drifting about made our eyes water a bit, but it had a nice smell. When we opened the door of the hut I thought I saw jewels glint as if illuminated by a ray of sunlight in the haze. And there was a sound inside the hut like the sound of the kaskawillas that our dancers wear on their legs, but here shaken without pause.

A hand led us children into the dark interior of the hut. When it touched my hand, I felt a indescribable excitement, even though I immediately recognized the calloused, curving fingers of my grandfather. Gently, he led us through the hazy darkness to a fire pit where a marvelous sight greeted our curious, innocent eyes. My mother and grandmother were seated by the fire, and so was my uncle, all of them dressed in a manner that I had never seen before.

The women wore jewels on their heads and their chests, and great braids of colored ribbons spilling down their backs. My mother's expectant eyes invited me to approach her and sit at her side.

We all sat down around the fire with our legs crossed, our hands holding the hands of the person to each side. This, I understood, was the sacred circle of the Millaguir family. My grandfather threw some special leaves on to the fire, the flames of which flared brightly, sending sparks whirling up to settle, eventually, in our hair or on our bare feet.

With each handful of leaves my grandfather spoke words that I was too young to understand, but still, even without understanding the words, we children intuitively encouraged him.

"Eeeey . . . eeeey," we said, at each flash of flames.

My grandfather did not respond to us, and his eyes seemed hardly to see us. I'm sure that at times he was unaware of our presence as he concentrated on the spirit work that he had learned from my aunt Chabela. As the smoke billowed, multiplying its peppery odors, I looked at my mother and found her present in body only. She still held my hand, but I could tell that her spirit was far away.

My heart pounded, my chest heaved, my pulse raced, my palms were sweating, and I felt as though I might burst. Abruptly, I pulled away from the fire, but I held on to my mother's hand. I knew that she would protect me even while her spirit was traveling to other places. My mother's hand squeezed mine, and I could feel her sweat on my skin and her tears in my hair.

And that's when it happened. Suddenly I could see what my mother's saw, understand what she knew, and feel what her heart felt. Little by little, my spirit rose out of my body like a spark rising out of the fire. A rainbow of colors surrounded me, melting into one another. Looking down, I saw my family dancing around the fire. I felt boneless, with no sensation of possessing legs or arms, or any body at all. Floating beside me was the spirit of my mother, my astral guide.

Up and up we floated, through the roof, converted into whisps of smoke or breeze, like transparent jellyfish in the night sky. I closed my eyes and began to sense the claws of a powerful lion with green eyes, reaching for me and sinking into my flesh, but I did not bleed or cry, and somehow I was not afraid. I was no longer me, a little girl, Charito. Instead, I felt myself sprouting feathers. Now I opened my eagle eyes and saw that I was soaring though the clouds on enormous wings. At my side was the green-eyed lion. It looked at me and roared. Somehow, I recognized my mother, she too had been transformed. I could tell that she was surprised to see me take on the form of my totem animal for the first time. We looked at each other deeply.

The sky belonged to the two of us. I flew into showers of colors and managed to brush the rainbow with my wings. We soared so high that I never wanted to come down. But it seemed we must descend, so down, down we floated like a couple of whisps of cotton, until we came to rest in an open field.

On the ground, my mother and I were still animals, but it seemed that we were invisible. Large trees surrounded us, and steaming pots, and structures of bamboo from which hung meat and the hides and body parts of various animals. Somehow I knew that this was a Mapuche encampment of the sort where my people had lived hundreds of years ago. There were several old women wearing the same sort of clothing that my mother and grandmother had put on for the ceremony in the fogón. They watched over babies wrapped tightly to wooden cradle boards that protected their heads, like little canoes. There were men, as well, and all the people spoke a language that sounded like the words my grandfather had used to begin the ceremony earlier that evening.

In the center of this field, too, was a place for ceremonies. There I saw *rewes*, like short totem poles with seven steps to connect the ground and sky, a sacred *canelo* tree, some chickens, and several cows that stood placidly watching and chewing their cuds. There was a man who drew my attention. He had dark skin and long black hair that reached his shoulders. He was thin and handsome, neither young nor old, though he wore clothes like my grandfather's, and his blue eyes made him stand out from the others.

The man with blue eyes walked toward us, and it seemed to me that he saw us. That can't be, I thought, because no one can see us here or know of our magical presence in this place.

But he did see us and walked straight to us, and it seemed that he carried all the light in the world towards us. The green-eyed lion who was my mother sank its claws into the earth. Neither of us could move.

The man walked between us and he ran his fingers through the lion's fur and through my feathers. His touch was hot with a heat that penetrated to the center of our beings. My mother's fur stood up and I felt my feathers fall away, one by one. Passing beyond us, the strange man turned and looked at my mother.

"I am Tadeo Millaguir," he said, "your grandfather."

Suddenly native riders on horseback appeared and swept around us in a circle, and now it was only me in the center of the circle, and I was no longer an eagle. Being an eagle had made me feel protected. I looked for my mother but she couldn't help me. She was outside the circle with her grandfather. The music of the star-crowded heavens struck a chord, and the circle swept into a universal dance that included everything and everyone I had seen that night. In the center of the circle, I felt protected again, and the dance drew me in. Together we danced under the stars until I was ready to collapse into the lush grass of that magical place in the mountains so full of meanings that I was only beginning to comprehend.

And then all the dancers, as if connected to one another by an invisible thread, crouched down at once until they could touch the toes of their bare feet, and all rose together and raised their arms skyward, and a voice said:

"These are your ancestors."

As my ancestors raised their arms, they became flames, and each person transformed, one by one, into a small ball of fire that rose gently into the air, as if carried by a breeze, although there was no breeze.

And each flame or being, each small ball of fire, entered my body, relaxing it. As my ancestors soaked into my chest, they brought a feeling of peace and calm, and I breathed deeply.

Now I was standing alone in the mountain field. My great grandfather Millaguir was walking away into the forest, a short man carrying a staff of authority in his hands, disappearing gradually from my sight. He was inviting everyone to the great dance, where all the animal spirits would be present. As he passed, all the trees of the forest—*lingues, coigues, tineos, canelos*—bowed before my great grandfather.

I wanted to find my mother and thought that she might have scratched me a message on the ground with her lion's claws, but there was none. I had lost all sense of the passage of time and had no idea what day or hour it might be. I only knew that I wanted the dream to continue, that I wanted to stay forever in this marvelous place that I was only beginning to discover.

Then, all at once, my lion mother appeared at my side and invited me to close my eyes, which I did. I felt nothing, but opened my eyes to find myself seated at the fire with my family, as if no time at all had passed.

We all looked at one another. I felt that everyone was looking particularly at me. I could tell by his face that my grandfather knew everything that had happened. But he didn't say a word, and neither did anyone else.

We slowly rose to our feet and filed out of the hut.

That night, we did not need to light candles or a lamp.

The house was illuminated all by itself.

Analyzing the Sources: Would you read this story the same way if it were written by an outsider to Mapuche life? How might your interpretation of it change?

UNEQUIVOCALLY BLACK

Shirley Campbell Barr

Shirley Campbell Barr is a Costa Rican poet of African descent who maintains a blog called Rotundamente Negra, *which means "flatly" or "unequivocally" black, a formulation of her own racial identity. Our selection of Campbell Barr's work includes a poem, presented here in a dual-language version by the bilingual poet herself. Following the poem is an essay that appeared on her blog as "Vivir Negro en El Salvador" in 2009. In it she describes a stay in that country's capital city, San Salvador. El Salvador, unlike most other Central American countries, lacks a sizable population of African descent.*

Source: Shirley Campbell Barr, "Liberada/Liberated," and "Vivir Negro en El Salvador," posted on *Rotundamente Negra*, rotundamentenegra.blogspot.com. The poem was first published in *Rotundamente negra y otros poemas* (Madrid: Ediciones Torremozas, 2013), p. 243N.

LIBERATED

I am no longer looking for reasons for my skin
no longer finding excuses nor explanations for the roundness
   of my butt
or the natural beat in my walking
I am no longer justifying my natural taste for drums
or the urge of my body   5
to dance to the sound that is played . . .

It's been a long time since I've stopped explaining ancestors
justifying my lips or my extraordinary nose
or this whole beauty that accompanies me since immemorial
   times
I do not justify my syncretism   10
nor my passions nor my sensuality
I do not grant reasons for being
I became myself
I learned myself
I am me   15

I am confident of myself and of my own people
I do not need endorsements to be
I'm not asking for permissions to live
I enjoy my blackness with elegance to spare
I wear it with honor, with confidence and distinction   20
I walk it through parks, markets and plazas
performing stages, simple conversations and big conferences
blackness fills my soul, my speech and my life.
I'm no longer trying to disguise it in my hair
my complexion, nor in my distinguished discourses   25
I've learned it by heart
from within, with history, and from the bottom of my soul

LIBERADA

Yo ya no busco razones para mi piel
no busco más excusas ni explicaciones para la redondez de mis
    nalgas
o la natural cadencia en mi andar
no justifico ya mi natural agrado por los tambores o la necesidad
    de mi cuerpo
de danzar al ritmo que le tocan . . .   5

Hace ya tiempo que deje de explicar antepasados
que justifiquen mis labios o mi extraordinaria nariz
o la hermosura incólume que me acompaña desde tiempos
    inmemoriales
no justifico más mis sincretismos
ni mis pasiones, ni mi sensualidad   10
yo ya no otorgo razones para mi ser.
Me convertí en mi misma
me aprendí
soy yo.

Tengo certeza de mi misma y de los míos   15
no necesito autorizaciones para ser
no pido ya permisos para vivir.
Hoy disfruto con sobrada elegancia mi negrura
la llevo con honor, con garbo y distinción
la paseo por parques, mercados y plazas   20
por escenarios, anfiteatros, simples coloquios y grandes
    conferencias
con placer me colma el alma
el discurso y la vida.
Ya no intento disimularla en mi cabello
en mi tez o en mis distinguidas alocuciones   25
la aprendí de memoria
desde adentro, con historia y desde el centro del alma.

Indeed
I do not need reasons to be
Because I discover myself clean   30
bright
victorious
intact
tested
blessed   35
brawled
black
without reasons, any more,
today I am myself
liberated   40

Por eso, ya no preciso de razones para ser
porque me descubrí limpia
brillante   30
victoriosa
incólume
probada
bendecida
batallada   35
negra
ya no,
no preciso razones
hoy soy yo
liberada   40

LIVING BLACK IN EL SALVADOR

We arrived in San Salvador after two years of living in Zimbabwe. Zimbabwe had been an attempt to find out who we really are. We always knew that the land of our African ancestors wasn't precisely Zimbabwe, but walking on any African soil was profoundly significant to us. In spite of all the differences among African peoples— cultural, historical, environmental or phenotypic—to be black in Africa just feels different from being black anywhere else. Everybody is some sort of black, and people don't automatically perceive you as not belonging.

So we arrived in San Salvador with an aura of pride and self-sufficiency and little desire to find ourselves once again members of a minority group, having to justify ourselves at every moment. The airport received us with lots of curious looks, the kind where the indiscreet lookers smile in embarrassment when you catch them looking. I saw about eight black people at the airport, the most that I ever saw in one place during my entire stay in El Salvador.

As we rode into the city my eyes looked for faces like mine, for dark skin and African features, without seeing any. Once in a while, seeing a person somewhat from behind I thought, "There's a black person," but looking closer I realized my mistake. Facial features are harder to read that skin tone. As long as I can remember, and sometimes even against my will, I have systematically scanned the faces of people I come across in the street, trying to decide who might be black. I suppose that it's an unconscious need for self-affirmation, to see myself in others. So I walk around saying to myself: "Look, that woman is black, and so is that fellow over there." I try to judge their facial features or the texture of their hair, or even the shape of their bodies.

It's not always possible. Nonetheless, it's a good exercise. I think I've developed a good eye for people's African ancestry. Sometimes the people see me observing them, and often they react in a way that, consciously or not, suggests a wish to deflect my attention or hide, a wish not to be identified as black. They don't want to be identified as black, because they don't want to identify themselves that way.

Our first days in El Salvador were not easy. Never before, except for an occasion a few years before, during a visit to Chile, had I been so watched by those around me. It's strange, especially considering that El Salvador shares a border with Honduras, where there are half a million people of African descent. In Central America as a whole, there have to be a million of us. But it's true that you don't see black people on the streets of San Salvador, and if you're black, everybody watches you. People assume that you are a foreigner and don't speak Spanish, and what's worse, they try their English on you.

The effect was magnified because there was not just one of us. We were a whole family, including a little girl of six years old and a little boy of four years old. The little ones created a sensation. School was eventful, too. Malcolm, the younger, attended a big school that ran from preschool through secondary school. His green eyes and dark skin attracted so much interest, his teachers used to tell us, that girls from the secondary school came to look at him, which embarrassed him no end.

Imagine you're driving, sitting at a red light beside a city bus, when you glance over to see every single passenger on the bus staring at you. That's what it was like.

Once there were black people in El Salvador. The Spanish brought slaves, as in the rest of Latin America. Various historical studies provide some details. In his book *The Population of El Salvador*, Rodolfo Barón Castro cites an unpublished document that even suggests the threat of rebellion. "In the province of San Salvador, during the year 1625, an uprising of two thousand blacks was planned for Holy Week, but word leaked out in time, some of the plotters were killed, and problems were avoided." Barón Castro indicates that the black population of the country was "never numerous enough to maintain its own characteristics." He says that the black population dissolved into the much larger indigenous population.

And that, as I've seen with my own eyes, isn't completely so. I was able to detect more than one Mandinga ancestor in Salvadoran physiognomies. In addition, subsequent work by Salvadoran scholars has shown that the historical presence of Afro-descendents in El Salvador has been greater than indicated by Barón Castro.

It never was large, though. And it is popularly recognized in El Salvador that the famous dictator Maximiliano Hernández Martínez, after repressing the indigenous people in 1932, and trying systematically to wipe out their culture, made a law in 1934 flatly denying blacks entry into the country. That law, even though not always strictly enforced, effectively ended immigration by anybody of African descent. The law remained on the books for half a century, until the 1980s.

Salvador's quasi-official definition of its national identity includes proud reference to Spain and indigenous America but explicitly excludes the possibilty that black people contributed to its racial, cultural, or ethnic makeup. A similar denial of blackness goes on across Latin America, even when the genes are clearly present.

Living black in El Salvador wasn't all bad, though. Our experiences sometimes made us uncomfortable, or even angry, but most of the time they just made us smile. The constant sense was of curiosity, not racism or persecution. I even remember thinking that I'd suffered more racism in Costa Rica, my own country, with a black population of about 10 percent, than I experienced in El Salvador.

The country was going through a bad time, involving rampant crime and street violence, when we lived there. There were gang wars, armed robberies, carjackings, you name it. We were clearly foreigners, and therefore presumed to have means. But we were never targeted.

We only knew one other black family in the city, Simba and Abby Machingaidze, our friends from Zimbabwe. If my family got a lot of attention, the Machingaidzes stole the show with their four children, including beautiful twins only a few months old. On more than one occasion I had to help them fend off a crowd of curious people who wanted to hold their babies. The Machingaidzes didn't speak Spanish and the crowds were well intentioned but unnerving. No kidding, a couple of times we had to flee from a store or public place to get away from the curious people. Our African friends were shocked. They had traveled internationally before, but never had they felt so isolated, or been regarded as so different, by the rest of the population.

A few black soccer players had passed through El Salvador. While we were there, a black Brazilian took Salvadoran citizenship in order to play on the Salvadoran team in international competitions. (Soccer, incidentally, is one of the reasons that I think Salvadorans, consciously or unconsciously, wish they did have a more blacks in the national population.) This player wasn't that good, but at least he was black. "So now there are even black Salvadorans," people joked. He didn't work out, though. The Salvadoran team did not make it to the World Cup, and the "black Salvadoran" drank too much and avoided child support. The sensationalist press had a field day, and people decided that there weren't any black Salvadorans, after all.

My partner Harold was sometimes taken for a soccer player. People pestered him for his autograph and often wouldn't believe him when he denied being a player. Sometimes he gave out autographs just to make them go away.

When Salvadorans tell you that there are no blacks in their country, sometimes they allow an exception. Once someone told us that to see black people in El Salvador, one had to travel to San Alejo, a small community in the eastern part of the country. We went there, and we didn't see anybody who looked like us, but somebody did recall "la negra Sonia and her family," who had once lived in San Alejo. Scoping around with my clinical eye, I saw more traces of African ancestry there than elsewhere in El Salvador.

A lot has happened for people of African descent in Latin America since I lived in El Salvador thirteen years ago. The social marginality endured by so many people in Latin American countries with a black population (which means all of them except El Salvador) has been revealed, and specifically black social movements have been strengthened around the region.

I'd like to think that black people on the streets of San Salvador no longer appear to Salvadorans as beings from another planet. Why that was so even thirteen years ago seems a little mysterious to me given frequently televised images of blacks, especially the musical and sports heroes of young people.

I'd like to think that things are changing in Latin America, and that the emphasis on European-indigenous mestizaje can be widened, everywhere without fuss, to include in the idea of an African contribution to our culture and gene pool.

I'd like to think that even El Salvador is not far from recognizing and celebrating the African blood that flows in Salvadoran veins. Several times, while in the country, I was invited to read my poety and discuss the plight of black people in Latin America. I met bright, tough people who seek wider horizons and do not accept the exclusionary racist discourse of the ruling class.

My family and I left wonderful friends in El Salvador, people who work tirelessly to change the political situation, and with it, old values and attitudes. Meanwhile, the people of El Salvador, even after the long war of the 1980s, continue their daily battle to survive.

Analyzing the Sources: What aspects of Campbell Barr's description seem similar to US racial identities, and what aspects seem different?

CREDITS

Ciro Alegria: From *El mundo es ancho y ajeno*. Reprinted in translation with permission of the Estate of Ciro Alegria.

José María Arguedas: "Runa Yupay" from *Agua y otros cuentos indígenas*. Reprinted in translation with permission of the Estate of José María Arguedas.

Shirley Campbell Barr: "Liberada" from *Rotundamente negra y otros poemas* 2013 and "Vivir Negra en El Salvador" from rotundamente-negra.blogspot.com by Shirley Campbell Barr. Reprinted by permission of the author.

Simon Bolivar: "A Patriot War Diary" and "Bolívar's Vision of an Orderly Republic," from Simon Bolivar, *Latin American Independence: An Anthology of Sources* (trans. John Charles Chasteen, ed. John Charles Chasteen and Sarah Chambers), copyright 2010 Hackett Publishing Company. Reprinted with permission from the publisher.

Eduardo Hughes Galeano: From *Memory of Fire: Century of the Wind*. Copyright © 1986 by Eduardo Galeano; Translation copyright © 1988 by Cedric Belfrage. Published in English by Nation Books. First published by Siglo XXI Editores, Spain. By permission of Susan Bergholz Literary Services, New York, NY and Lamy, NM. All rights reserved.

Rómulo Gallegos: "Los derechos de Mister Peligro" from *Doña Bárbara* (Madrid: Ediciones Catedra, 1929), pp. 235-238.

Federico Gamboa: From *Santa: A Novel of Mexico City* by Federico Gamboa, translated by John Charles Chasteen. Copyright © 2010 by the University of North Carolina Press. Used by permission of the publisher. www.uncpress.unc.edu

Ana Patricia Martinez Huchim: "It's No Use," *K'aaylay: El canto de la memoria, Revista de cultura maya* 2:31 (2008) by Ana Patricia Martinez Huchim. Used in translation by permission of the author.

337